WITHDRAWN

Charles T. Griffes

Charles T. Griffes

A Life in Music

Donna K. Anderson

Smithsonian Institution Press • Washington and London

Copy Editor: Aaron Appelstein
Supervisory Editor: Duke Johns
Designer: Linda McKnight

Library of Congress Cataloging-in-Publication Data

Anderson, Donna K.
    Charles T. Griffes : a life in music / Donna K. Anderson.
        p. cm.
    Includes bibliographical references and index.
    Includes discography: p.
    ISBN 1-56098-191-1
    1. Griffes, Charles Tomlinson, 1884–1920. 2. Composers—
    United States—Biography. I. Title.
    ML410.G9134A8 1993
    780'.92—dc20
    [B]   92-21844

British Library Cataloguing-in-Publication Data is available

Manufactured in the United States of America
00 99 98 97 96 95 94 93   5 4 3 2 1

⊗ The paper used in this publication meets the minimum re-
quirements of the American National Standard for Perma-
nence of Paper for Printed Library Materials Z39.48-1984

Contents

Preface

The name Charles Tomlinson Griffes, although not universally known, is certainly familiar to music lovers in the United States and Europe. Since his death in 1920, Griffes's music has maintained a presence in the concert hall and teaching studio. Anyone interested in his music has access to a large body of recordings, ranging from old 78s to modern compact discs. And it is propitious that C. F. Peters Corporation (Henmar Press Inc.) has undertaken several Griffes publications since 1967, and that G. Schirmer, Inc., is currently reprinting many of its Griffes works—songs and piano music that have been out-of-print or unavailable for some time. Both publishers are also issuing "new" works by Griffes, thus ensuring the availability of and providing scholars, performers, and musicians with more published works by Griffes than ever before. The 1984 centennial celebrations of Griffes's birth resulted in numerous performances, recordings, and articles—a true resurgence of interest in the man and in his music. This renewed attention is further reflected in many valuable master's theses and doctoral dissertations. One can hope that the interest in Griffes will continue to grow and that his music will remain a treasured part of our musical heritage.

My study of Griffes began when I was in high school, just beginning piano lessons with an artist-teacher, Denise Barrette Norton. She assigned me a piece called *The White Peacock,* with which I was to accompany a dancer in an upcoming recital. That was the first I had heard of Charles Griffes, but his music fascinated me immediately. At the MacPhail College of Music in Minneapolis, I had the good fortune to study piano with Lenore Engdahl, whose performances of Griffes's music inspired me to continue my own exploration of the composer and his music. As a doctoral candidate at Indiana University in Bloomington, I investigated the feasibility of writing a dissertation on Griffes and was encouraged to proceed with my project after a long phone conversation with author and Griffes biographer Edward Maisel. A man of many talents, Maisel has, since his Griffes biography, written on such diverse subjects as tai chi for health and F. Matthias Alexander and the Alexander technique. He has promoted Griffes's music since the mid-1940s. While I was living in New York City, Harriett Johnson, who was, until her death in 1987, music editor and critic on the *New York Post,* took an interest in my work. We remained friends over the years, and she was always generous in promoting Griffes's music. Over the past two decades, my research on Griffes has resulted in a descriptive catalog of his works (based on my dissertation and published by UMI Press in 1983); an annotated bibliography-discography of works about Griffes (published by Information Coordinators—now Harmonie Park Press—in 1977); editions, translations, and reconstructions of several Griffes works for piano and for voice and piano; articles, program notes, and jacket notes; and premieres of several of the composer's unpublished compositions. I am delighted for this opportunity to contribute to the Smithsonian Studies of American Musicians.

When Charles Griffes died in 1920, the family, under the guidance and steady hand of its matriarch, Clara Griffes, took charge of Charles's extant papers and memorabilia. After Clara's death in 1946, the responsibility of caring for this material passed to Charles's youngest sister, Marguerite. For almost forty years Marguerite attentively and lovingly watched over her brother's legacy. The family eventually deposited much of the material in three libraries. The New York Public Library received several autograph manuscripts, sketches, and sketchbooks; about four hundred letters and postcards (equally divided, the former mostly from Griffes's Berlin years); original drawings, watercolors, and etchings; albums of photographs taken by Griffes; career scrapbooks kept by Griffes and, after his death, by his family; and published scores by other composers once owned by Griffes. The Music Division of the Library of Congress acquired several autograph manuscripts, letters, and photographs, and the Gannett-Tripp Library at Elmira College received a few autograph manuscripts, a sketchbook of juvenilia, several dozen Berlin letters (mainly those written to Mary Selena Broughton), more than fifty books once owned by Griffes, and career scrapbooks kept by Griffes and, after his death, by his family.

Beginning about 1964, I met, interviewed, and corresponded with all of Griffes's siblings except Florence, who died in 1963, and with many of his nieces and nephews. The Griffes family has been most helpful and generous to me. Marguerite Griffes's trust, support, and friendship, especially, over a period of almost two decades, were invaluable to all my Griffes research. Before her death in 1983, she transferred to me all her legal rights and interests in Griffes's unpublished manuscripts, letters, photographs, and so on and placed into my possession all the remaining Griffes material, including the composer's five extant diaries, several autograph manuscripts, family photograph albums, original programs, publishing contracts, royalty records, books, a scrapbook, and other assorted memorabilia. This material will eventually be placed in the New York Public Library and the Library of Congress.

In this book I quote extensively from Griffes's diaries and letters, from interviews with members of his family, and from material provided to me by Griffes's students, friends, and acquaintances. They speak eloquently for Griffes. I also cite substantial excerpts from music reviews and articles written about Griffes during his lifetime in hopes that the reader will feel the immediacy of the highs and lows of Griffes's struggle for recognition and acceptance, and will get a flavor of the prevailing view of American music during that time.

Anyone interested in Griffes is indebted to Edward Maisel's biography of the composer, first published in 1943 and reissued in 1984 in commemoration of the composer's centenary. During the latter part of Griffes's life and in the years up to 1943, several articles discussing various aspects of Griffes and his music had appeared, but Maisel's work was the first full-length biography and for almost half a century remained the only one available. The text of the 1984 revision is basically the same as that of the 1943 edition (with some minor corrections), but Maisel added substantial source notes, a new introduction, and a list of works. Maisel's biography is a staple of the literature on Griffes. Filled with detail, it scrutinizes Griffes's interaction with friends and associates, both professional and personal, and explores for the first time his homosexuality (the 1984 source notes are especially useful in this regard). With the exception of a chapter devoted to the Piano Sonata, however, there is little analysis of Griffes's musical style.

Why another biography of Griffes? After so long a time, there is certainly room for a reevaluation, a "new look," if you will. I approach the subject from the vantage point of a trained musician with a lifetime of study of Griffes—his music, his life, and his times. Over the years I have collected new material and kept abreast of Griffes publications, performances, and recordings. Although no startling revelations have come to light, a large body of Griffes literature is now available. My biography, the first new full-length study in almost fifty years, brings past and current Griffes research up to date. My investigations and publications have been undertaken with the desire to provide a foundation for further Griffes scholarship and to stimulate performance of Griffes's music. Included in this biography, for example, are a comprehensive works list identifying media, poets, dates of origin, publications, and first performances; a works chronology to provide a quick overview of Griffes's compositional activities; and a complete discography (up-to-date as of July 1992) arranged by composition. I have also included much discussion of Griffes's music and devote a chapter to an overview and analysis of his musical style. What I have sought in this book is to present a new perspective of Griffes—an objective, exhaustively researched, and fully documented portrait of the life and career of this remarkable American composer.

Many people have assisted me in the preparation of this book. My deep appreciation goes to Fay D. Rose, whose genealogical fact-finding, cataloging, and charting forms the basis for most of the information on the Griffes family history, and whose sense of humor and encouragement were invaluable; to Vincent Picerno, State University of New York College at Cortland, retired, and Robert Carrol Smith, Indiana State University, for reading the entire manuscript and offering valuable and incisive comments and corrections; to Marjorie Griffes Harper, Charles ("Bud") and Janet Griffes, Bill and Helen Roake, for providing photographs, identifications, memories, and genealogical information; to Edward Maisel for providing me with copies of Griffes's letters to Gottfried Galston and for verifying certain dates and other information contained in Griffes material once in his possession and now in the possession of Professor David A. Reed of Muhlenberg College; to noted pianist Joseph Bloch for sharing with me his expertise on all matters musical; and to Natalie Burfoot Billing and Gary Burfoot for providing previously unknown information about Emil Joël and his family and photographs of the Joël family.

Thanks are due to several State University of New York College at Cortland colleagues who provided me with assistance and advice: Lauren Stiles and the staff of the Memorial Library; Stephen B. Wilson for making corrections and suggestions to the final chapter; Victoria Stiles for assistance on many German questions; Gerald Surette for helping verify Consumer Price Index information; James Palmer for directing me to sources about the American theater; and Deborah Yacavone for secretarial support during all stages of this project.

For their help in searching out and verifying people, places, dates, and other facts of all kinds, I wish to thank Richard Jackson and the staff of the New York Public Library for the Performing Arts; Mark Woodhouse, Gannett-Tripp Library at Elmira College; JoAnne E. Barry, the Philadelphia Orchestra Association; the staff of the Library of Congress; Lee Vial at the Historical Society of the Tarrytowns, Inc.; and Timothy Decker, formerly Chemung County Historical Society.

Thanks also to Fredrick Smith, Harvey Stevenson, and W. Houston Kenyon, Jr., former Hackley students, for their memories of Griffes; to Headmaster Peter Gibbon, Hackley School, and Beth Eggar, formerly of the Hackley School, for information on Griffes's tenure there; to Robert D. Swisher, a discography wizard who provided me with numerous items and information for the Griffes discography; to Gunhilde Lischke for assistance in the translation of Griffes's German diary entries and German letters; to Eugene Griffes, Lois Kortering, Shirley B. Goerlich, the Huntington Historical Society for genealogical information; and to New York State/United University Professions Professional Development and Quality of Working Life for a travel grant that aided my research during the midphase of the book.

Finally, I want to express my deep gratitude to the late Martin Williams of the Smithsonian Institution Press for his patience and support during the early stages of the project; to Aaron Appelstein for the great care and wisdom he brought to the editing of this book; and to Duke Johns, Linda McKnight, and the staff at the Smithsonian Institution Press for their expertise.

Acknowledgments

The author wishes to thank G. Schirmer, Inc., and Henmar Press Inc. for permission to excerpt the following copyrighted music.

G. SCHIRMER, INC.

"Symphony in Yellow," copyright 1915 by G. Schirmer, Inc. Copyright renewal assigned 1943 to G. Schirmer, Inc. Used with permission. All rights reserved.

"Tears," copyright 1917 by G. Schirmer, Inc. Copyright renewal assigned 1945 to G. Schirmer, Inc. Used with permission. All rights reserved.

"Phantoms," copyright 1918 by G. Schirmer, Inc. Copyright renewal assigned 1945 to G. Schirmer, Inc. Used with permission. All rights reserved.

"Waikiki," copyright 1918 by G. Schirmer, Inc. Copyright renewal assigned 1945 to G. Schirmer, Inc. Used with permission. All rights reserved.

The author also wishes to thank the Gannett-Tripp Library, Elmira College, and Natalie Burfoot Billing for permission to reproduce photographs so identified in the captions. All other photographs are from the author's collection.

1

Birth in Late Nineteenth-Century Elmira

For most residents of Elmira, New York, 17 September 1884 was just an ordinary day on Main Street. Not so, however, for Wilber Gideon Griffes and his wife, Clara, who celebrated that day not only their eleventh wedding anniversary but the birth of their son Charles Tomlinson Griffes. Charles was the third of five Griffes children. The couple had had two daughters: Katharine, born in 1874, and Florence, born in 1880. A third daughter, Alice Marguerite, would be born in 1886, and a second son, Arthur, in 1892.

Experiences in several cities played a significant part in shaping Charles Griffes's life and career: Elmira, the city of his birth, his youth, and his first musical training; Berlin, where he studied piano, theory, and composition from 1903 to 1907; Tarrytown, New York, where he taught at the Hackley School from 1907 until his death in 1920; and New York City, where he spent every spare minute between 1907 and 1920 promoting his music and enjoying the rich cultural life and freedom that the city offered. Several premieres of Griffes's music took place in New York. But perhaps the most important premiere of all—that of *The Pleasure-Dome of Kubla Khan* on 28 November 1919—occurred not in New York but in Boston. That performance by the Boston Symphony Orchestra, conducted by Pierre Monteux, and the Carnegie Hall performances that followed in December drew rave reviews placing Griffes in the top echelon of young American composers. His death less than five months later, was a cruel twist of fate that diminished American music. One more city must be mentioned to complete Griffes's story—the city where he lies buried, Bloomfield, New Jersey. There, in the Bloomfield Cemetery, his final resting place is marked by an unpretentious tombstone that reads simply, "Charles Tomlinson Griffes 1884–1920."

Griffes's hometown, Elmira, was a modest urban center. Its population had grown from about 4,000 in 1828 to 12,000 in 1864 to about 31,000 in 1890, just six years after Griffes's birth. By 1905, a year before the Griffes family left Elmira, the population of Elmira had more or less peaked at nearly 35,000. Although its motto had been "50,000 in 1910!" Elmira never reached such heights. Its population in 1988 was just over 35,000.[1]

During the Civil War, Elmira served first as a military depot, then, because of its excellent transportation network, as a draft rendezvous. On 6 July 1864 the infamous Elmira Prison Camp officially opened. During its one-year existence, the camp quartered 12,123 Confederate prisoners, 2,963 of whom died. Griffes's mother, Clara, remembered how as a child of ten, she walked by the prison camp and watched the soldiers through the fence.[2]

Elmira could not have prospered had it not enjoyed excellent transportation facilities. The Chemung Canal, connecting Elmira and Watkins Glen on Seneca Lake to the north, a distance of twenty-three miles, began operation in October 1833 and reached its peak of tonnage in 1854, the year Griffes's mother, Clara, was born in Elmira, and just when railroads were beginning to grow in importance.[3] The Erie Railroad, for example, began serving Elmira in

1849, and by 1867 as many as 30–40 freight and passenger trains stopped in Elmira every day. By the 1890s 2,500 Elmirans worked for the Erie.[4] The smaller Delaware, Lackawanna & Western Railroad opened for business in Elmira on 21 April 1882, just two years before Griffes was born. In August 1903 Griffes took this smaller railroad on the first leg of a journey that would take him to Berlin, Germany, where he would live and study for four years.[5]

Transportation within Elmira proliferated and improved as the village grew into a city. A horse-drawn trolley system had been established in Elmira in 1871 and was electrified in the 1890s.[6] Marguerite Griffes fondly remembered the trolley parties that were popular when the Griffes children were growing up.

> We lived about a block from one of the streetcar railroads. Crowds of people would get together and hire a trolley and decorate it with colored lights. . . . They'd go all over the city, bells ringing, people singing, and ice cream and cake served right on the trolley. . . . Someone would say, "Trolley party," and we'd all run to the corner to see the trolley go by.[7]

The first wooden sidewalks appeared in 1885, the year after Griffes's birth. The main business streets in Elmira were paved with brick or stone by 1894, and Elmira got its first asphalt paved street two years later in 1896. The first automobile appeared in Elmira in 1899, and the Griffes family all rushed out to see it.[8]

America, especially in the years following the Civil War, was gradually changing from a rural to an urban society. Besides the increased ease in moving goods and people from place to place, this change brought about an improvement in the quality of education, a benefit enjoyed by Charles and the other Griffes children in Elmira. At the time of Charles's birth in 1884, Elmira boasted several excellent private, parochial, and public schools, including Elmira Female College, which had opened in 1855, the first woman's college in the United States to grant degrees of full

academic standing equal to those given men.[9] Charles attended
the No. 2 School (built in 1869) from about 1891 to 1899.[10] The
school, located at West Second and Davis streets, "on a beautiful,
dry and airy lot" not far from the Griffes home at 422 West First
Street (the family having moved from Charles's birthplace at 128
North Main in 1888), was one of several numbered elementary
schools in Elmira covering grades 1–8.[11] Elmira's only public high
school (until 1924) was the Elmira Free Academy, called affec-
tionately "EFA" by all who went there.[12]

Established as the Elmira Academy in 1836 and incorporated
four years later, the Elmira Free Academy began as a private
institution serving a paying clientele.[13] By the mid-nineteenth
century, such institutions came under increasing pressure to "go
public" so that everyone, not just the wealthy, could enjoy the
benefits of a secondary education. The Elmira Academy followed
the national pattern.[14] In 1859, with the establishment of a board
of education, the Elmira Academy became the Elmira Free Academy, offering free public education to "all those who could use
it."[15] The responsibility for education now belonged to the tax-
payer. This would prove to be an important development for
Charles Griffes, because it is doubtful whether his parents could
have afforded to send him to a private high school.

When Charles attended Elmira Free Academy, it was located
at East Clinton, Lake, and William streets, about ten blocks from
the family home at 422 West First Street.[16] The Griffes children
usually walked the distance, although they could have taken the
streetcar if necessary.[17] Among the subjects Charles studied were
English and English reading (literature), German, French, Latin,
Virgil, psychology, zoology, botany, algebra, geometry, English history, and New York history.[18] Elmira Free Academy served the
Griffes family well. Charles's Uncle Charlie graduated in 1878,
Katharine in 1893, Florence in 1899(?), Charles in 1903, and Marguerite in 1905.[19]

The growth of colleges and universities in the United States from the post–Civil War period to the turn of the century was impressive. Between 1870 and 1905 the number of such institutions rose from 536 to nearly 1,000.[20] Among the best of these institutions was Elmira Female College, known as Elmira College from 1890.[21]

Elmira College played an important role in the lives of the Griffes family. Griffes's mother, Clara, enrolled there during the academic year 1869–70 in the classical academic program (preparatory to the regular collegiate course). She was just fifteen. Clara continued the classical academic program during 1870–71, but the following year, her last at the college, she switched to the English preparatory program, for students who had not completed algebra and "whose parents desired them to omit the study of Latin."[22] Clara's cousins Fannie and Louie (not Louise) Rice and Ella Birdsall attended the college in the 1870s.[23] All three of Charles's sisters also matriculated there. Katharine graduated from the School of Music in 1898, Florence received her bachelor of arts degree in 1902, and Marguerite was a special (nondegree) student during the academic year 1905–6.[24]

But most important to Charles T. Griffes was the arrival at the college of Mary Selena (also spelled Selina) Broughton, who joined the faculty as a teacher of piano during the 1891–92 academic year. Miss Broughton was born in Picton, New Zealand, in 1862 of English ancestry.[25] Her parents, Lieutenant Brian Sneyd Herbert Broughton and Selina Downes, died when she was a child, and a governess in the home of relatives in Auckland, New Zealand, directed her early education. She was eventually sent to Ambleside, Grasmere, England, to live with her grandfather, Dr. Briggs. From there she went to Berlin, where she studied piano with Karl Klindworth, a pupil of Franz Liszt. Klindworth recommended Miss Broughton for a position as piano teacher in the School of Music at Elmira College, and when offered the position

"Professor of Piano Playing," she accepted.[26] Miss Broughton's title and duties changed as she climbed the academic ladder. For example, in 1894–95 she taught harmony as well as piano; in 1903–4 her duties included teaching music history; and in 1904–5 she became head of the piano department.[27] From the academic year 1917–18 until her death, she was listed as professor of Spanish and was no longer affiliated with the School of Music.[28] Miss Broughton also earned bachelor of music and master of arts degrees from Elmira College in 1905 and 1914, respectively.[29]

Many Elmirans considered Miss Broughton somewhat eccentric. Among themselves, the Elmira College girls sometimes called her "horseface," in that typically student way that implies no disrespect but that gives the student a feeling of affectionate familiarity with the teacher, almost always unbeknownst to the teacher.[30] Miss Broughton could be brusque and demanding, as demonstrated by a story told through the years in the Griffes family of how at the dinner table she would demand to know, "Is there any reason why I can't have some bread?"[31] But she was warmhearted and "a good sport." Twelve-year-old Arthur Griffes once invited Miss Broughton to accompany him on the train from Elmira to Corning with his canoe and to float back down to Elmira on the Chemung River with him. She said she would love to go with him. She did, and they had a wonderful time.[32]

Charles's oldest sister, Katharine, studied piano with Miss Broughton at Elmira College. After her graduation in 1898, Katharine joined the faculty of the School of Music as a piano teacher and taught there for three years before she left to marry Stephen A. Roake in June 1901.[33] Katharine was a fine pianist and was Charles's first teacher. According to family lore, Katharine first introduced her brother to the finer points of piano playing about 1894 when he was ten—Katharine's first year at Elmira College.[34] In about 1899, when Charles was fifteen, he began to study with Miss Broughton herself.[35] Miss Broughton immediately recognized the rarity of Griffes's raw talent, but to her eternal credit she wasn't "dazzled" by the young Griffes. She could have crippled him with indiscriminate praise, but as an experienced musician-teacher, she knew when to encourage and when to discourage, when to give praise and when to withhold it—traits she herself would later admire in Griffes's first piano teacher in Berlin, Ernst Jedliczka.

From the beginning Charles was interested in composition as well as piano performance, and his goal was to become an "all-round musician."[36] About the time he first began to study with Miss Broughton, Charles wrote his first compositions (not surprisingly for piano), and he appropriately dedicated these pieces to Miss Broughton: Six Variations in B-flat Major, which Griffes numbered "Opus 2" and dated 1898; Four Preludes, which he numbered "Opus 40" (a flight of fancy?) and dated 1899–1900; and a Mazurka, undated but undoubtedly from the same period.[37]

The careful and thorough musical training Griffes received from Miss Broughton from about 1899 to 1903 provided the foundation for his distinguished musical career. His progress under this remarkable woman in those four short years must have been startling—so much so that when he graduated from high school in 1903 and had to make a career choice, Miss Broughton encouraged him to study in Berlin and was even willing to help underwrite much of the cost. Had she not felt that Charles was ready and that he had the talent to succeed, she would surely have suggested he continue with her until he *was* ready, or she would have bluntly told him to choose another career.

Miss Broughton did not restrict her interest in the young Griffes to music. She also corrected his grammar, advised him on his manners and his dress, and nurtured his love of literature and art. She was a powerful mentor and must have seemed to the teenage Griffes a most sophisticated woman indeed, unlike any he had ever known. In fact, the entire Griffes family admired Miss

Broughton and, except for young Arthur, was somewhat in awe of her as, apparently, were a good many Elmirans. She was, after all, from another country, keenly intelligent, highly educated, and widely traveled. That Miss Broughton was unmarried and had no family of her own strengthened the bond between her and the Griffes family. She was a frequent guest at their home for dinner and for family outings. When Charles was in Germany studying music, Miss Broughton went to the Griffes home every Sunday to share his latest letter and have a piece of chocolate cake (her favorite) and a glass of milk.[38] Both the Griffeses and Miss Broughton prized the enjoyment and pleasure they derived from these shared moments.

Charles Griffes, the "eternal self-improver," gratefully accepted Miss Broughton's suggestions, musical and otherwise.[39] With youthful fervor he set out to rid himself of provincialism and naïveté. He wrote to her from Berlin: "My language must be very bad indeed to occasion five pages of lecturing. However, I am very glad to have it. . . . I think 'beastly' is a very pretty word but suppose I must drop it if it isn't good. I shall be very much obliged to you if you will tell me of any other 'provincial' expressions which I may happen to use at any time."[40]

As Charles grew and matured as a person and as a musician, especially after his return from Germany, the student-teacher relationship of the early years ripened into a lifelong friendship between peers, with respect and admiration on both sides. Interestingly, though, Griffes always addressed her as Miss Broughton, and she referred to him as Charles or Charlie.[41] Perhaps this was due to the difference in their ages—Miss Broughton was just eight years younger than Griffes's mother. Shortly after Griffes's death in 1920, Miss Broughton wrote to Clara Griffes:

> When I got your letter it came to me again that I should never
> see Charlie's most individual writing again. It used to be some-

thing to look forward to and there was always something to make me proud and glad. It is heart rending the way people forget but I really think they have remembered Charlie longer than most. In a few years we shall all be forgotten[.][42]

Miss Broughton died of valvular heart disease at Gleason's Health Resort overlooking the valley of Elmira, on 7 June 1922, just two years after the death of her beloved pupil.[43] She is buried in Woodlawn Cemetery in Elmira. Her tombstone reads, "Selina Mary Broughton, born in Picton, N.Z., 1862–1922, A Professor in Elmira College, 1892–1922."

Elmira never lacked for culture and entertainment. The Opera House, Elmira's first "real" theater, opened on 17 December 1867 and over the years presented such works as *Our American Cousin* with Laura Keene (1867), *Davy Crockett* with Frank Mayo (1873), Shakespeare's *Julius Caesar* with Edwin Booth (1889), and lectures by such notables as Mark Twain (1869). Remodeled in 1898, the Opera House changed its name to "Lyceum," and for the next several generations until it closed in 1929, the Lyceum presented such entertainment and public luminaries as Lillian Russell, Anna Pavlova, Billie Burke, William Jennings Bryan, Theodore Roosevelt, and many others. Several other theaters operated in Elmira and presented a tantalizing variety of vaudeville, minstrel shows, musicals, lectures, and plays.[44]

Marguerite Griffes described theatrical extravaganzas that occasionally came in from New York or were "got up" in Elmira with local talent. She and Charles both participated in at least two of these homegrown productions as children. Miss Griffes recalled one such event presented in about 1892 in which she and Charles joined forces as blossoms inside a giant water lily. Charles, who was about eight, was chagrined to be consigned beneath a stuffy flower model until it was time to emerge as a blossom.[45] A photograph of a disgruntled Marguerite, taken at the time, reveals that she wasn't too happy about it either.

During Griffes's youth there was a great deal of musical activity in Elmira: numerous glee clubs and choruses; a long succession of bands that performed on summer evenings and at parades; and concerts downtown, in local churches, and at the college. Elmira also had a long tradition of women's clubs devoted to stimulating interest in music and culture.[46] Griffes's first public appearance as a pianist (14 February 1901) took place under the auspices of one such group, the Elmira Woman's Musical Club. The program was typical of the "enlightening" quality expected of such groups and included Griffes's performance of compositions by Carl Maria von Weber and Frédéric Chopin, a performance of Edward MacDowell's "Dervish Vigil," sung by a Mr. Young, and a "Paper on Current Topics," presented by a Miss Beckwith.[47]

The Griffes family owned two pianos: a square Steinway grand given to Clara by her father, Solomon, when she was about fourteen (possibly earlier), and Katharine's Chickering grand.[48] Clara, Wilber, Katharine, Florence, and Charles could all play by ear and provided music for a variety of neighborhood parties and dances. Charles could play any piece after hearing it once. He also knew when other pianists were faking and wouldn't tolerate that even to be polite. After one of his fellow students had played some familiar piece at an Elmira Free Academy program, a woman turned to Charles and said, "Didn't he play that beautifully?" Charles replied, "No, he left out eight bars."[49] Such comments did not endear him to his peers.

Katharine and Charles not only could play by ear but were, of course, "expert" pianists as well. Charles, however, was never comfortable playing "serious" music at informal gatherings. He never wanted to go any place where a piano was available because he knew that the host and hostess would ask him to play. If he did consent to play and people talked, he would never play for them again.[50] He wrote in his diary after one such invitation:

> In the evening Marguerite and I went over to the Briggs' house.
> . . . I wish such people would have the taste not to beg me to
> play. One can never go anyplace without [having] to play
> against ones [sic] will on pianos that are frightfully out of tune
> and before people who have no idea of music and don't know
> good from bad playing. It is an insult! Only to please Mar-
> guerite I played the "Liebestraum."[51]

Charles, Katharine, and Florence shared an interest in pho-
tography and developed their own "blueprints" at home in Elmira
in the bathroom.[52] After he returned from Germany, Griffes often
took pictures of the New Jersey countryside, where his sister
Florence was living; scenes around Hackley School, where he was
teaching; and scenes in New York City. Marguerite Griffes
recalled:

> He liked pictures of trees and didn't care about having any
> people in his pictures. I remember one time at my sister Flor-
> ence's [in Ridgewood] . . . there were a lot of fields and daisies
> and things, and Charlie wanted to take a picture of the fields.
> And he thought it would be better if he had a *figure*. So I got
> into his picture, quite a long ways off, just a little figure in the
> picture. He thought it would be graceful if there was somebody
> standing among the daisies.[53]

Griffes also created many fine etchings, drawings, and delicate
water colors, generally, as in his photographs (except for candid
shots), scenes of nature or buildings—rarely of people.

In the post-Elmira and post-Berlin years, Griffes also became
a movie fan. He often went to the cinema in New York and, in
fact, the 1919 premiere of his *The White Peacock* for dancer and

orchestra took place at a New York movie house, the Rivoli, on a program that featured the full-length silent film *The Secret Service*.[54] Griffes once attended a movie at the Rialto in New York "where they had 3 or 4 minutes of the weirdest stuff I ever experienced. The pictures were of the munitions pier explosion and the director had arranged as accompaniment a combination of full orchestra, organ whistles, etc., which was so strangely thrilling that it made my hair stand on end."[55] No doubt Griffes would have attended the movies in Elmira, but the city's first all-movie theater, the Dreamland, did not open until 1905, by which time Griffes was already in Berlin.[56] His mother and grandmother probably would have frowned upon this infant, "vulgar" medium of entertainment anyway, as did many respectable people at the turn of the century.

The Griffes family did not often take advantage of the plays, lectures, theatrical events, and concerts in Elmira because they could not afford to do so except on special occasions. Even so, Charles tried to take in as many musical events as he could, sometimes accompanied by Howard Conant, principal of Elmira Free Academy.[57] While studying in Berlin and later on his trips to New York, Charles seemed to be making up for lost time by constantly attending the opera, theater, concerts, dance, lectures, and circus and by visiting museums, zoos, and parks.

Although the Griffes family could not afford to attend entertainment events regularly, they did what most people in their situation did—entertained themselves. The family would gather around the piano in the evenings and on weekend afternoons or invite the neighbors in for a party. Everyone would dance while one or another of the Griffes family played popular music of the day. "We didn't spend much money, you know. When we had a party we didn't always have refreshments. We just had a good time. Somebody would say, 'let's have the neighbors in tonight,' and we'd go and fetch them."[58] The Griffes children also presented "dress up" plays and masquerades with their friends, and they enjoyed family picnics for which Wilber Griffes would make the sandwiches and drinks. Since they did not own a car, the Griffes family took no long trips.[59] But on every holiday they would have a picnic at home, walk the four blocks to Wisner Park, or take the trolley out to Eldridge Park, their lunch packed in Arthur's old wicker baby carriage. Miss Griffes fondly recalled, "I can still see my father filling the milk bottles with coffee."[60] During one picnic in their backyard, Wilber built a fire in a large washtub that served as a barbecue pit. The flames shot into the air, and a little neighbor boy came running over in a panic, shouting, "The flames are rising higher and higher!" Everyone was greatly amused by the incident, and years later members of the Griffes family would greet each other with, "The flames are rising higher and higher!"[61]

As was common in those days, even families of relatively moderate means were able to afford some domestic help.[62] The Griffeses were no exception. Marguerite Griffes recalled: "Everybody generally had their washing done at home. And they'd have a colored girl come and do the work. . . . Sometimes she wouldn't come, and my father would have to go down to the railroad area to hunt her up."[63] The Griffes women did the ironing and other household chores. Wilber used to pitch in and do the dishes, but Charles never did. In later years, when he visited his mother and Marguerite in New Jersey, he did consent to wipe dishes but insisted that the kitchen curtain be drawn so no one would see him.[64]

Charles, more so than the other Griffes children, seemed to feel the lack of money and once remarked that people should not have children if they couldn't afford to give them all the extras.[65] He seemed especially prone to feelings of "deprivation" when he was in Germany studying. He would have liked to have traveled more extensively—to Paris, for example, a city he was never able to visit.[66] Marguerite Griffes remarked: "We never felt we didn't have everything. We had everything we needed to wear, we had good meals, very good meals."[67] Clara was an excellent cook; she also sewed beautifully and made most of the children's clothes.[68]

Wilber and Clara were sensitive to Charles's teenage need for privacy and had a room built for him over the kitchen.[69] The Griffeses never owned their own home, but apparently their landlord, Daniel Pugh, had no objection to the construction.[70] To help furnish the room, Charles was given his late Grandfather Solomon Tomlinson's desk—the icing on the cake of his own private domain, a "hide-a-way" he treasured.[71]

Theirs was a close-knit, happy family, infused with warmth and laughter. Money was not the key to their happiness. In 1920 when Charles was dying and his sisters and mother rallied by his bedside, he came to appreciate that family is far more important than money. He remarked to Marguerite how amazed he was that they were all with him, and she pointed out, "Well, that's what families are for." Charles replied, "Yes, but I never knew that before."[72]

Ancestry

Charles Tomlinson Griffes was born into a solid, hard-working Protestant family. His ancestry can be traced back on his father's side to Richard Pengriffin (Griffith), born in Wales about 1465 (a soldier of Henry VII, present at Bosworth Field in 1485), and on his mother's side to the Reverend William Tomlinson, born in England about 1775, and the Reverend John Crandall, born in England, near the Welsh border, in 1612 (came to America in 1634).[1] Recorded variously as Griffin, Griffith, Griffiths, Griffis, Griffen, Griffing, and so on, the Griffes name originated from "Griffith," a variant of "Griffin," which meant "the son of 'Griffin' or 'Griffith,'" the names of many Welsh princes. According to family lore, one of the Griffith ancestors (Charles's great-great-grandfather William) pronounced *th* as *s,* and, not wanting to be embarrassed when his name was copied down by the county clerk, allowed his name to be spelled "Griffis."[2] Although the lisp usually works the other way around, it is a charming story. Eventually, "Griffes" became the spelling for the line that led to Charles T. Griffes.

Griffes's maternal grandmother, Delinda Perry Rice Tomlinson, was the daughter of John Rice and Margaret Crandall. John Rice was born in Pomfret, Windham County, Connecticut, in 1782 and died in Middlefield, Otsego County, New York, in 1833. His wife, Margaret Crandall, was born in Pittstown, Rensselaer County, New York, in 1789 and died in Elmira, New York, in 1868.[3] John Rice was one of six children born to Daniel and Zeruiah Rice. Daniel's birth date is unknown, but he died in Middlefield on 27 March 1827.[4] All we know about Daniel's wife, Zeruiah, is her first name and that she died on 9 April 1834. Margaret Crandall was one of sixteen children born to John Crandall and Margaret O'Brien. John Crandall was born in Chatham, Columbia County, New York, in 1765; his date and place of death are unknown. Margaret O'Brien was born in Swansey, Massachusetts, in 1769. She died in 1842 and is buried in the Middlefield Cemetery. John Crandall and Margaret O'Brien, the composer's great-great-grandparents, were married on 9 March 1783 when they were not quite eighteen and fourteen years old, respectively.[5]

Delinda's parents (and Griffes's great-grandparents), John Rice and Margaret Crandall, were married on 3 March 1814.[6] They had nine children, all born in Middlefield: Amanda (1814–1904), Selina (1817–44), Melissa (1819–1910), Adrian (1822–55), Daniel Owen (1824–1917), Milo Smith (January 1826–September 1826), Unity (1827–?), Delinda Perry (26 April 1832–1 March 1915), and Francis (January 1834–June 1834). When John Rice died on 6 September 1833, Margaret was pregnant with their ninth child, Francis. Delinda was just over a year old.[7]

Margaret Crandall Rice was remarried about 1846 to Elisha Lathrop (1774–1865) of Unadilla, New York (a small village about forty miles southwest of Middlefield), and lived there until the death of Mr. Lathrop on 7 February 1865 at the age of ninety.[8] Elisha Lathrop was fifteen years older than Margaret and had been married before, to Mary (Polly) Lathrop, who died in 1845. He had a large, grown family of his own.[9] Given that Margaret was about fifty-seven and Elisha about seventy-two when they married, they could hardly have had children of their own. This was more likely a marriage of convenience. Still, they were married almost twenty years, and Lathrop provided generously for Margaret in his will, bequeathing her rents, use and profits of the fifty-acre home lot on which he and Margaret resided, one horse ("providing there is one belonging to my estate at my decease"), two cows, ten sheep, all the farming tools and utensils for use during the term of her natural life, and all the furniture, beds, bedding, clothing, and other property Margaret owned when she and Elisha married. The will directed that upon Margaret's decease everything would go to Lathrop's children and grandchildren.[10] Margaret Crandall Rice Lathrop died in 1868 and is buried in her son Daniel's plot in Elmira's Woodlawn Cemetery.[11]

Apparently, sometime after the death of her father, John Rice, in 1833, Delinda went to live with her older sister Melissa ("Lissy").[12] Delinda may have attended a Miss Rockwell's Academy in Unadilla before leaving for Elmira as a teenager, to visit or live with her brother Daniel Owen Rice, who had himself arrived in Elmira in 1847, and who operated a grocery store on the corner of Railroad Avenue and East Church Street.[13]

In Elmira, Delinda eventually met a young lawyer, Solomon Byron Tomlinson, who declared when he first saw her, "She is the prettiest, smartest girl in Elmira and I'm going to marry her."[14] However, before that happened, Delinda apparently attended Miss Clarissa Thurston's Elmira Seminary (at age sixteen or seventeen?).[15]

"For seventeen years, from 1847 to 1864, Miss Clarissa Thurston's Elmira Seminary or Elmira Ladies' Seminary educated the daughters of Elmira's finest families and many other young ladies from towns and cities in New York and other states."[16] The purpose of Miss Thurston's school was "to furnish young ladies with an opportunity to acquire a thorough scientific education, and at the same time to aid them in the formation of such a character as shall fit them for the active duties of life."[17] The 1851 catalog stated: "The Bible is a text-book for all classes, and daily instructions are drawn from its sacred pages. . . . Much general instruction is given, and such as is calculated to impart lessons of practical wisdom, to awaken thought and elevate the mind, to produce refinement of manners and firmness of character."[18] For a short time before she married, Delinda apparently ran a small private school for girls, and she desperately wanted to continue teaching and not get married— ever. But getting married was the thing to do, besides which, as Lissy pointed out to her, Solomon was an up-and-coming lawyer and a "prize catch." Delinda always claimed that it was Melissa who "egged her on" to marry Solomon and never quite forgave her.[19]

Griffes's grandfather, Solomon Byron Tomlinson, was born at Anderson, Cheshire, England, on 28 March 1828.[20] Solomon's father, grandfather, and three of his uncles were all Methodist ministers. Charles Griffes's great-great-grandfather, the Reverend William Tomlinson (b. ca. 1775), and William's wife, née Mary Nixon (b. ca. 1779), were natives of Cheshire. The date and place of their deaths is unknown. William and Mary had six children (all born in Cheshire): James (b. ca. 1801), John (b. ca. 1803), Thomas (Solomon's father, ca. 1805–68), William, Jr. (b. ca. 1807), Margaret (b. ca. 1809), and Rebecca (b. ca. 1811).[21]

Solomon's father, the Reverend Thomas Tomlinson, married Mary Donald (b. 1803 in Oldham, Lancaster, England; d. 1890 in Forks Township, Pennsylvania) in 1824. Thomas Tomlinson and Mary Donald had six children: Esther (b. 1825), Sarah (b. ca. 1827), Hepzibah (b. ca. 1829), Solomon (1828–87), Jabez (b. ca. 1833), and Joseph (b. ca. 1835). The entire family emigrated to America in 1843 when Solomon was about fourteen.[22]

Solomon settled in Elmira, where he studied law in the office of Judge E. P. Brooks, later becoming his partner. He also practiced law as a partner with Rastus Ranson, later with E. P. Hart, and, finally, with Uriah S. Lowe.[23] Solomon served as district attorney from 1856 to 1859, county clerk from 1861 to 1864, and alderman of Ward 2 in Elmira from 1867 to 1872 and again from 1874 to 1876.[24] He died in Elmira on 18 June 1887 of endocarditis-edema of the lungs, after an illness of five months. His obituary characterized him as an "able lawyer and a leading citizen."[25]

Solomon and Delinda were married in Elmira on 7 September 1853.[26] They had two children: Clara Louise (Charles Griffes's mother), born in Elmira on 3 July 1854, and Charles Henry, born in Elmira on 20 May 1858.[27] One of the joys of Delinda's married life was teaching Bible class at the Baptist church; the church was everything to her, and she had strong prejudices against smoking, drinking, playing cards, and dancing. In fact, years later she used to say, "When I first saw this young man [Solomon] as he came across the street, he threw away the cigar he had been smoking, and I should have known [about him] right then!"[28]

Solomon and Delinda were the least suited couple imaginable; they disagreed on almost everything.[29] Whereas Solomon loved jewelry, fancy dress balls, social gatherings of all kinds, and elegant clothes (he wore white suits that had to be ironed perfectly or he would toss them aside and insist that they be redone), Delinda found such things frivolous and would not accept gifts of jewelry and clothes from her husband, especially since there were "so many people going hungry."[30] Delinda's attitude did not change with age. Marguerite Griffes recalled with amusement: "Uncle Charlie was always wanting my grandmother to visit him [in Albany]. So Grandmother would write to him and say, 'I'd like to come and visit you for a couple of weeks.' And he'd say, 'I'm glad you're coming. Buy yourself a new dress.' And that was the end of it. She would always say, 'I already have a dress. Why should I buy another one?'"[31] Since Delinda refused to accept gifts from Solomon, he often gave them to his daughter, Clara

Louise. One of Clara's most cherished gifts was the square Steinway piano Solomon bought her when she was a girl. She kept it all during her married life.

Over the years Solomon carried out many real estate transactions on his own behalf (as opposed to for his clients).[32] Once, without consulting Delinda, he bought a house he thought would be nice for the family. Delinda liked neither the house nor the neighborhood and refused to move in.[33] Solomon changed law partners and residences several times over the years, indicating a restless spirit and no doubt reflecting some measure of the domestic instability of his marriage to Delinda. The Griffes family remembered him with fondness but also as something of a spendthrift.[34]

Griffes's grandmother Delinda was a victim of her time. She did not fit the mold of "True Womanhood" as expressed in contemporaneous women's magazines or as defined from the pulpit and in nineteenth-century religious literature. Of the four virtues by which every woman was judged—piety, purity, submissiveness, and domesticity—the latter two did not interest Delinda.[35] The lowliest man could vote and hold office, but women were fettered by taboos of every sort.[36] Delinda never realized her dreams and lived under a cloud of regret and disappointment all her life, mourning a past she had never had, before finally slipping into a world of gentle madness.

Delinda began to suffer from what the family called "her spells" shortly after the birth of her second child, Charles Henry. Clara recalled that, when she was a child, she often slept with her mother and held on to her nightgown so she wouldn't get up and wander off.[37] After Solomon died in 1887, Delinda's son-in-law Wilber Griffes, whom Delinda loved as if he were her own son, was the only one who could comfort and calm her.[38] At night she would often wander through the house, haunted by the past and crying, "Why didn't I do this?" "Why did this happen?" Wilber was the one who would gently take her arm, talk to her, calm her, and lead her back to bed. When Wilber died in 1905, Delinda "wasn't well at all,"[39] and it became impossible for Clara to deal with her mother's illness. On 26 July 1906 Delinda was committed to the state hospital in Binghamton, New York, suffering from major depression with melancholia. She remained there until her death on 1 March 1915.[40] Charles rarely spoke of his grandmother. In 1915, two days after her death, he wrote in his diary: "Letter from mother, saying that Grandma passed away at 11.30 Monday night—after all these weary years at rest, as mother says. . . . Too bad the end had to come in such a place."[41]

Delinda and Solomon wanted both their children to have as much education as possible. As a young girl Griffes's mother, Clara, attended the Galatian sisters' Young Ladies Seminary, one of the private, select schools that flourished in Elmira in competition with the public schools from the 1830s to the early 1900s.[42] The Galatian seminary was similar to the female seminary Delinda had apparently attended as a girl. An 1854 Galatian advertisement proclaimed: "The course of instruction embraces all those branches usually taught in Select Schools, while at the same time particular attention is paid to the common English branches. . . . The year commences September 1st, and continues 'forty-four weeks."[43] Tuition and board for the full term was $120. For a small extra charge, students could study music on the piano ($10), drawing ($3), painting in water colors ($5), and painting in oils ($8)—all subjects that interested Clara.[44] A faded Miss Galatian's Select School Certificate dated 21 June 1867 rated Clara a top number 1 ("Worthy of Commendation") for all her academic subjects—arithmetic, geography, spelling, reading, writing, comprehension, and grammar—and for general industry and general amiability. However, she fell to a number 2 rating ("In good standing") for general behavior.[45]

Clara continued her education at Elmira Female College for three years (1869–1872). Besides "regular courses" such as Latin,

English grammar and analysis, arithmetic, and higher arithmetic, she studied music and painting.[46] Clara learned enough piano to be able to play for the Griffes parties years later, and one of her paintings, a little duck eating pea pods, was the source of much teasing from Charles and the other Griffes children because the pea pods were just as large as the duck.[47] Unlike her mother, Clara had no desire to be a teacher, and she thrived as a wife and mother. The match between Wilber Griffes and Clara Tomlinson turned out to be a very successful and happy one.

Clara's brother, Charles Henry ("Uncle Charlie" to all the Griffes children), was educated at No. 2 School and Elmira Free Academy, and then took a collegiate and law course (most likely in Elmira). For a time (1880–82?) he practiced law with his father, Solomon, and lived at the family home with his parents and Clara and Wilber. He finally settled in Albany about 1887 (possibly earlier), where he practiced law until his death in 1917, for most of the time with the firm of R. G. Dunn.[48]

Uncle Charlie never married, perhaps because he felt a strong family obligation to support his mother, Delinda, after his father's death in 1887.[49] His obligations multiplied when Wilber Griffes died in 1905, and from that time on he felt it his responsibility to keep a watchful eye on Clara and her children. Marguerite Griffes recalled, "My uncle did a lot for my mother—helped her a great deal."[50] Always mindful of his sister's and mother's welfare, Charles Tomlinson made out his will on 9 January 1906, leaving Clara his entire estate. At the time of his death in 1917, the estate, including proceeds from the sale of 425 shares of Anaconda Copper and 200 shares of Brooklyn Rapid Transit Company, amounted to nearly $19,000 (comparable in 1990 currency to about $195,000).[51]

When young Charles Griffes declared in 1903 that he wanted to go to Germany to study music and that he intended to make music his career, Uncle Charlie strongly opposed the idea. He thought Charles should go to college (and would have helped pay his way) because, as he said, "No one can make a decent living in music."[52] He felt so strongly about the subject that, even knowing that Wilber and Clara could not afford to help their son financially, he contributed only occasionally to Charles's studies abroad.[53] When Charles returned to the United States in 1907 after his four years of study in Berlin and immediately landed a job as director of music at the Hackley School, Uncle Charlie had to admit that maybe a musician could earn a living after all.[54]

Uncle Charlie and Charles did not see too much of each other because they were pursuing their own careers in cities more than 150 miles apart. But, since Uncle Charlie had always spent Christmas and Thanksgiving in Elmira with his mother and the Griffeses, and since both he and Charles joined Clara in New Jersey for all the major holidays after 1906, they did see enough of each other to become friends; although, as Marguerite said, not awfully good friends.[55] A shared sense of humor seemed to draw them together. "Uncle Charlie was a great kidder, and he was always kidding Charlie and they had good times when they *were* together. Charlie visited him [in Albany] once or twice, I think."[56]

Charles Tomlinson's death occurred suddenly and unexpectedly (after a three-day illness) in Albany on 10 January 1917. Cause of death was acute endocarditis, contributory cause arteriosclerosis.[57] He was buried in the Tomlinson family plot in Elmira's Woodlawn Cemetery. "Mr. Tomlinson was unmarried and had devoted his life to those whose relation to him placed upon him some responsibility through kinship or friendship. He was a devoted son and brother and a faithful friend."[58]

Turning now to Charles's paternal ancestry—Griffes's great-great-grandfather William Griffes (1733–78) of Huntington, Long Island, married Abiah Gates (1742–?) on 27 January 1756.[59] William and Abiah had eleven children.[60] Their son Nathaniel (1768–1842),

Charles's great-grandfather, married his first cousin Esther Gates (1778–1848). The fifth of their ten offspring was Charles's grandfather Stephen Griffes (1805–50), who married Mary Whitney (1810–77) on 24 March 1832. Stephen and Mary raised seven children, the youngest of whom, Wilber Gideon Griffes, was Charles's father, born in Niskayuna, New York, on 2 February 1847.[61] Two of Stephen's and Mary's children died in childhood—Katharine (1837–41) and Julia Ann (1844–48). When Stephen Griffes died on 22 February 1850, he left his widow, Mary, and five children. The surviving children were Nathaniel (1833–81), William Whitney (1835–1905), James Allen (1839–98), Almira, also known as Myra (1842–77), and Wilber (1847–1905).

Stephen Griffes had inherited "the use and enjoyment" of the family farm in Niskayuna when his father, Nathaniel, died in 1842. Nathaniel, however, had directed that upon Stephen's death one-half of the farm should go to Stephen's oldest son, Nathaniel, the other half divided among the rest of Stephen's children.[62] Stephen Griffes died without a will, and his son Nathaniel was forced to go to court in 1856 in order to take possession of his half of the farm.[63] In 1856 or 1857 Mary Griffes moved to Schenectady, a fairly large city a few miles west of Niskayuna.[64] It may be that William (age twenty-one) and James (age seventeen or eighteen) stayed with their brother Nathaniel and his wife, Mary Consaul Griffes (whom Nathaniel married on 12 October 1853), to help run the farm. Wilber and Almira, the two youngest children, most likely went to Schenectady with their mother. Both William, who married Kate Nichols in 1858, and James, who married Julia Harkness in 1860, also eventually went to Schenectady.[65] In any case, Mary may have decided to make the move to Schenectady to enhance Wilber's educational opportunities.[66]

Wilber wanted very much to go to college, but lack of money ended his formal education after he graduated from high school.[67] For at least one year (1867–68), while living in Schenectady with his mother (at 127 Liberty), Wilber was in business with his brother William as "W. W. Griffes & Bro. Dealers in Pictures, Oval Frames, [Books,] etc."[68]

Wilber moved to Elmira about 1868 and conducted a custom shirt establishment under the firm name of Waldron & Griffes. The "Waldron" of Waldron & Griffes was Wilber's brother-in-law David T. Waldron, who married Almira Griffes on 15 April 1868.[69] The 1868–69 *Gazetteer and Business Directory of Chemung and Schuyler Counties* described Waldron & Griffes as "dealers in gents' furnishing goods and agents for Eliptic Lock Stitch sewing machine, 7 Baldwin."[70] The firm lasted about ten years, located variously at 7 Baldwin, 112 Baldwin, 202 Baldwin, 108 Baldwin, and 135 East Water.[71] The frequent changes in location may reflect some of the competition the business faced. In 1870, for example, Elmira had twenty-two clothiers, and by 1890 that number had increased to forty-eight.[72] Although not all of these clothiers specialized in men's furnishings, competition for business was obviously fierce.

David and Almira had three children—William Boyd Waldron (1869–72), Wilber ("Willie") Waldron (b. 1873), named after his uncle, and Henry ("Harry") Boyd Waldron (b. 1875).[73] Mary Griffes left Schenectady and moved in with her daughter Almira and son-in-law David about 1871. Julia Griffes (1814–90), Wilber's and Almira's maiden aunt, came to live with the Waldron's in about 1875. And Wilber himself lived with David and Almira beginning in 1869 and was still living with them when he married Clara in 1873. However, Wilber and Clara left to move in with Solomon and Delinda Tomlinson about a year after the birth of their daughter Katharine (1874).[74]

Wilber Griffes and Clara Tomlinson were married in Elmira by the Reverend Thomas Tousey on 17 September 1873 at the Tomlinson home at 58 Main Street.[75] Ironically, it was Delinda, forgetting her sister Melissa's interference in *her* own life, who played matchmaker for Clara and Wilber Griffes. As Marguerite Griffes told it, "[My grandmother] always said that she made the marriage between my mother and father, and she always used to say, 'Wilber should have been president of Elmira College.'"[76] The couple's first child, Katharine Clara, was born on 21 October 1874; Florence Beatrice followed some five years later on 5 February 1880. In 1884 the Griffes and Tomlinson families moved to 128 Main Street, where Charles was born on 17 September 1884 and Alice Marguerite on 1 April 1886. Solomon died in 1887, and the family moved once again (1888), this time to 422 West First Street, where Wilber and Clara's last child, Arthur Raynes, was born on 17 April 1892, and where Charles and his three sisters and brother grew up.[77]

The Griffes and Tomlinson families maintained a large extended family, all looking out for one another. On 19 January 1877, at age thirty-five, Almira Griffes Waldron fell victim to a tumor.[78] In a poignant letter written to two-year-old Harry Waldron, Julia Griffes explained the painful circumstances of his mother's death.

> As you were too young to remember anything definite about your own "dear mamma," when God saw fit to take her away from you, I will try and write some particulars that you can read as you grow older. . . . All through her protracted illness, she always had a smile and pleasant word to greet every one that came in her presence. . . . You know she died three days after having a tumor removed from her bowels, that weighed thirty five pounds. . . . On the morning of the operation, altho' she had not slept any all night she came out and sat down to the breakfast table as usual eating but little, but still wore a smiling countenance. After breakfast Uncle Wilber with hand sleigh with a box on, came and she superinted [sic] getting Willie ready and fixed in the sleigh . . . the last she saw her dear boy, or he his mother. . . . Then she and the nurse went into the sitting room till the [nine] doctors began to come. . . . [The

operation, which lasted two hours, took place on the kitchen table.] The next day she asked to see her dear little Harry, but she was so altered he refused to kiss her. The next morn, the doctors let her Mother [Mary Griffes] go in, your dear Grandma, and the next morn, he let me. . . . At noon Uncle Wilber went in, when she inquired after Willie. . . . About noon your Father went into the room. . . . Then asked for her Mother [who comforted], "My dear child, the Lord is able to raise you up yet, but if not, put all your faith in the Saviour." She said, "I do Mother, I do." When I went in her eyes were fixed. . . . She continued talking incoherently and soon ceased to breathe.[79]

This letter is illuminating because it indicates how traumatic Almira's death must have been for everyone. Her courage in facing a primitive operation, agonizing pain, and what she must have known was certain death was remarkable. When Wilber took his nephew Willie home to look after him during the crisis, he must have felt a wave of fear for his own wife, Clara. The letter also illustrates the importance of religious faith in the Griffes family. Almira's death struck without pity, and the family could not have endured without a deep faith in God. Wilber's mother, Mary, had this faith, and Clara's mother, Delinda, had it; in their own quiet way, so did Wilber and Clara. (Wilber had been brought up Dutch Reform, Clara a Baptist.)[80] That faith seems to have been diluted somewhat for the younger generation, however. For example, although Charles was baptized, along with Marguerite, on 30 April 1899 at the First Baptist Church in Elmira, and attended Sunday school as a youngster with the rest of his siblings, he maintained no interest in formal religion as an adult.[81]

Mary Griffes died on 9 April 1877, less than three months after the death of her daughter Almira. After the deaths of his infant son, wife, and mother-in-law, David Waldron lost his taste for the gent's furnishings business. He eventually became a traveling salesman, remarried, and left Elmira for good in about 1886.[82]

After the demise of Waldron & Griffes in 1880, Wilber apparently worked a year on his own before joining the employ of Sidney Fairlee, who had taken over the business. Wilber worked for several years for John Cushing, who took over the business when Fairlee died, and from 1902 until his own death, for E. H. Colburn, who had taken over the business from Cushing.[83] Wilber designed men's shirts, and all his custom-made shirts included a monogram tab that Katharine or Marguerite were often called upon to embroider in red cross-stitch. Marguerite remembered that "most of the time my father probably earned about $25 a week." Not a lordly sum but comparable to about $19,200 in the inflated market of 1990.[84]

Wilber taught Sunday school at the YMCA—which must have pleased his mother-in-law, Delinda—and often brought home less fortunate souls for a square meal and a little family comfort.[85] Among the most interesting of these visitors was Jack Raynes, a young English actor. Marguerite Griffes recalled:

> Everyone liked him. He would go off with his troupe, and they'd wander around until they went broke, and then they'd come back to Elmira. One night he came home about 12 o'clock. He opened the side window and then he sat down at the piano and played "Home, Sweet Home." And the whole family got up—including Grandmother—and welcomed him home. . . . Jack had a cot in the living room, and he came and went.[86]

Jack became "one of the family," and Clara and Wilber named their last child, Arthur Raynes, after him.[87]

Clara and Wilber were well suited to each other and, as Marguerite described it, "calm with themselves and calm with everybody else."[88] Theirs was a most happy marriage. The children were dependent on Clara and used to ask, "Mama, what should I wear?" "Mama, should I wear my raincoat?" "Mama, is it going to snow?" It became an in-family joke, and years later when Jim Aitken, Florence's husband, tipped over his canoe on a family outing, he stood up in the knee-deep water, looked at Clara, and asked, "Mama, what should I do now?"[89] But, although Clara was the dominant parent, as her mother had been before her, Wilber was a strong, calm presence on the scene. For example, when Florence began teaching in New Jersey after her graduation from Elmira College in 1902, she "couldn't stand it" and wrote to Wilber to come and take her home. Wilber, in his typically calm and reasoned manner, told her to wait for a little and "if you don't like it, I'll come and get you." Sure enough, after a few days Florence decided to stick it out.[90]

One day in early November 1905, Wilber came down with what seemed to be a common cold. He had always been a healthy man, so neither he nor anyone in the family took much notice. But complications set in, and, despite constant medical attention, and much to the family's shock and dismay, in three short days Wilber Griffes was dead.[91] His death came on 10 November 1905 as a result of pleurisy complicated with pneumonia (due to cardiac weakness).[92] He was fifty-eight years old. Clara did not want to worry Charles, who was in Berlin studying and who obviously could not get home. Rather than break the distressing news to her son in a cable, she sent him a long, reassuring letter.

The Griffes children grew up with a strong sense of security, in a home filled with love, warmth, and humor. Their bonds of love were forged early and lasted a lifetime. Yet they rarely demonstrated their love overtly. Marguerite Griffes recalled how as a child she would meet her father at work and walk home with him for lunch. They passed a high hardboard fence along the way, and he always lifted her up so she could see the flowers on the other side. She said wistfully, "Sometimes I used to think it would be nice if he took hold of my hand, but he never did."[93]

Humor was the way the Griffes family most easily expressed their feelings. They all loved to laugh, including Charles, who often "roared" when something struck him funny. With casual acquaintances and strangers, they maintained a certain reserve, but within the family and with their close friends, they were open, friendly, and full of fun. Those who later thought of Charles as aloof simply did not know him.

Personality: A Perspective

A photograph of Charles Griffes taken when he was about six months old shows a healthy, chubby, bright-eyed baby with an appealing smile. From early childhood Charles exhibited an acute awareness of color. Orange was among his favorite colors, and he kept an old dead branch covered with orange fungus in his room at home in Elmira.[1] Later, as an adult, he kept an orange tie on his tie rack, although he didn't wear it often because he thought it was a little too bright.[2] Griffes had a keen, observant eye and liked to express precisely what he saw. For example, he described the following scene in a letter to his mother written on the ocean leg of his trip to Berlin:

> We got up about 3.30 [in Cherbourg harbor] to see the sun-rise and we felt well paid. It was the most beautiful sight! First there was a streak of light pink against the gray, then it grew to a bright rose and then became a sort of orange; the sun really came into view however about 5.30 in the shape of an immense

fiery ball. Outlined against the pink sky was a fort, which only increased the beauty of it all.[3]

Griffes once remarked in a conversation with artist Elmer Garnsey that a beautiful color is lovely in itself quite aside from any part it plays in the design of the picture. Garnsey had just been commissioned to do some paintings for the Customs House in New York City, and Griffes was pleased to note that his statement corresponded exactly to Garnsey's ideas. "He himself puts a great deal of importance on the coloring and has some exquisite colors in his pictures and sketches. He seemed pleased at my remark, too."[4]

Griffes's visual responsiveness to color is often reflected in his music, especially in mature works such as the orchestral versions of *The White Peacock, Clouds, Bacchanale, The Pleasure-Dome of Kubla Khan,* and the *Poem for Flute and Orchestra.* Here, as in his watercolors, the shades of color are subtle and delicate, not sharp, bright, or garish. According to Edward Maisel, Griffes associated certain colors with certain keys in music. "The key of E-flat, for example, was yellow or golden. C major was an incandescent white light, the most brilliant key in the tonality. It was his favorite key."[5] Griffes, however, used C major infrequently. The key appears as the clear, overall tonality only twice in his oeuvre (excluding works with oriental scales, compositions with marginal tonality, and the Arthur Tomlinson pieces for children): in "Le Réveillon" for voice and piano (*Four Impressions,* no. 4, set to a stirring Oscar Wilde text about the coming of the dawn) and in the early, unpublished song "Ich weiss nicht, wie's geschieht" (set to an Emanuel Geibel text about love). Griffes also cast the section just before the epilogue in act 3 of *Salut au monde* in C major as the chorus sings "Hail freedom of nations!" *Salut* ends in A-flat major, a key that, according to Maisel, had much the same quality for Griffes as C major, "but it was more tempered and removed from the absolute."[6]

Like his grandfather Solomon and his Uncle Charlie before him, Charles was fastidious in his dress. Griffes's nephew Wilber ("Bill") Roake, named for Charles's father, remembered "Uncle Carl" well. "He used to come over for dinner quite often in the summer. He'd practice on our piano. He was pretty well-dressed, wore a tie and suit—and dark, usually brown. I remember his wearing yellow shirts once in a while, and a green tie."[7] Griffes's sister-in-law, Charlotte Griffes, with a practiced female eye, remembered Charles as always being neat, well-dressed, and well-groomed.[8]

Charles also had definite ideas about how others should dress. For example, he informed his mother and Marguerite that, because of the shape of their faces, they should wear either very small hats or very large hats—never anything in between. And on one occasion when Charles invited Marguerite to visit him at Hackley, he specifically asked her to wear a green plaid dress that she had made, because he was especially fond of it and because she looked so good in it.[9]

As a youth in Elmira, Charles enjoyed dressing up in fancy costumes for neighborhood parties. In their back room the Griffeses had an old trunk filled with a fascinating assortment of cast-off clothes, some of which had belonged to Grandfather Solomon—hats, shoes, dresses, vests, suits, coats, dusters, ribbons, everything under the sun—and whenever they had a "fancy dress party," everyone, including the neighbor children, would run to the Griffes trunk to put together a costume.[10] The Griffes backyard was quite large, and the neighborhood children gathered there to play games and climb the fruit trees. An old barn behind the house was filled with all sorts of intriguing junk left behind by the family who had lived at 422 West First before the Griffes family moved in.[11] It was a child's paradise, and Charles spent many happy hours there as a youngster romping with his family and friends.

Everyone enjoyed the Griffes parties. The neighbors would gather and dance through the large house, starting in the living room, going through the back parlor, into the front parlor, down the hall, and back to the family room, while Charles, Clara, Wilber, Florence, and Katharine all took turns playing the piano or dancing. Charles always had a wonderful time, although he wasn't especially fond of dancing, despite the few lessons he and Marguerite had taken as youngsters.[12] To add to the festivity, Wilber would often string candle-illuminated Japanese lanterns around the backyard. The lanterns were collapsible and could be used over and over unless, of course, they caught fire, which they sometimes did.[13] The Griffes family knew how to make their guests feel comfortable and welcome. Their friend and landlady, Mrs. Daniel Pugh, once asked her son Reese why he didn't invite the kids to *their* house once in a while. He replied, "Oh, we don't have as much fun here. We have a lot more fun at the Griffeses."[14]

Charles was a keen observer of people, and his comments and evaluations about those who caught his attention were sometimes harsh and blunt. He wrote to his mother in 1904: "[Frau Hamburger,] a German lady who lives in the room across the hall from mine . . . does some rather odd things when she eats. Some of the Germans eat more like animals than anything else anyway."[15] Griffes had an almost overreactive fear of being naive or gauche during his years abroad and was very concerned with his own table manners (and behavior in general), so it is not surprising that he would scrutinize everyone else, including his family, with an unforgiving, razor-sharp eye.

Every time I stop to think of it, I begin to tremble for fear I have done or shall do something which isn't in good taste. . . . I never thought so much before about how great an advantage it is to be brought up in the best society and to do everything right from habit. When Miss Broughton was here, she corrected me for not laying my knife and fork right together on the plate when I was through. It was rather mortifying but I always take special pains to do it now. Please teach Arthur to do that if he doesn't already. And let no one ever say "I was to a place" instead of "at a place," or "he don't" or "she don't." I think I have noticed the first in letters.[16]

As blunt as he could be with others, Griffes could just as easily laugh at himself. May Roberts, a family friend who had attended Elmira College with Katharine and who taught at Elmira Free Academy, visited Charles in Germany in 1905. "The first thing May said when she came into the room was, 'Why, you look just the same as ever,' so I seem doomed to keep my same old style of beauty."[17]

All his life Griffes maintained a certain distance between himself and all but his family and close friends. A letter Charles wrote to Marguerite in 1903 illustrates his attitude. "It seems to me that those people at the Lutheran Church must be getting extremely familiar suddenly to call me [by my first name] . . . and those not by my wish, I am sure."[18] Years later a friend of Charles's gave a party in New York and invited several musicians, including a woman from Elmira who remarked about "Charlie Griffes" being at the party. Charles heard about her remark and muttered: "Well, she's got a nerve. I never allow anybody but my own family and special friends to call me 'Charlie.'"[19]

From his grade school days at Elmira's No. 2 School through his high school days at Elmira Free Academy, Griffes was an excellent student. While in high school, in addition to piano lessons with Miss Broughton, Griffes took a few organ lessons with George Morgan McKnight, organist and choirmaster at the Trinity Episcopal Church in Elmira from about 1890 until his death in 1941, and who was also associated with Elmira College as professor and head of the School of Music from 1894 to 1936.[20] Griffes earned a little money and experience playing the organ at one of Elmira's two Lutheran churches a year or two before he went to Germany in 1903.[21] And, according to Marguerite Griffes, Charles took German lessons from a local minister in Elmira "at a little Methodist church" in exchange for playing the organ.[22] Charles directed a choir at the church and tried to convince his younger brother, Arthur, to join. Typically for Arthur, and to the chagrin of Charles, Arthur did not mind singing in the choir but refused to attend rehearsals.[23]

Another of Charles's musical activities in Elmira was playing the piano for Sunday afternoon services at the YMCA.[24] One of his jobs was to accompany the occasional soloists who sang at the services, an excellent experience for the young Griffes.[25] Griffes developed friendships with Herbert Lansdale, general secretary of the Y until 1902, and then with Henry N. Hansen, who replaced Lansdale.[26] Hansen was still general secretary when Charles left for Germany in August 1903 and saw Charles off at the train station in Elmira. "They were both awfully nice men, and Charles was fond of both of them and he went around with them quite a little and knew their families."[27]

Marguerite Griffes described her brother as "a boy that kept to himself a great deal. He had lots of friends and boys that he used to play with. But he was kind of apart. He liked things that boys didn't."[28] Like his parents and siblings, Charles was undemonstrative. As a youngster in Elmira, he rarely shared his thoughts with his family or friends.[29] However, Charles's delightful sense of humor was a perfect foil for the serious, introspective side of his personality. He often found humor in things that escaped others, as, for example, when he wrote home from Berlin, tongue-in-cheek, "I think it must have been real exciting that day at school when so many were frostbitten on the way; I read about it in the paper which came this A.M., and [Marguerite] also mentioned it in her letter."[30] Griffes's nephew Bill Roake recounted: "I remember that he used to be quite fond of my sister Virginia, and he used to kid her. One of his expressions was 'a poiple boidy on thoidy thoid street.' He always came out with that, and she'd always laugh at it. Everytime he'd come over, he'd pull that one on her."[31]

Most likely in his midteens Charles began to sense his homosexuality—to recognize that he was different from his peers. In the atmosphere of sexual repression in America at the time, Griffes had no one with whom he could feel at ease discussing his homosexuality, without generating at least shock and embarrassment, if not censure. Compounding his dilemma Charles chose music as his career, and that, in itself, was suspect. One of Griffes's students at the Hackley School put it well: "What is hard for a young person today to visualize is an atmosphere in which any boy with real interest in the arts was considered as definitely queer ['odd']—a situation that then persisted even at Yale."[32] Griffes had no sexual revolution from which to benefit, and he would always have to live with the specter of discovery. It is highly unlikely that he had any sexual encounters in Elmira. His first actual physical experience may have taken place while in Germany, with Emil Joël, his mentor and friend in Berlin.

During his tenure at the Hackley School, Griffes had "crushes" on certain boys (and vice versa), but it is doubtful whether these ever culminated in physical intimacy. Griffes would have been dismissed from Hackley had he been discovered in such a liaison. Even today, the prohibition in most high schools and colleges against teachers entering into sexual relationships with their students is stringent. In the early twentieth century, it was a strict taboo, most especially a relationship between a male teacher and a male student. There is no reason to deny that such relationships existed, but, if discovered, the consequences were fatal. Griffes even treaded a thin line by singling out special friends among his students. One should remember that when he started teaching at Hackley, Charles was only twenty-three years old, not much older than some of the students. It is likely that the most Griffes ever shared with a Hackley student was furtive kisses. About one infatuation Griffes wrote:

> It seemed lonesome around tonight. I couldn't help thinking of a year ago at this time. Then I was in ———'s room until 12 o'clock—great as that infraction of rules may seem—and when I left, he called me "dearest" and "sweetheart. . . ." He was as fascinating as I have ever seen him and when he left me finally to go down to the gym, I caught him to me and kissed his lips— a kiss which he eagerly returned. The next afternoon was a little ice-cream spread in my rooms for several of the boys. In the evening I gave him his Christmas present and he kissed me again with the greatest tenderness. Never shall I forget the unspeakable charm of those two first kisses from this lovely and fascinating boy. But how things have changed since then! Now I never exchange a word with him except a greeting in the halls. For me he exists only as he was then and our relations now cannot efface the charm of our former ones. But they could not last. [33]

Only with one other Hackley student did Griffes indulge his feelings.

> [Dostoyevski's *Crime and Punishment*] made me intolerably morbid. Fortunately I got hold of ——— for the afternoon and he cured me completely. After all that is the most powerful remedy. If he knew what a magical effect he is capable of on me, and what a beautiful afternoon he gave me! . . . The feeling that I have his confidence and that he is not indifferent to me make me very happy at times. [34]

Two years later Griffes was in the same student's room.

> Had a most charming and unexpected talk with ——— this evening. . . . I went into his room and sat on the bed with him

until almost 12 o'clock. . . . [Now in German:] [W]e have seldom spoken so intimately to one another. He was charming, and spoke as openly and nicely as a child. I would like to have sat all night like that. We also talked of our relationship to one another.[35]

Despite such encounters and the openness with which Griffes and this student often spoke, Griffes was a realist and must have known that he could never establish a mutually satisfying and intimate relationship with any Hackley student. He could dream, somewhat adolescently, but he knew that such dreams were illusory. The inevitable truth was that he was the one at risk, that he would be the one left behind, and that he would be the one left frustrated and disappointed. It could not be otherwise.

Naturally enough, Griffes formed friendships with many Hackley boys because he found them to be more interesting, intelligent, and sensitive than the normal run of students. Such friendships often extended to the students' families as well. It would be naive to think that there were "romantic" impulses behind every Hackley friendship.

During Griffes's lifetime, as today, New York City had a well-established homosexual network. Griffes cultivated a wide circle of gay acquaintances there and frequented popular homosexual gathering places, among them the Produce Exchange Baths at 6 Broadway and the Lafayette Baths at 403–405 Lafayette Street (just south of Cooper Union).[36] Griffes was attracted to men in uniform, such as policemen and streetcar and train conductors, and he pursued his interests with an enormous amount of energy and ingenuity.

In his diary Griffes often referred to the policemen he encountered in New York by the streets they patrolled, referring at various times to "42-5th," "46th-5," "37-5," and "34-5." He also used initials and symbols ("X," "∅") to identify his homosexual contacts. Griffes felt no shame about his homosexuality; rather he expressed frustration that homosexuals could not meet openly. After a visit to the Lafayette Baths, he wrote, "It always angers me that one can't meet these people anywhere but there, but they all seem to be afraid."[37] Griffes also obviously believed that it was necessary to take precautions when writing about his homosexual encounters, and almost all of those diary entries are in German.

Throughout his life Griffes kept a careful record of almost everything he did. His Berlin letters, for example, give practically a minute-by-minute account of his activities. In fact, he gave orders that they be saved because he thought he might someday write his autobiography.[38] His diaries are no less rich in information about Griffes the man and Griffes the musician. Among other things, his sexual perambulations, preferences, and strategies are revealed with fascinating clarity. It is worthwhile, therefore, to quote several entries from his diaries referring to New York City. The excerpts are all translations from the original German.

> A certain streetcar driver between W. P. [White Plains] and T. [Tarrytown], whose looks interested me for a long time, greeted me and spoke to me for the first time today. With patience you can get anything. (28 February 1914)

> He [39th-5th] was especially friendly and readily accepted cigarettes from me. (28 March 1914)

> This morning I talked to 39-5, and maybe went too far because I asked him to go to the theater with me some evening. He didn't say no but he told me that next week would be better. I felt that I had made a fool of myself and left. (1 April 1914)

> Was there [at the Lafayette Baths] for 3½ hours. It disgusts me and attracts me at the same time. (3 October 1914)

> A rather sadistic person interested me, but he hurt me. (21 October 1914)

Not very interesting but I left [the Lafayette Baths] with a German C. L. whom I found very interesting. . . . He told me a lot of interesting things about H. S. in Mexico, and so on. (21 April 1915)

Talked to Pol[iceman] 42-5th at 11.15 P.M. He was very amiable. (28 April 1915)

I was rather disappointed in [C. H., a train conductor]—he doesn't look *at all* attractive in civilian clothes. One can see by that how much certain clothes, like a uniform, matter. (27 May 1915)

At 7.45 I was again with J. M. and stayed until 8.30. At 8.50 I picked him up again and we went to the Grand Central for dinner. Both of us talked about our feelings and that we have known each other for years already. Time seems too short for us. (29 May 1915)

Of the various encounters and acquaintances alluded to above, one, "J. M.," stands out above the rest. "J. M." (or "42-5th") was John Meyer of Corona, Queens, whom Charles first met on 28 April 1915 and with whom he formed a permanent relationship. Meyer was thirty-eight—more than seven years Griffes's senior—married, and a father.[39] On 2 June Griffes was in New York again with John. "The whole evening was very enjoyable. . . . We already called each other by our first names. All these little things happen so naturally and unaffectedly with us that sometimes I'm amazed at how much feeling he has for it. Can this really be a policeman and have we really known each other for such a short time? I would hardly have thought it possible. . . . I would like to re-live this evening again."[40] Shortly after, Charles's and John's relationship had progressed to the point where John was offering advice on Griffes's career. "Talked awhile with J. M. in the afternoon. Had an appointment with him for the evening and we went to the Grand Central for dinner again. I showed him my corrections [for the op. 5 piano pieces] and we talked about music as a profession and how much money one can make on it. He thinks I ought to earn more."[41]

Griffes visited John's family in Corona in July 1915. "John, the 2 older girls and I went over to the beach for a swim and staid [*sic*] most of the P.M. I took 5 pictures of J. and the girls and J. alone and he got one of me. . . . He took me all over the house with great pride, even down cellar. The 2 girls played for me and then I had to play for them!"[42]

Charles continued to see a great deal of John, while making new contacts and nurturing old ones. One new acquaintance was a young musician, William Earl Brown.

> [He] asked me to drop by 46th Street. I agreed and had a very interesting morning. He really wants me to move into his studio. I would pay half the rent ($35) and have his Steinway grand for practicing. He is a singing teacher with only 3 or 4 students at the moment. He and the whole matter please me very much and, above all, the location on 12 W. 46th is wonderful. . . . W. E. B. interests me in every respect.[43]

Griffes decided to accept Brown's offer, wrote him to that effect, and moved in on 24 June.[44]

Charles was sometimes involved in brief but, for him, searing encounters, such as one that took place on 21 August 1915.

> This afternoon went to the Laf. and left in an unhappy mood, as usual. I had finally succeeded in introducing myself to someone who had interested me the whole afternoon. He accepted my invitation to keep company with me tonight—but then he backed out. . . . I was very humiliated and could think of nothing else. John, who came round later on for dinner,

guessed that I was in love and learned that it was without prospect. He believed that he could give me an explanation for the whole affair but I don't believe he can!!! A nasty night![45]

Griffes's sexual encounters in New York were frequent and varied. Fortunately, his relationship with John, which lasted until Griffes's death, provided him with some stability, emotional fulfillment, and happiness. But John was married and had a family, and Griffes could never be the major focus of his life.

Two diary entries illustrate some of Griffes's thoughts on homosexuality. In November 1912 he was at the New York Public Library reading André Gide's *Oscar Wilde: A Study*. Griffes commented, "He mentioned a thing which has often struck me in the descriptions of 'cases' and otherwise—namely that when of the two parents the husband is weak-willed and less energetic than the wife, the son is frequently inverted."[46] Griffes was likely thinking of himself here, since, although Wilber Griffes was by no means "weak-willed," the Griffes household had been a matriarchal rather than a patriarchal one. In December 1912 Griffes wrote:

> [Robert Sherard in *The Life of Oscar Wilde*] says interesting things about the traits of Wilde's parents and other relatives, and their part in his inherited nature. . . . But it is not quite clear to me whether Sherard considered Wilde as from the start inverted, or one with whom the homosexual nature broke forth only under outward impulse. The tendency sometimes does not appear until later in life, but Oscar Wilde certainly had from childhood on many traits of inverts.[47]

Griffes may have been searching for parallels between Wilde and himself here. There were few to be found, except for Griffes's apparent belief that homosexuality was an "inherited nature," as he says in the December comments about Wilde.

Griffes's family suspected that he was homosexual. Marguerite Griffes commented: "He did have moody spells sometimes, but you'd hardly know it. He just felt a little down or something, but he never said anything. But we felt that maybe it was the condition that, that—you know, his life—that bothered him at times."[48] However, the family did not come to a full realization until they read the diaries sometime after his death.[49] After Charles died, the family found a letter he had written to Edward Carpenter(?) "asking about that but I guess we threw it away."[50] The suspicion and then knowledge of Charles's homosexuality did not diminish the family's love for him. Still, it is sad that Griffes could not share this important aspect of his life with his family. It is even sadder to contemplate that his mother, Clara, said, not long before her death, "Maybe it's just as well he died. He might have been very unhappy."[51]

4

Graduation from High School and on to Berlin

Even before Charles graduated from Elmira Free Academy in June 1903, he had no doubts that music would be his career. However, there was much discussion among Clara, Wilber, Uncle Charlie, and Miss Broughton about whether or not music would be a suitable career for Charles, whether he could make a decent living as a musician, and how his studies could possibly be financed. In the end Charles's determination and Miss Broughton's verbal and financial support won out.[1]

Charles could not have been happier, and once the decision had been made, the entire Griffes family shared in their pride and excitement for him.[2] There was little question of where Charles would be sent to study. Where else but Imperial Germany, America's musical mecca, and where else but Berlin, where Miss Broughton had studied with Karl Klindworth years before. This decision was a turning point in Griffes's life. His Berlin studies moved him to the threshold of his professional career.

On 21 May 1903 Griffes played a farewell concert in the Elmira College Chapel. The program included compositions by

Claude Dacquin, Felix Mendelssohn, Frédéric Chopin, Franz Liszt, and Johannes Brahms, as well as the premiere of Griffes's songs "Si mes vers avaient des ailes" and "Sur ma lyre l'autre fois," both written in 1901.[3] Baritone George Morgan McKnight and two of his voice students, William Pomeroy Frost and Mrs. William Barron, assisted Griffes. Barron sang the two Griffes songs accompanied by the young composer.[4] Three Elmira papers reviewed the concert, all giving high praise to Griffes. The *Elmira Telegram* summed up the evening as follows:

> At Elmira college Thursday night one of the most interesting of concerts attracted a large and cultivated audience. The occasion was a testimonial benefit in honor of Charles T. Griffes, a young pianist, who has won great fame in his native city by the remarkable quality of his work. Mr. Griffes contemplates going shortly to Germany for further study. . . . The playing of Mr. Griffes was at his highest mark and gained the closest attention and unlimited praise. His compositions were also greatly admired, and brought for him prophesies of a career that will do him the highest credit among artists accepted as leaders in their profession. . . . His extraordinary powers of memorizing and ability to produce with perfect literalness are rarely equalled. This is the more amazing in view of the fact that he has been a regular student at Elmira free academy, and is now about to be graduated. Musicians will appreciate what an endowment is his who can carry successfully two lines of important work.[5]

After this big success, Griffes had much to do to prepare for his journey—clothes to be readied, gifts from family and friends to be packed, letters to be written, finances to be sorted out, and good-byes to be said.

Then, at last, the time was at hand. On 11 August 1903 family members and friends accompanied the excited eighteen year old to the Delaware, Lackawanna & Western passenger terminal in Elmira. Charles and his sister Florence bought their tickets ($6.10

one way), boarded the train, and were on the way to Hoboken, New Jersey, where Griffes's ocean liner, the *Grosser Kurfürst,* was docked.[6] Rex Sturdevant, a friend from Elmira working in New York, met the two in Hoboken. Charles wrote to Clara that evening from New York to give her a rundown of what had happened so far: "It is about 9 o'clock and we have at last gotten two rooms. Mrs. Pickens could not take us but sent us to a house around the corner where the lady finally gave us two rooms on the 4th floor at 50¢ a night. Rex met us all right at Hoboken and is with us now."[7]

The next day Uncle Charlie arrived in New York, and in a letter home Charles provided a detailed account of their activities:

> We have been going busily since our arrival. . . . But this morning we decided that we would . . . stay at the Victoria tonight, for Florence's bed was so full of insects that she got bitten up. . . . After our breakfast we went through Brentano's book store and then went over to Hoboken. My baggage was there all right and was to be put on this morning. We went all through the steamer and I was delighted with it. I couldn't see much difference between the first and second class state rooms. . . . Tonight I think we shall go to Chinatown. Rex is coming over and if Uncle Charlie has no other . . . plans he wants to take us there. This afternoon we are going to Mrs. Young-Fulton's [a teaching employment agency] and up to Macy's. . . . It was awfully nice as we came over on the ferry last night. On the New York end there is a long pier going out into the water with a pavillion above over the whole thing.[8]

On Thursday, 13 August, Charles boarded the *Grosser Kurfürst* and wrote to his mother at 5:30 P.M.

> You can't imagine how perfectly beautiful it is out here on the ocean. We left all sight of land about 2 hours ago and begin to feel quite on the way. It was quite stirring as we left the Pier for

the band on board played and everybody was waving flags, etc.,
but I was glad none of you were there.[9]

The next day, Charles noted that he had received a steamer letter
from Mr. Hansen of the YMCA. He described the activities of the
ship's orchestra and band and detailed the size and shape of his
stateroom.[10]

Griffes continued to write home almost daily for the dura-
tion of his trip. On Saturday, 15 August, he described in great
detail some "dandy Berlin fritters" he had eaten for dinner and
regaled his mother with descriptions of some of his traveling
companions. The following day he wrote: "We had a service this
A.M. in the dining room conducted by a minister who is head of a
German orphan asylum out west. . . . If they had not already asked
their pianist I should have offered to do it for this one they had
played abominably. . . . We stop at Plymouth in about 5 or 6 days
and I will have this letter ready to mail there. I hope the pencil
writing won't fade before it goes the rounds."[11]

On Tuesday, 18 August, the weather turned dreary. Charles,
following his tendency for sharing minute detail, reported home
that he had tasted his first zwieback and had begun to paint a
bridge scene for Miss Broughton in his stateroom. The next day
the weather improved, but trip fatigue had already set in: "We
shall all be glad when we get to Bremen for we are getting awfully
tired of the monotonous life. I was looking at the chart a few
moments ago and at 12 o'clock this noon we had gone 2021 miles."
And, betraying a bit of homesickness, Charles continued: "Someone was playing that old piece of yours last night, 'Le Lever du
soleil.' It is in that big book, I think, and it sounded so familiar."[12]

And so it went. The *Grosser Kurfürst* arrived at Plymouth,
England, at 4:00 P.M. on Saturday, 22 August: "We get into Bre-
merhaven (Bremen Harbor) about 4 o'clock tomorrow P.M. and
from there we take a 2 hours' [*sic*] train ride before we come into

the city. So I shall no doubt stay over night in Bremen with the other Berlin people and take the first train for Berlin the next morning."[13]

As he had anticipated, Griffes stayed overnight in Bremen and took the train to Berlin the next morning, arriving there at 1:12 P.M. on 25 August. He had expected to be met by Miss Broughton, who was in Europe for the summer and who had arranged her trip so she could help Charles get settled. But when he arrived,

> she was nowhere to be seen, so I got my trunk and took a [horse-drawn] droschke or cab which brought me, baggage and all to Frau Werner's [at Kurfürstenstrasse 48]. I had to pay 2 Marks, 25 Pfennigs (56¢) but that wasn't bad. Miss Broughton wasn't here just then but soon got here and I guess was glad to find me here, for she had begun to think I hadn't come at all.[14]

When Griffes left Elmira that day in August 1903, he joined many other young American music students who had flocked to Germany often to settle in Berlin, which in 1903 was one of Europe's largest cities and among its preeminent musical centers. Most of the young musicians emerged from their studies forever bound to Germany's musical philosophy and "speech." It is not surprising, therefore, that when Griffes returned to America after *his* four years in Berlin, he, too, "spoke" the German musical language. What is surprising, I believe, is that he spoke it so fluently. More important, in acquiring this fluency Griffes did not sacrifice his own musical individuality. For example, while his early German songs, such as "Auf geheimem Waldespfade," reveal the influence of Brahms and Strauss, they also clearly exhibit Griffes's own sensitivity to harmony and his wonderful melodic gift.

With the establishment of the German Empire in 1871, Berlin became its capital, and the city's population soon rose from 826,000 in 1871 to 2,033,900 in 1905.[15] One can only imagine how exciting and formidable this large city must have seemed to Griffes in comparison with his home town of Elmira. Berlin was the principal residence of the German emperor, the seat of the imperial parliament (Reichstag), and of the state offices of the empire, all except the supreme court of justice (Reichsgericht) located in Leipzig. Moreover, it was an essentially modern city:

> The bustle of the modern commercial city has superseded the austere dignity of the old Prussian capital. . . . [Berlin] has become the chief pleasure town of Germany; and, though the standard of morality, owing to the enormous influx of people bent on amusement, has become lower, yet there is so much healthy, strenuous activity in intellectual life and commercial rivalry as to entitle it, despite many moral deficiencies, to be regarded as the centre of life and learning in Germany.[16]

The "main street" of Berlin, the famed Unter den Linden, with its double avenue divided by a promenade, ran about one mile from the royal palace to the Brandenburg Gate. The city was filled with beautiful parks, including the Tiergarten and the Lustgarten, and was flanked by a thick belt of pine woods, the Jungfernheide, the Spandauer Forst, and the Grunewald.[17]

Berlin could base its claim as one of the leading centers of intellectual life in Germany on the Friedrich Wilhelm University, the Royal Academy of Sciences, and the Royal Academy of Arts; on its fifteen *Gymnasia* (classical schools "for the highest branches of the learned professions"), its commercial schools, and its public high schools for girls; and, of course, on its music conservatories, including the Hochschule für Musik, directed by Josef Joachim, the Klindworth-Schwarenka Konservatorium, and the Stern'sches Konservatorium, where Griffes enrolled.[18] Most of these names and places became familiar to Griffes during his four-year sojourn in Berlin. No less familiar to Griffes were Berlin's many museums, zoological gardens, theaters, art galleries, opera houses, and concert halls—quite a cultural banquet for the hungry young man from Elmira, New York.

Berlin's musical life was dominated by Richard Strauss, who was general music director and conductor of the Royal Court Opera from 1898 to 1918. Strauss also conducted concerts with the Berlin Tonkünstler Orchestra and later the Berlin Philharmonic Orchestra.[19] Most of the world's great singers, instrumentalists, and conductors performed in Berlin, and Griffes took advantage of this musical cornucopia on every possible occasion.

Charles, Miss Broughton, and Kate Pigott, a friend of Miss Broughton's who served as English governess for the Landau family in Berlin,[20] began making the rounds of museums and concerts immediately. On 27 August 1903, just two days after Charles's arrival, they visited a museum where they saw several Rembrandts and Titians. Later that evening they went to the Berlin Theater to hear Franceschina Prevosti in Verdi's *La Traviata.*[21]

Griffes traded his original room at Frau Werner's for a quieter one in the back and had a piano brought in so he could practice there.[22] On 1 September, Griffes got his first look at the emperor and empress and the "little Princess Victoria and the Prince Oscar."

> Everybody of course waved their handkerchiefs and took off their hats . . . but Miss Broughton says they were not near so enthusiastic as the people in England are. . . . Sunday P.M. Miss Pigott and we went to the Zoological Garden and took in the sights and music. The animals were of course all out in the open cages. . . . Among the peacocks was a pure white one— very curious.[23]

This image of the white peacock found expression twelve years later in what was to become one of Griffes's best-known compositions, *The White Peacock* for piano.

On 2 September, Charles and Miss Broughton called on Ernst Jedliczka, piano instructor at the Stern Conservatory. Charles reported: "His lessons begin tomorrow A.M. and he told me to come around then and play for him. . . . I shall play the Mendelssohn Prelude and Fugue." Charles was also pleased to tell Clara that "composition lessons at the Conservatorium are $50 extra but Miss Broughton says for me to take them just the same."[24]

Thursday, 3 September 1903, was an important day for Griffes.

I went and played for Dr. Jedliczka . . . and we [Charles and Miss Broughton] were very much relieved when he said he would take me, for he had already said his classes were full. He said some very nice things about me and seemed pleased with my playing. . . . I have my piano lessons Monday at 11, forty minutes each time; but you can come any time you want to and listen to the others and that is what they mean by class lessons. Thursday A.M. he gave me 2 pieces to get and look over for Monday—a Sonata in g minor by Schumann and an Etude by Rubenstein [sic]. The Schumann Sonata is gorgeous. . . . I shall do 2 [hours of practicing] in the A.M. and 2 in the P.M. . . . I have a regular composition lesson Thursday A.M. with Herr Professor [Philippe] Rüfer and come to listen at another of his classes Monday A.M. Counterpoint with Max Loewengard comes Wednesday A.M. and ensemble playing also Thursday A.M. This [sic] lessons are of course all in German so I shall perhaps find it hard at first.[25]

Griffes dropped ensemble playing because he didn't enjoy it and because it took too much time. Besides, "[I]t isn't worth while for me to go there and just play over those Haydn symphonies."[26]

The time soon came for Miss Broughton to leave Berlin to begin her journey home for the fall term at Elmira College. "She went Thursday night [3 September] at 10 o'clock," Charles wrote home, "and you can imagine how sorry Miss Pigott and I were to have her go; I guess she felt awfully to go too. We had such a nice time when she was here." In the same letter a somewhat nostalgic Charles remarked: "The Sundays here seem awfully queer to me after my two services and Y.M.C.A. in the P.M. Do you know, I really miss those Y.M.C.A. Sunday meetings very much—[*sic*]."[27]

Griffes, however, was already making friends at the Stern Conservatory, notably with a "Mr. Henry," who also studied with Jedliczka and lived at the same pension as Griffes.[28] In his letters home Charles generally referred to the people he met as "Mr. Henry," "Miss Hunt," and so on. His repeated references to Mr. Henry must have aroused his father's curiosity: "What made father ask what Mr. Henry's first name is? It is Harold."[29] Charles was also grateful for the continued friendship of Kate Pigott and the Landau family. He especially enjoyed evenings at the Landaus because Dr. Landau was a fine violinist, "a fiend on music," and owned a Bechstein piano that Charles loved to play, often in duets with the doctor.[30] Charles was always welcome to share dinner with the family.

Griffes quickly settled into the routine of lessons at the Stern Conservatory.

> My first [piano] lesson is at last over and I am settled down to my four hrs. a day. Dr. Jedliczka is awfully nice at the lessons— doesn't fly into passions or anything like that. . . . Every once in a while he puts his arm around you and when you come to a big crescendo he sort of pinches your shoulder. . . . If I didn't give a note its full value he would say, "Don't swindle now." . . . He was also kind enough to say to the other pupils in the room as I went, "He is very gifted." . . . This A.M. I had my first Counterpoint lesson. It is going to be real hard for me until I get to understand German better, for of course everything is in German. . . . There are about 12 in the class.[31]

Reporting on his first composition lesson with Philippe Rüfer, Griffes noted: "This A.M. [Thursday, 10 September] I had my

first composition lesson and you ought to have heard how he
picked to pieces my poor little Victor Hugo song ["Si mes vers
avaient des ailes"]. There was hardly a bar which did not have
some mistake in it or some place where Herr Rüfer said was
awkward."[32]

Apparently the flow of letters from home since his arrival in
Berlin had been less than what Charles would have liked. He
scolded his sister Marguerite: "You people at home must write as
often as you can; I suppose you don't realize it, but I have been
here almost 3 weeks now and have heard from you only twice.
And I have written faithfully twice a week, I think."[33] He also
admonished his family to be sure to put enough postage on the
letters they sent so he wouldn't have to pay the postage due
himself.[34] Charles was on a strict budget, and comments about
the price of everything from opera tickets to laundry to food
appear often in his letters.[35] However, he almost certainly was
exaggerating the precariousness of his financial situation when he
exclaimed in 1905: "This morning Emil and I were in the first
[Arthur] Nikisch [orchestra] rehearsal of this winter. We got taken
or else I am afraid we should neither of us have been there, for we
are both at a stage when we just about have to beg on the
street."[36]

Griffes celebrated his nineteenth birthday on 17 September
1903 with presents from home, a vase of scarlet flowers from
Harold Henry, a German dictionary from Miss Broughton, and an
evening dance in the pension dining room—his landlady Frau
Werner's present to him. It was among the most pleasant birth-
days he had had for a long time and only lacked someone from
Elmira with whom to enjoy it.[37]

Time flew by quickly. Charles attended a wide assortment of
musical performances, visited numerous churches, museums, and
parks, took in a parade every chance he could get—there were
many in Berlin—and worked hard every day practicing and pre-

paring his lessons. He was also soaking up German life and customs, some of which amused him greatly.

> When the Germans go and come to the table they always say
> Mahlzeit which seems so funny as it is hard to see the applica-
> tion; it means literally meal or dinner. . . . It seems as if the
> Germans are terribly fond of eating. . . . It is so funny at the
> Conservatory to see pupils and even professors standing around
> in the halls or elsewhere eating the second breakfast which
> [they] have brought with them.[38]

Among the friends mentioned by Griffes in his correspondence was Leslie Hodgson. On 4 October 1903 Griffes wrote his
mother: "[I] got my counterpoint lesson with Mr. Hodgson, one
of the other students in our class. He is from Canada and has
been here a year already; I like him very much. He is also
studying with Dr. Jedliczka and I imagine must play very well
from the pieces he has."[39] Leslie Hodgson and Griffes became
lifelong friends.

In a letter home dated 16 October 1903, Griffes mentioned
Emil Joël for the first time. What the frugal Charles reported
with pleasure was that Herr Joël had enabled him to see
Mozart's *Don Giovanni* at a greatly reduced ticket price:

> I got my ticket in a very nice way. Mr. Joel [*sic*], a German
> whom Miss Broughton will remember as the one who was very
> polite to his mother, goes to the technical Hochschule here and
> all the students there have the privilege of getting tickets in the
> 75¢ part for 30¢. He had a ticket for Don Juan but in the end
> couldn't go, so he gave me his for the same price, 30¢.[40]

In that same letter of 16 October, Griffes wrote of three
more American acquaintances, who "have come to Frau
Werner's—isn't it awful? A mother and 2 daughters, one to study

violin, and one to study German. And they practically can't speak German at all. It is horrid, but I suppose we shall have to stand it." The three Americans were the Shooberts from San Francisco. A wonderful friendship developed between Charles and the two Shoobert girls, Alicia ("Fanny") and Lillian ("Babe"), a friendship that continued after they all returned to the United States. Griffes thoroughly enjoyed the jokes they shared, the parties they organized, and the concerts, parades, excursions, and other activities they shared.

For Christmas 1903 "the older Miss Shoobert [Fanny] gave me an awfully cute little cotton swan," Charles wrote Clara. "We have a joke about the swan in Lohengrin and use the phrase Mein Lieber Schwan, which Lohengrin sings, as a sort of signal. The other Miss Shoobert [Babe] gave me a duck which refers to Cosmuddle [Cussmoodle], the duck in Lovey Mary, a nickname which has been given to me for some reason or other."[41]

In spring 1904 Griffes described another outing with the Shooberts as "one of the pleasantest days I have had for a long time."

> I went out with the Shooberts to Grunewald; it is first a suburb where there are lots of gorgeous villas and beyond where they are is the forest where we went. It is an immense place and awfully wild and beautiful. . . . And oh! the lovely piney smell of the woods! You felt like a different person from in the city and just wanted to get down and roll on the ground or do something like that.[42]

The fun Charles shared with the Shooberts was reminiscent of the good times he used to have at home. Their companionship allowed him to "loosen up" and enjoy the openness and acceptance true friendship brings. The Shooberts left Berlin on 1 July 1905, and Griffes wondered if he would ever see any of them again.[43] In later years Charles and Babe (who lived in California) kept in touch by letter. In 1914 Babe was in New York visiting her sister Ethel ("Pod") and brother-in-law Dr. Fred Bancroft, and it is possible that Griffes confided in Babe about his homosexuality. Marguerite Griffes remembered: "I think in his diaries he spoke about that one night they took a long walk and told each other things they had never said before. So I had an idea that they knew about Charlie."[44]

5

The Berlin Years

Spring 1904–Spring 1905

The most important relationship Griffes established during his Berlin years was with Emil Joël, a young German whom Griffes met not long after his arrival in Berlin in August 1903. Emil, seven years Charles's senior and a civil engineering student at the Technische Hochschule in Berlin, was someone whose musical judgments Griffes could value and respect, someone who could advise him on matters concerning everyday German life, someone upon whom he could depend for encouragement, and someone who could help satisfy his emotional needs. Emil eagerly discharged his role as adviser and mentor, offering advice on every conceivable matter, and as their relationship flourished, Emil's influence could be detected in practically everything Charles did. It was in concert with Emil, for example, that Griffes decided to concentrate less on performance and more on composition. But Griffes himself had strong convictions, and had he not agreed with Emil's judgments and advice, he most certainly would have done things the way *he* thought they should be done.

The degree of physical involvement between Emil and Charles is a matter of conjecture.[1] Emil was married in 1908, a year after Griffes left Berlin, and he raised a family of three children. Griffes returned to Berlin in 1908 to attend the wedding and while there stayed with Emil. Charles described Emil's fiancée, Elly Bock, as rather pretty, with lovely hair, extremely lively, and well up on everything; he declared her "an agreeable disappointment."[2] Emil and Elly were married on 22 August, and Charles actively participated in all the proceedings.[3] Two years later, in the summer of 1910, Griffes returned to Berlin once more, this time to act as godfather for Emil's and Elly's first child, a son, Helmer Karl, named after Charles. After a five-week holiday on the island of Rügen with Emil, Elly, the baby, and Elly's brother, Charles reported from Berlin: "The baptism will be very soon. . . . They call the baby by its first name Helmer now, but think they may later use the 2 names Helmer Karl together. They don't like the name Karl alone or Emil said they would have chosen that as the first name instead of Helmer."[4] Charles seemed to take Emil's and Elly's marriage and the birth of their first child in stride and enjoyed his role in Emil's newly formed family.

During the years that Charles was a student in Berlin, however, especially from 1904 on, the attraction between Charles and Emil was a strong one. Emil may have been drawn to Charles because of the latter's youthfulness and lack of experience. Another factor in their relationship was that Emil lived with his widowed mother (in various pensions) and was more or less subservient to her needs and wishes. His relationship with Charles allowed Emil to assume a dominant role and to find an emotional outlet for what must have been, at times, an intolerable situation. For his part Charles was delighted to find someone like Emil who could introduce him to the life and culture of Germany and who could give him a sense of stability and "belonging."

Mention of Emil (or Herr) Joël (Charles referred to him both ways) became a regular part of Charles's letters home. He described Emil to a curious Griffes family in a letter dated 28 February 1905:

> I have in him a friend such as I never dreamed of finding in Berlin, and one who I think will stick by me. You ask how he looks and about him. But I can't tell you much except that he is decidedly German in character—and therefore very different from the Americans—and wears his hair pompadour, according to the German fashion. He is twenty-eight now but he never seems half so old as that to me.[5]

Griffes's letters continued to be filled with Emil, so much so that Charles, having mentioned Emil seven times in a letter of 1–2 May 1905, remarked: "I am sure that if you laughed before at the frequent mention of him in my letters, you will roar at this one. But really he is the only one with whom I have been doing anything special and if I don't write about that there is nothing. Frau Joël said once in fun she was going to fix me a bed in their rooms so that I could stay all the time."[6]

Music was an important part of Emil's life, as it was for most Germans at that time, regardless of their profession, and he had strong opinions on all musical matters. Griffes commented in a letter to his mother: "I didn't finish my letter last night because I was down in Herr Joel's [*sic*] room most of the time. He is a crank on the subject of opera and the orchestra, in fact music in general. Last night I played part of Die Meistersinger, of Wagner and he sang some of the time. I nearly roared right out, for it was too funny."[7]

Griffes went to Berlin in 1903 primarily to study piano. The plan was for him to stay for two years. Those two years passed quickly. In fact, Griffes remarked even before *one* year had gone by: "I can't realize that I have been here over 6 months. . . . And I suppose next year will go more quickly still and I shall be home again before I know it."[8]

Charles studied a variety of piano literature with Ernst Jedliczka at the Stern Conservatory, including the Schumann Sonata in G Minor, which he loved; études by Anton Rubinstein; J. S. Bach's *Well-Tempered Clavier* and Chromatic Fantasy and Fugue; several works by Chopin, including the Nocturne, op. 32, no. 2, several études, and the Concerto in E Minor; Franz Liszt's *Waldesrauschen*, which Griffes hated and disliked practicing; Ludwig Beethoven's Thirty-two Variations on an Original Theme in C Minor and the *Les Adieux* Sonata (the latter Charles found "quite simple" after studying the Schumann sonata); compositions by Moritz Moszkowski; Peter Tchaikovsky's Nocturne, op. 19, no. 4; études by Josef Pischna; and *Virtuoso Studies* by Christian Louis Heinrich Köhler.[9]

Griffes progressed so well in his piano studies that at the end of his first year he was chosen to appear at one of the conservatory's year-end concerts on 19 June 1904 in the Beethovensaal.[10] A proud Charles wrote to his mother, "I should feel very much flattered for only the very good pupils play at these, and one must be generally very talented to play the first year."[11] Griffes performed Beethoven's Thirty-two Variations on an Original Theme in C Minor, which he had begun to work on earlier that year. Miss Broughton, in Berlin for her summer vacation, attended the concert and seemed pleased with her former pupil's performance. However, Charles warned his mother: "But right here I must impress upon you at home that you *must not* imagine that there is any wonderful improvement in my playing. Miss Broughton says she couldn't make you understand that she wasn't especially anxious to hear me play and wasn't expecting anything very different from last year."[12]

Jedliczka died on 3 August 1904, and Griffes informed his mother that he was "teacherless."[13] At the time, Charles was enjoying a six-week summer holiday in the Harz Mountains with Miss Broughton and Kate Pigott.[14] On 26 September 1904, shortly after the start of the new term at the conservatory, a memorial program for Jedlizcka (arranged by Dr. Gustav Hollaender, director of the Stern Conservatory) took place in the Beethovensaal. Charles found it

> very disgusting and out of taste. . . . [E]ight of the pupils played a funeral march from one of Wagner's operas and eight the Chopin Funeral March—on four pianos. It was so flat and silly to hear these things done on four pianos. . . . Mr. Henry, Mr. Bertram and I were to have played with them, but they both decided they didn't want to do it, and as there were no other boys in it and I didn't want to sit up there and play with fifteen girls, I quietly backed out too. . . . I hate such things, for they always seem so sort of constrained and empty.[15]

Griffes continued piano studies at the Stern Conservatory with Gottfried Galston, a young Leschetizky pupil. Miss Broughton was not happy about this turn of events, and in a letter written to Griffes's mother from Berlin (while Jedliczka was ill), she expressed her concern:

> I am dreadfully worried about Dr. Jedliczka. I fear there is small chance of his recovery. . . . Charlie took some lessons the last four weeks from a young man called Galston, who is a splendid pianist, but who in my opinion lacks experience. . . . With Mr. Galston teaching is a secondary consideration, his own playing comes first.[16]

Charles had no such qualms. He wrote to Miss Broughton on 26 September 1904, shortly after she had returned to Elmira from Berlin: "I am real enthusiastic about Galston's method. It is going to be a fine thing, I think, and it seems to me already that I have more strength and surety in my fingers."[17]

Galston assigned his new pupil an étude by Leschetizky, Bach's *Well-Tempered Clavier,* and some Carl Czerny études and

Muzio Clementi studies to build up the strength in his fingers. Later assignments included Beethoven's Rondo a capriccio, op. 129 ("Rage over a Lost Penny"), *Waldstein* Sonata, and Concerto in G Major; Domenico Scarlatti sonatas; Liszt's Fantasie und Fuge, which helped build up the endurance in the left hand; Chopin études; and the Bach-Busoni Toccata and Fugue in D Minor.[18]

Galston played a concert in Berlin on 17 October 1904, which Griffes attended, although he was annoyed because Galston did not give out free tickets: "Perhaps Galston prefers a small audience to giving tickets away. . . . He played awfully well and I enjoyed it much better than I expected. . . . I had a lesson this afternoon and he seemed awfully distracted and uninterested—as I might have known he would on the day after. From now on he will be travelling a great deal."[19] Unlike Dr. Jedliczka, Galston was an active recitalist and was on the road a great deal fulfilling concert engagements, just as Miss Broughton had predicted.

Griffes was diligent in all his classes at the conservatory. His first composition assignment from Philippe Rüfer in September 1903 was to make some corrections in the French songs he had written in Elmira in 1901 and to write a four-part mixed chorus of about 25–30 measures (not more than one page).[20] Rüfer was pleased with Griffes's chorus and told the young man that it was "not at all bad but very good indeed. And he said to write another mixed chorus and also a short male chorus for next time."[21] Additional assignments included composing a minuet, and then arranging it for string quartet.[22] Griffes continued to hone his skills writing string quartet movements, and on 6 December 1903 he informed Miss Broughton:

> I have about finished my Adagio for the String Quartet and I think it will be quite respectable. . . . After the Andante I begin the 1st movement and then I am to have some fun, I know. It seems as if I am going terribly slowly, but I suppose the 1st

String Quartet must necessarily be a rather slow process. . . . I
think it is getting easier now to sit down and write something
in spite of lack of inspiration; perhaps I am not quite so particular as at first.[23]

Herr Rüfer must have been an excellent composition teacher.
Among Griffes's first assignments was to write a minuet—a genre
with specific structure, meter, key and theme relationships, and a
great deal of straightforward repetition—a perfect type of composition for a novice. Only after that did Rüfer assign movements
that would require the working out of themes. That Griffes was
finding it easier to sit down and write without "inspiration"
shows that he was acquiring the technical craftsmanship necessary
to become a fine composer. Rather than being "less particular," he
was beginning to master his art.[24]

Over time Charles became less specific in his letters about
his composition assignments, but he did complain shortly before
the end of the 1904 school year: "I never saw such people for
holidays as the Germans. The 12th of this month was Ascension
Day and I lost a composition lesson."[25]

On 19 August 1904 Charles and Miss Broughton visited Karl
Klindworth, Miss Broughton's former piano teacher in Berlin, who
was now retired as head of the Klavier-Schule Klindworth. Charles
reported to his mother: "We asked him about the teachers here and
he said to go to a Portuguese by the name of [José Vianna] da Motta;
I heard him play last year but didn't care much for him. When I
have a chance to practice a bit more I want to play for Busoni, a very
well-known player and teacher. For composition I shall keep right
on with Prof. Rüfer in the Conservatory."[26]

Griffes began orchestration studies with Rüfer in January
1905, and Emil figured prominently in his work.

Since I have begun orchestration in my composition work, I
just have to begin to study up scores and especially to learn to

play from score—for which Herr Joël furnishes the music and a good part of the incentive. He simply insists on it. . . . I know I shouldn't get half such a broad and general music knowledge from the advantages here if it weren't for Emil. . . . It is rather a fault of piano students and especially of Americans that they know nothing except the piano and its music. . . . And of course a real musician has got to be a great deal more than a piano player.[27]

Charles reported to Miss Broughton on the progress of his first large-scale orchestral work:

My ouverture [Overture in B Minor] is almost finished in the sketch and now soon I have to begin working out the instrumentation in detail. Prof. Rüfer says the Conservatory orchestra will give it in the Beethoven Saal [sic] at one of the June [1905] performances but, I am sure I don't know whether it will be feasible for such an amateurish and unpracticed orchestra. Herr Joël says it is really very interesting and not a bit Wagnerian—which is very pleasing, I think, as I hate orchestral compositions which sound only as if they were patterned after Wagner. However I am no doubt not yet far enough along to know how to use the Wagnerian effects. Prof. Rüfer said at once it was at least ganz orchestral gedacht [idiomatic for the orchestra].[28]

Discussing the Overture with his mother, Griffes wrote:

Miss Broughton sent the advertisement of a prize contest to me, and I suppose I might send my overture on to the Paderewski contest. . . . There would hardly be a possibility of my getting anything, as, judging from the names of the first prize-winners 4 years ago, old and already experienced and known musicians are among the competitors. And then of course one's first orchestral work is hardly apt to be so

strikingly orchestrated that it would take such a big prize. But I
don't know that it would do any harm to send it on if it is
ready.[29]

Griffes was enough of a realist to recognize that his skills as an
orchestrator were still in an embryonic state (the Overture was, as
he pointed out, his *first* orchestral work), but in that recognition
he also demonstrated a willingness to take a chance on submitting
the work. This, I believe, is the quintessential Griffes, always
aware of what he didn't know but always eager to press on and to
address and overcome limitations he perceived in himself.

Charles did not finish his Overture in time for the
Paderewski contest or for the 22 June 1905 performance featuring
compositions by conservatory students, at which Griffes played
instead the first movement of his Sonata in F Minor for piano,
written about 1904. He was disappointed with his performance
and acknowledged that he hadn't practiced enough. He also admitted to Miss Broughton that he hadn't thought of his own hands
when he composed the sonata and found the piece none too
easy.[30]

Griffes continued to work on the Overture, intending to
finish it in private lessons and thinking perhaps he would hear it
performed the next year.[31] He did complete it, most likely sometime late in 1905 (the manuscript is not dated), but the first performance did not take place until half a century later.[32]

Griffes also composed several songs during his Berlin years,
reflecting the German style he then admired. In February 1904
Charles wrote his mother about an informal musicale he attended:

> Most of the evening we had music and among other things Miss
> Cap [an American guest] sang the Rosary to her own accom-
> paniment. We all roared inwardly when she began that, for it
> and a few other songs such as "Violets" . . . are standing jokes. I
> have heard so many of the fine German songs—in fact only

them—since I have been here, that those sentimental American songs seem terribly silly.[33]

Counterpoint and fugue lessons with Max Loewengard at the conservatory also occupied Griffes's attention, although his letters do not include as many details about those lessons as they do about his piano and composition studies. Griffes reported to Miss Broughton after one class in December 1903:

Last week Herr Loewengard gave the Counterpoint class a regular blowing-up. They evidently had made very bad exercises, for he said, "Das ist Dilettantismus und Sie wollen Musiker sein" [that is dilettantism, and you want to be musicians]. Really I think we Americans are about the only ones who know anything and generally we can't say a word when he asks any of us a question. Every German word you ever knew, takes flight immediately on his putting a question.[34]

Griffes was annoyed that his counterpoint lesson on 27 January 1904 had been canceled because of the kaiser's birthday— another German holiday.[35] Missing lessons was always a sore point with Charles, and it was one of the reasons he gave for leaving the Stern Conservatory in 1905.

Max Loewengard left Berlin for Hamburg in October 1904 and was replaced at the conservatory by Wilhelm Klatte.[36] On 23 January 1905 Charles wrote to Marguerite: "Saturday morning was Fugue class, but I was the only one there, so Herr Klatte, the teacher, and I just talked for a while. It was awfully interesting, for he is musical critic on one of the papers here [the Berlin *Lokal-Anzeiger*] and knows everybody and everything."[37]

As a critic Herr Klatte received free concert tickets and often gave away those he couldn't use. Charles was the recipient of Klatte's generosity on at least one occasion but only grudgingly accepted: "[Herr Klatte] gave me a ticket to a comic opera company which gives its first performance tonight. I don't imagine it will be anything much, and I really don't want to go especially, but the seat is in the second row downstairs and he said I must tell him about it next lesson, so I shall probably go."[38]

Even as Charles was completing the 1904–5 school year at the Stern Conservatory—the year in which he was to wind up his Berlin studies—he was writing home conveying an almost desperate desire to stay and continue his studies. He wrote to Miss Broughton on 5 January 1905:

> I don't know what to do about next year except that I am crazy to stay. I don't feel ready to come home really. For this year I shall stay with Galston and get as much technique as possible; and then I should like to go to someone else like Ansorge for interpretation. . . . Busoni would be splendid, but I am sure it would do no good to go to him.[39]

Ferruccio Busoni was a renowned pianist and sought-after teacher, and Griffes did not believe he could get into his class. According to Charles, Busoni only accepted extraordinary students who had achieved a very high standard of technique. Therefore, he believed that studying with Busoni was entirely out of the question.[40] Continuing his letter to Miss Broughton, Charles remarked:

> [Herr Joël] insists that I stay another year and go to Ansorge or some such one, after staying this year with Galston. He has another project for my composition, and that is that I try to get with [Engelbert] Humperdinck, the composer of *Hänsel and Gretel*. Humperdinck takes pupils only upon recommendation, but Herr Joël seems to think it might be accomplished, tho' I don't exactly see how myself. It would be simply dandy if I could [study with Humperdinck] for of course in Germany he is almost like Richard Strauss and is regarded as one of the very best teachers.[41]

Griffes went on to explain how he could try to earn some money himself for another year's stay—teaching, accompanying, moving to a cheaper room, and going back to renting an upright piano instead of a grand for practicing in his room at the pension. He then concluded his letter, saying: "I awfully want to stay another year now that I am here. I should love to come home in the summer, but I am sure I should never get back if I once got home, even for only a visit."[42]

In a soul-searching letter to his mother on 12 February 1905 (written not long after the 5 January letter to Miss Broughton, which the Griffes family had no doubt already read), Griffes again expressed his intense yearning for another year in Berlin and spoke of his hopes for the future:

> You ask whether I feel that it would be of more benefit to have another year here now or later, and so far as I am concerned, I feel decidedly that one more year now would be of more value. I realize now that I knew absolutely nothing about music in general when I came over and that tho' I could perhaps play a little better than some other people in Elmira, it was very small indeed compared to really finished playing. . . . A composer nowadays has to be able to write for the orchestra. . . . With me, who never heard an orchestra in my life but three times in Philadelphia and twice in New York, and who didn't know one instrument from another, it takes a long time to get even a slight knowledge of the different instruments and of what can be done with the orchestra. . . . I don't want to become merely a piano teacher. And I feel sure that I shall never become a great concert player and virtuoso, for I realize now that to be such one has to begin much earlier than I did and has to devote much more time to it than I ever did at home. So I want to be an all-round musician who can do something else beside[s] teach and play the piano. Not that I want to play any other instru-

ment than the piano, for it would always be my specialty. But I want to know music in general and especially if I want to do anything with composition, I feel that I ought to have a good foundation. And I guess now there is nothing more to say.[43]

This letter indicates the direction Charles felt his career should take. Clearly he was no longer considering a career as a performer—a decision no doubt influenced by discussions with Emil, by Griffes's growing interest in composition, by his desire to be a well-rounded musician, by his awareness of the difficulties and sacrifices required to build a career as a concert performer, and by his own realistic assessment of his capabilities as a pianist. Charles often despaired about the size of his hands and once wrote to Miss Broughton, "My hands are a fearful nuisance; I should like to exchange them for a decent pair."[44]

Not long after the 12 February letter, Charles again pressed his case to stay on in Berlin. This time he wrote to his mother about financial considerations:

> If [Miss Broughton] can give me the money for next year with-out its being a sacrifice to her I should be willing to do it. I mean that I shouldn't hesitate about the borrowing for another year as I could pay it all back in the end surely and would stand so much the better chance of doing so soon. . . . Oh dear! it is such a misfortune not to have any money when there are so many who could easily spare it. I wish we could find out exactly how it is with Miss Broughton. If only somebody like Uncle Whitney [Wilber Griffes's brother, William Whitney Griffes, who died in January 1905] were able to help me. Now he is gone and whatever he had I suppose will go to Aunt Angie [Whit-ney's second wife, Angelica] who doesn't need it and who has no children to leave it to.[45]

Fortunately, Miss Broughton agreed that Charles should re-main in Berlin to continue his studies, and a happy Charles wrote to her on 19 March 1905: "Do you really want me to stay another year? And I wouldn't want you to think of it if you would have to make the slightest sacrifice on my account."[46]

Charles was on the mark in his letters to Miss Broughton and to his family. If his studies had been terminated in 1905, he would have returned to America without the musical foundation he needed to pursue a career.

6

The Berlin Years

Summer 1905–Summer 1906

Charles moved to Motz Strasse 64, Gartenhaus, "bei Frau Hilpert" (his landlady), on 15 June 1905. He described the advantages of his new location in a letter to his mother dated 6 June:

> [I]t is in a Gartenhaus, which is a house in behind the street house and separated from it by a court generally with a garden in it. . . . They have the advantage of being quiet and are generally cheaper. . . . It is a dandy big [room] with two windows which get the morning sun. . . . [T]he best part of the place is that it is so convenient for my dinners, for the Joël's Pension where I shall take them, is in this same street, No. 70—you see only a couple houses off. . . . They have 3 dandy big rooms. . . . They take as good care of me, as if I belonged to them, or at least they try to. They always say that I belong to the family and am the youngest son, so you see I don't lack for good friends.[1]

Charles was in wonderful spirits at this juncture. The specter of his having to leave Berlin had been banished for another year, and he was delighted with his new room. That Emil lived only a couple of houses away and that Charles took dinner with Emil and his mother at their pension made everything perfect.

Griffes was also looking forward to his summer vacation. The previous summer (1904) he had gone to the Harz Mountains with Miss Broughton and Miss Pigott, but this year Miss Broughton would not be coming to Germany, and Charles would have to make his own plans.

On Sunday, 2 July 1905, Charles and Emil went on an excursion to Sassnitz on the island of Rügen. Charles was entranced by Sassnitz and decided to return in early August for his summer vacation. Besides the beauty of the place, there was the further attraction that Emil and his mother had vacationed there nine or ten times previously and planned to return again that summer.[2]

Many of Charles's friends and acquaintances were leaving Berlin—either for good, like the Shooberts, or for the summer, like the Landaus. Griffes wrote his mother on 17 July 1905, "I should be real lonesome if it weren't for No. 70 [the Joëls], I think, but they don't leave me any time for that."[3]

Charles arrived in Sassnitz on 28 July and found a room at the Villa Carl Hauer (having been instructed by Emil where to look), a room that was

> the best and cheapest I could find. . . . After supper I went along the beach to one of the lovely benches scattered every once in a while near the water and watched the most beautiful sky of pale pink and blue. The water was of a green the color of poppy stems and leaves with the pink of the sky reflected in it and you can imagine how beautiful everything was.[4]

Until Emil and his mother arrived in Sassnitz, Charles was left to his own devices. He attended concerts, read, wandered through the woods and along the water's edge, went swimming (he had learned to swim that June in Berlin), painted (completing four sketches in all), composed music to a short Goethe poem (unidentified) and sent it to Emil, went on pleasure excursions, and reveled in the gorgeous sunsets and the wonderful sounds of the trees and the water.[5]

Of course, Charles did not know anyone on the island, although soon after his arrival he introduced himself to Fraulein Klotz, a girl "Emil met up here 4 or 5 years ago. . . . Emil had a card from her about a week before I came, and he said if I liked her looks I could introduce myself to her as his friend. So after meeting her different times on the beach (I had seen her picture) I went up and spoke to her."[6]

Emil and his mother arrived on 12 August, and a delighted Charles wrote home: "The Joëls arrived yesterday afternoon at 3.30 and are here at the Villa Hauer with me. Emil and I have just come from the bath where we had a lot of fun. It is dandy that we can be here together, for they are so fond of it, too, and know every stone almost."[7] Charles was concerned about not being able to practice and was pleased when a friend of Emil's from Prague arrived because his accommodations included a piano. Charles intended to "work the poor beast hard."[8]

The days and nights on Rügen were filled with activity. Charles and Emil were reading *Ships That Pass in the Night* by Beatrice Harraden in order to improve Emil's English; the sixty-eight-year-old Frau Joël recited English poems by memory, amazing the young Griffes; Emil and Charles took long walks together, went on excursions (sometimes with Frau Joël), attended concerts, and spent time with friends of Emil's.[9]

"The evenings are so beautiful here. The moon rises late and it is enchanting to see it gradually appear above the water," Charles wrote home. "It is always a bright orange at first and then it gets yellow as it goes higher. . . . Everything is transformed by moonlight and the simplest things look lovely. I think one first learns to appreciate moonlight where there is water to reflect everything."[10] For Charles this tranquil scene was no doubt tarnished by the presence of Fraulein Klotz. He remarked to his mother: "This Frl. Klotz was a sort of flame of Emil's five years ago here in Sassnitz. . . . However there is nothing serious this time. She is a Hungarian with black hair and eyes and very fascinating in her way, but I haven't cared much for her from the beginning on."[11] Charles's lack of fondness for Fraulein Klotz is not surprising. She was a rival, if not a very serious one, for Emil's attention.

Emil and his mother left Rügen and returned to Berlin on Wednesday, 30 August, and Charles followed them two days later after a wonderful five-week holiday. Griffes then made a critical decision not to reenroll at the Stern Conservatory. He explained his reasons in an important letter to his mother dated 4 September 1905:

> We [Charles and Emil] have finally decided that I might as well stay with Galston, so I shall do that, but with private lessons. Miss Broughton seems to think it better to be in the Conservatory, but I feel that I have had enough of the Conservatory. I think you get twice as much from private lessons and you don't miss lessons all the time which you have paid for. . . . About composition, I don't know yet. For this last year I need some one [*sic*] more modern and who will give me more incentive [than Rüfer]. I think Emil is of the same opinion and Galston also told me that last June. . . . I do hope you will be satisfied with what I do.[12]

Despite Miss Broughton's reservations, Charles's decision to leave the Stern Conservatory was a valid one. It led to his taking lessons from Engelbert Humperdinck (albeit only about nine in a period from late October 1905 to late April 1906); it allowed him the freedom and responsibility to work more on his own; it prompted him to begin to accept a few pupils of his own (in piano and theory)—a great learning experience as well as a way to earn a little extra money; it encouraged him to perform in public as an accompanist and soloist (sometimes for a fee); and it made him begin to think about seeking employment when his Berlin studies were over.

For Charles things could not be better. He spent a wonderful day on 17 September celebrating his twenty-first birthday with Emil and Frau Joël. In addition to a large cake with candles, there were presents of music from Emil. Emil's birthday was coming up soon (25 September), and Charles was thinking of composing something for him. For Charles, who could not afford to buy Emil anything, this was a perfect way to repay Emil's generosity.[13]

Charles noted in a letter of 15 October that he would be moving from Motz Strasse 64 because his landlady, Frau Hilpert, needed his room for a relative. The move did not upset him because he was sure he could save money at a new location. He moved to Motz Strasse 16, Gartenhaus 1, "bei Frau Wesche," on 1 November and was, to his delight, still only a stone's throw from Motz Strasse 70 and the Joëls. Motz Strasse 16 would be Charles's home until he left Berlin for good in June 1907.

Griffes had always been fussy about his lodgings. He was continually on the lookout for a small pension because he would have more personal attention from the landlady; he insisted on good meals served at his convenience; he did not want too many other music students around because they interfered with his own work; he desired a room that was light and sunny; and, of course, he wanted a place that was not too expensive. As he admitted to his mother, "So I am afraid I am rather hard to suit."[14] He was indeed hard to please and lived at five different addresses in Berlin between August 1903 and June 1907.[15]

Griffes started composition lessons with Engelbert Humperdinck in late October 1905. "I took my first lesson at Humperdinck's last Friday [27 October]. . . . It is going to be much more difficult with him, of course, than with Prof. Rüfer, as he requires more and is stricter. Then of course I want to do more."[16] Charles naturally wrote about the lessons in greater detail to Miss Broughton:

> [W]ith fear and trembling I took them [counterpoint and fugue exercises] out to him, but he hardly looked at them. In the beginning of the first book were two or three exercises that I had done with you those couple of weeks I studied a little counterpoint, and in one of them were parallel octaves. . . . I said I had done that in America when I didn't know much; then he laughed and said "Octaven sind wohl in Amerika erlaubt, ja?" [So, octaves are okay in America?] I have [i.e., had] my first lesson Friday P.M. at 4. . . . [H]e has given me some chorales to harmonize and put counterpoint to.[17]

Griffes wrote to Miss Broughton again in January 1906, describing in detail how his assignments in chorale writing were progressing: "I am still doing chorales, but each lesson they get harder. . . . Now I am doing them with text in each of the voices, so that they have to be singable. I brought him a Scherzo for string-orchestra the first lesson after the vacation, and he wants me to go on and make a suite of it with 4 or 5 movements."[18]

In addition to his lessons with Humperdinck, Charles was busy practicing for his "first real appearance in Germany," an evening of arias and lieder at the Friedrichs Gymnasiums in Berlin on 11 November 1905 featuring tenor Hans Kalinke, who was, as Charles described him, "a sort of protégé of a friend of Emil's."[19] Although Charles would not be paid for the concert, he felt it well worth doing because it was "splendid practice and I must seize every opportunity."[20] Charles was not the only recipient of Emil's musical advice. Although Kalinke had his own voice instructor, Emil took over preparation of the concert, practicing with Herr Kalinke and giving Charles and Kalinke advice on how to act onstage. In addition to accompanying Kalinke in several arias and lieder, Charles played two groups of compositions by Chopin, chosen because "everybody seems to admit that 'Chopin liegt mir sehr gut' [Chopin suits me very well]."[21]

The concert on 11 November went very well, and Charles, for the first time in his life, was satisfied with how he had played:

> Emil was pretty well satisfied with most of [the accompaniments], and he always declares that I do not accompany especially well as a rule. He turned over the leaves for me. . . . It has been simply splendid practice for me, not only the solo-playing, but also the accompanying; for if I do not always accompany well, it lies in a lack of practice and familiarity with the various songs.[22]

Griffes eventually became an excellent accompanist and performed as soloist, accompanist, and ensemble player all his life. Soprano Eva Gauthier, with whom Griffes premiered his op. 10 songs in New York in 1917, characterized him as a "magnificent pianist."[23] Griffes had definite ideas about what constituted good piano playing. Comments in his Berlin letters and, later, in his diaries reveal that he disliked pianists who played too loud and too fast, who were sloppy or careless in execution, and who emphasized technique over interpretation. He admired those with temperament and feeling, those who played with both delicacy and power, and those with control.[24] Griffes's sister-in-law, Charlotte, who studied piano at the Cincinnati College of Music, remembered that Charles played beautifully with a lovely touch and technical facility. His playing was exciting but not flamboyant.[25] One document of Griffes's actual playing exists—a Duo-Art piano roll of *The White Peacock* (reproduced on New World Records NW 310–11).

Griffes continued his intense musical activity into late November and December 1905 and was disappointed that Humperdinck would be gone for four weeks on a trip to America.[26] He commented to Marguerite in a letter written just after the New Year (1906), that his work was taking so much time he had "gotten out of the habit of writing letters."[27] He also continued his numerous sight-seeing and social activities. On 22 November 1905 a carefree Charles wrote to his mother: "Last Sunday P.M. the Joëls had a company of about 18 in the afternoon to coffee and then to supper. . . . I feel quite German being around so much in German society; it is always sort of interesting to feel that you are the only foreigner there."[28] He added a few paragraphs to the letter on 23 November and ended by casually remarking: "It is a long time since Papa has written. I suppose he is so busy and then perhaps there is nothing to write any way [*sic*]."[29]

What Charles could not have known was that his father had died unexpectedly almost two weeks before, on 10 November. Clara Griffes decided not to cable Charles. Instead she broke the news to him in a letter written the day after Wilber's death, a letter that did not reach Charles until 25 November.

> Your letter came Saturday morning a little while before dinner and I don't need to write how I felt; I don't know how you settled down to write as much as you did. . . . You have evidently decided that I ought to stay and Miss Broughton seems also to think that I couldn't be of any very practical use at present. . . . I feel as if I were neglecting my duty over here and as if everybody else must feel the same way about me. Emil and Frau Joël have been doubly kind to me now and have hardly left me a minute to myself. . . . I ought to be very thankful for such a friend, for you may imagine that I never felt the need of one as now. . . . As Miss Broughton says, it is hardly possible for me to realize it all over here. I read about it but yet I can't think that it is any different from when I left. Perhaps it is better so.[30]

Charles was shaken by the terrible news. His father's death posed some unsettling questions. Should he go back to Elmira immediately? What could he do if he did go home? How would it affect his last year in Berlin? Fortunately, Mrs. Griffes had already answered at least some of those questions for her son. On 4 December, Charles wrote home again, having just received another letter from his mother.

> Your letter today was a great comfort. I was very much relieved to see that you were inwardly at rest. . . . At first I wanted to come home, but the more I think of it, the more it seems to me that when I am once here now and just in the midst of my development I had better stay as long as I can and make the most of everything and then be all the readier and more confident when I do come home. Emil is strongly of the same opinion and also everybody else who knows anything about it. . . . I am glad Papa left so peacefully and without realizing it himself; on the whole I am sure we could hardly have wished him a more agreeable end. . . . I hope your Christmas will be a pleasant one even if it is a quiet one.[31]

Even before the death of his father, Griffes had feared his studies in Berlin would end the summer of 1906. And not long after Wilber's death, he and Emil began thinking of ways to extend Charles's stay yet another year, into 1907. Even in his 4 December letter, for example, Charles gingerly broached the subject, writing that Emil might be able to get the money for him to stay another year. On 18 February 1906 he pressed the issue further: "It is also quite clear to me that whatever I do next year I want to and ought to come home for the summer. Whenever we talk about it Emil always insists that I shall surely come back again next fall. . . . Emil thinks also that it would be practically impossible under the conditions here to do much toward paying my own expenses."[32]

Both Galston and Humperdinck were sympathetic to Charles's predicament. In December 1905 Galston assured Charles that money made no difference with the two of them, "that so long as I was in Berlin and wanted to have lessons with him I could have them and pay just what I could, and if I couldn't pay anything at all, why that was all right too and he would simply arrange the lessons a little more conveniently for him."[33] In January 1906 Charles told Humperdinck that he would not be able to pay his price for lessons, and Humperdinck responded that "I needn't let that disturb me, as the money didn't make any difference."[34]

Miss Broughton continued to help Charles financially, but she also believed that he should try to contribute something toward the cost of his Berlin studies if he wanted to stay another year. Charles wrote that he thought it would be practically impossible for him to earn enough on his own to make much difference in what he would need "from America."[35] Miss Broughton generously continued to help Charles as much as she could during 1906 and into 1907, Griffes's last year in Berlin.

Charles continued his lessons with Humperdinck and Galston during the first five months of 1906.[36] His final lesson with Humperdinck, although Charles did not realize it at the time, took place on 27 April 1906. Griffes spent June–August 1906 in Elmira. When Charles returned to Berlin, Humperdinck was too busy to give him lessons in September and October and was away in early November.[37] Finally, in a letter dated 25 November 1906, Charles reported, "I finally had an answer from Humperdinck that he was extremely busy now and didn't feel able to spare me the time for lessons."[38] Emil and Charles decided that he should continue to work on his own, which is just what he did for the remainder of his stay in Germany.

Charles's piano lessons with Gottfried Galston were more regular than his composition lessons with Humperdinck, even though Galston often was away on tour. Those lessons continued throughout 1906 and into 1907, until Charles left Berlin for America. Griffes and Galston enjoyed a friendly, warm relationship that lasted after the Berlin years. Galston was only five years older than Charles, having been born in Vienna on 31 August 1879. Charles attended concerts with Galston and his wife, Sandra Droucker, who was also a pianist, and he received encouragement from Galston in his composition efforts.[39] Charles went to Galston's *Musikabends* (often with Emil), and the two men often discussed music and a variety of other subjects. When Griffes visited Berlin in August 1910, he and Galston resumed their friendship,[40] and when Galston came to New York in 1912 for his American debut, he and Griffes spent several hours together.

Because Griffes did not know whether he would be going home for good in June 1906, he was busy gathering recommendations and writing letters looking for a teaching position. He decided to get new pictures taken in Berlin and wrote to Miss Broughton: "I am sure I look some older now. . . . Herr Joël at any rate maintains that my face has a much maturer and manlier look now, than last year. Don't get anxious for fear I shall grow a mustache, for there is not the slightest danger."[41] Griffes did grow a mustache while he was in Berlin and wore one for the remainder of his life.

Griffes wrote to five conservatories in Berlin (unidentified), to the Cincinnati Conservatory, the Chicago Musical College, the Pittsburgh Conservatory, and Peabody Institute. He obtained letters of recommendation from Humperdinck (who recommended him as an orchestral conductor), Galston, Klatte, Rüfer, and Miss Broughton and was hoping to secure letters from Professor McKnight (Elmira College) and Howard Conant (Elmira Free Academy). He also intended to get a letter from Emil or at least to include his name as a reference.[42] In spite of this job-related activity, Charles and Emil kept up their campaign to convince Mrs. Griffes that Charles should return to Berlin after spending the summer in Elmira.[43]

Apparently Clara Griffes did *not* favor another year in Germany for Charles. On 23 May 1906 he replied to a letter she had sent, which, unfortunately, is no longer extant: "Of course I was sad to read what you say about coming back here for next year, but I can't deny that your reasons have weight and that they have already occurred to me also. I told Emil in the very beginning that you might feel you would need me in America and that it would look queer and cowardly of me to outsiders."[44]

To complicate matters, Emil's mother was very ill, and Emil had to spend most of his time looking after her ("she is at present in a sanitarium in a suburb and that takes Emil's time still more, as he goes out to her everyday from his work and stays until after supper").[45]

Griffes left Berlin for Elmira on 1 June 1906, not knowing for certain whether or not he would ever be back. He sailed from Hamburg on the *Kaiserin Augusta Viktoria* on 7 June and arrived in New York on Friday, 15 June.[46] In Elmira the family and, no doubt, Miss Broughton talked things over, and Griffes was relieved and happy when his mother agreed that, after spending a few weeks at home in Elmira, he could return to Berlin for one more year.

Among the highlights of Griffes's summer in Elmira was a concert he presented in the Elmira College Chapel on 24 July. The program included works by Bach, Beethoven, Liszt, Chopin, Strauss-Reger, and Strauss-Pfeiffer, as well as Griffes's arrangements of two of his own compositions—Nocturne for String Orchestra and "Si mes vers avaient des ailes," the latter originally written for voice and piano—and of Richard Strauss's *Wiegenlied*.[47] The reviewer from the *Elmira [Daily] Gazette and Free Press* commented:

> Mr. Griffes is one of the finest pianists who has visited Elmira for some years. His playing has force, vitality and individuality.

His tone, never overstepping the limits of his instrument, is remarkably powerful. His use of the pedal in sustained passages is skillful and his poetic and mental grasp of the composition remarkable in so young a man. The audience enthusiastically recalled Mr. Griffes six times.[48]

Two days after Charles's successful concert, his grandmother, Delinda, whose mental condition had deteriorated severely after the death of Wilber Griffes, was committed to the Binghamton State Hospital in Binghamton, New York, about fifty miles east of Elmira. Grandmother Tomlinson's commitment caused Clara and the Griffes family much anguish and sorrow, and Charles must have had second thoughts about leaving his family again to return to Germany in the face of such a tragedy. But his plans had been made, and nothing could deter him. Shortly after Charles left for Germany in August 1906, Clara, Marguerite, and Arthur moved from Elmira to Trenton, New Jersey, to live with Katharine and her family. Clara chose to close up the house and leave the packing until the summer of 1907, when Charles would be home again.[49] For all intents and purposes, after August 1906 the Griffes home in Elmira no longer existed.

$$7$$

The Final Year in Berlin

August 1906–July 1907

After spending the summer in Elmira, Griffes sailed for Germany on 18 August 1906, arriving in Berlin via Hamburg on 26 August 1906.[1] Emil met him in Berlin and helped him move into a new room at his old address, Motz Strasse 16. Griffes's new room, although noisier than the one he had vacated in June, two floors below, was larger and better lit and had a nice balcony.[2] Charles was ecstatic that he would have at least another year of study in Berlin and another year to enjoy the intellectual, cultural, and social opportunities that Berlin and Germany had to offer. From the day he first arrived in Germany in August 1903, Griffes knew that the key to his education was availing himself of these opportunities. In so doing, he fueled his lifelong interest in people, places, music, literature, theater, dance, painting, food, nature, parades, and so forth and defined himself as a man and as a musician.

Shortly after Griffes returned to Berlin, he informed his mother that "Frau Joël has been pretty badly off this summer, in fact at one time about a week before I came they didn't know but

what she might go at any moment. Emil has a pretty hard time."[3]
Frau Joël's condition grew progressively worse. On 16 September
she and Emil gave up their rooms at Motz Strasse 70 and moved to
Wiesbaden, almost three hundred miles southwest of Berlin. This
was the last thing that Griffes could ever have imagined, and an
angry and frustrated young man described his feelings to his
mother on 17 September 1906, his twenty-second birthday:

> Frau Joël wasn't getting any better and the doctor said she must
> have a change, so as usual, everything else was set aside on that
> account and they have stored their furniture so as to be entirely
> free. Of course Emil has given up his position and it is abso-
> lutely uncertain whether he will try to get something in that
> neighborhood or whether they will come back to Berlin after a
> few weeks. It is of course a great sacrifice for him and one
> which others as well as myself feel that he ought not to make at
> all, but Frau Joël has gotten so in the habit of expecting him to
> do everything for her that she doesn't seem to think it anything
> unnatural. It exasperates me fearfully sometimes to see how
> absorbingly selfish she is and how Emil gives in to her slightest
> whim.[4]

Charles spent his birthday with Emil's brother Philipp and his wife.
In Emil's absence he eased his loneliness by spending much of his
time with them and with a cousin of Emil's who had recently
moved to Berlin. He considered their friendship of inestimable
worth and realized how fortunate he was to be accepted as part of
the Joël family.[5]

Emil returned to Berlin from Wiesbaden for one day on 29
September to see about a position, and a delighted Charles found
out that Emil and his mother would be returning to the city at the
end of October.[6] This is not to say that Charles could not get
along without Emil. On the contrary, Griffes kept up his usual

flurry of activity, but without his friend the joy and pleasure in everything was greatly diminished.

Emil and his mother came back to Berlin on 28 October 1906, after an absence of about five weeks. Charles breathed a sigh of relief and reported to his mother on 29 October, "Their being in Wiesbaden didn't make any difference about Emil's helping me, and now of course he will be here again and have a position, too."[7]

Frau Joël, whose health seemed to have improved from her stay in Wiesbaden, soon celebrated her seventieth birthday. She and Emil moved into two beautiful rooms in a new, small pension with an elevator, on the edge of the city. Then, on 18 November 1906, Charles informed his mother that Emil had moved in with him at Motz Strasse 16 because Frau Joël required twenty-four hour nursing care, and Emil's room at home was needed. Charles and Emil did not share a room for long, however, because Emil and his mother moved back into the Poltrock pension at Motz Strasse 70 on 1 January 1907. Although Emil would have preferred staying with Charles, he felt his mother would get better care at their old pension, and Frau Joël wanted Emil back with her.[8]

Frau Joël's condition deteriorated rapidly, and she died on 8 January 1907. Charles described the end in a letter to his mother dated 13 January 1907:

> It was a dark, dreary day and it was still drearier sitting in Emil's room waiting for the end to come. . . . For the first time in my life I was at a deathbed and saw some one [sic] dead whom I had known so well in real life. I thought so much that afternoon and evening of you and how it must have been a year ago November.[9]

The death of Emil's mother drew Charles and Emil even closer than before, and Charles could let Emil depend on him in some things, such as choosing the books and pictures that Emil would get from his mother's belongings and helping Emil arrange the furniture in his new room at Motz Strasse 70.[10]

Griffes's last year in Berlin went by swiftly, as he feared it would. He apologized to his mother for the irregularity of his letters, saying, "I think you understand from your own experience how the days go by so quickly."[11] Griffes continued all the activities in which he had been engaged since August 1906: working on composition, studying piano with Galston, teaching piano and harmony to a handful of students (including Emil), performing as a soloist and accompanist in occasional concerts (including music evenings at Emil's pension), attending a variety of musical and cultural events, enjoying the beauties of Berlin, and, of course, spending as much time as possible with Emil.

Griffes also continued to seek a teaching position. Although teaching did not earn him much money (not nearly enough to support himself), Charles did seem to enjoy his pupils in Berlin.[12]

Griffes was an admirer of Richard Strauss and remarked to his mother in March 1906: "It is really a wonderful privilege which one has here hearing him direct at the opera. . . . I don't know what I shall do in America without all these things."[13] Charles attended performances of Strauss's opera *Salome* (which had its Berlin premiere on 5 December 1906) at least four times before he left Berlin.[14] Three weeks after the American premiere of the opera at the Metropolitan Opera House (22 January 1907) a disgusted Griffes wrote:

> There were very absurd things about the work in the New York papers which I had from Uncle Charlie. . . . The opera lasts only a little over an hour and a half and Strauss, foreseeing that some directors might therefore be tempted to give a ballet or some other thing beforehand, forbade them giving anything else on the same evening. . . . [O]f course in New York the fashionable subscribers would have kicked up a row at a performance that lasted only an hour and a half saying they hadn't gotten

their money's worth. . . . [S]o [Heinrich] Conried [manager of the Metropolitan Opera] came upon the idea of giving a concert beforehand with an extremely miscellaneous programme. . . . It is too ridiculous and one cannot wonder that musicians in a place like this make fun of the music in America.[15]

Griffes enjoyed performing at the weekly music evenings in Emil's room at Motz Strasse 70.

I am sending you one of the very finely gotten up programmes—as a surprise Emil had it copied out. . . . Marguerite will translate anything . . . you might want to know. . . . At the Pension, Emil excluded, I go generally by the name of Mr. Griffes, but otherwise I am always called Herr Griffes. Emil generally writes "Karl" instead of "Charles" too.[16]

And he continued to meet new people: "There are five [Norwegians] at the Pension at present and at table we hear Norwegian on all sides. . . . Frl. Juel [a singer] was with me last night."[17] Charles apparently admired Fraulein Juel enough to dedicate one of his German songs, "Nacht liegt auf den fremden Wegen," to her.

Charles also had moments of sheer fun. "Tuesday afternoon I was out in Grunewald with [four friends]. . . . We have had so much snow lately that we came upon the idea of going out there where everything was clean and having a snow-ball fight. . . . [We] snow-balled all the sleighs that came by, coasted down a hill on a sled borrowed from some boys who were doing it, and had our fight besides. . . . We almost got into a fight with one sleigh whose occupants were angry because we threw snow-balls at them."[18]

In May, Griffes finally got to meet Ferruccio Busoni.

Thursday I had an interesting afternoon. I had a lesson with Galston in the morning and then he asked me to go with him to

Busoni's in the afternoon. So I am finally introduced there. It was one of his "days" but there weren't more than twelve people there. . . . I laughed to hear myself introduced as "Monsieur Griffes, un élève de Monsieur Galston" [Mr. Griffes, a student of Mr. Galston].[19]

This meeting with Busoni would prove helpful to Charles in the future, since Busoni's recommendation in 1915 helped convince G. Schirmer to publish six of Griffes's piano compositions.

Amid these activities Charles dreamed of remaining in Berlin yet another year. On 28 April 1907, for example, almost the eleventh hour of his return to America, Charles wrote to his mother: "You seem in your last letter to be very uncertain where I am going to stay next year—that is, whether it will be here or in America. I suppose I ought really to have written the agencies before, but time has gone by so frightfully quickly this winter that I simply didn't realize that it was already so late."[20] This vacillation by her son must have alarmed Mrs. Griffes. But Charles was realistic enough to know that his German days were drawing to a close, and his letters began to reflect the plans he was making for his return to America.

Charles's inquiries to employment agencies seemed to have paid off, since he related to Mrs. Griffes on 27 May 1907:

I have accepted a position from here which I hope and think I shall get. . . . It is as head piano teacher in a conservatory in Wichita, Kans., the Wichita College of Music. . . . I shall have guaranteed $1000 and a certain percentage of all lessons given beyond that. . . . Thanks for the money, which arrived a day or two ago. . . . It will at last [least?] be enough for everything that has to do with the journey, such as baggage from here, etc., and also some over.[21]

On 20 June, Charles informed his mother that the Wichita job had not worked out. He would be returning to America without a position for the fall. Charles moved out of his room on 19 June and stayed with Emil until leaving Berlin about a week later. He was booked to sail on 26 June from Bremen on the North German Lloyd steamer *Barbarossa* and would arrive in New York on 6 July.[22]

And then, that which he and Emil had tried for so long to postpone—the day of his departure from Berlin—was at hand. Griffes's sadness at leaving was not all prompted by the fact that he knew this would be the end of his formal studies. He cherished the sense of "belonging" that he felt in Germany, and he knew that when he left Berlin he would, in all reality, be leaving behind forever Emil's valued friendship and love. Emil's friendship was the source of much of Charles's happiness, as well as a compelling influence on his musical, cultural, and emotional growth during the Berlin years. Griffes's last Berlin composition, *Symphonische Phantasie* (dated 26 August 1907), an ambitious work for orchestra, is dedicated to Emil with the inscription, "Dem einzigen Freunde widme ich diese Partitur, das Kind unserer Freundschaft, in un-vergänglicher Liebe. Cossi" (To my beloved friend, I dedicate this score, the child of our friendship, with undying love. Cossi [Emil's nickname for Charles]).[23]

After returning to the United States, Griffes continued to correspond with Emil and his family as well as with other Berlin friends,[24] and he often wrote about Emil and his family in his diaries. On 17 September 1912, for example, he wrote, "I hardly remembered that it was my birthday; I wonder if anybody in Berlin did?" They did. On 23 September, Griffes noted: "I had a card from Elly tonight with birthday wishes. A strange feeling I had when I saw it in my box! So they did not forget! On the card was a picture of Helmer." Griffes referred to his Berlin years as "that fatal time in Berlin—fatal and yet not fatal. It was a marvellous life."[25]

In August 1914 World War I broke out, and Emil was soon drilling recruits near Berlin and expecting to be called to the front at any time.[26] On 27 November and 4 December 1914, Griffes recorded in his diary that he had received mailings of pamphlets and newspapers defending Germany's position in the war. On 27 November he noted: "Received some pamphlets in defense of Germany mailed from Amsterdam. The address was complete and correct so I don't know whether they came from Emil directly or through the government."

Correspondence between Charles and the Joëls during the war was, naturally, sporadic—almost nonexistent.[27] In a letter to Clara Griffes written after Charles's death, Miss Broughton commented: "I do not understand why Herr Joel [*sic*] has not written. [I]n all my four letters I gave him your address and said 'I am sure you will not fail to write to the sorrowing mother' or something like that. When I sent the newspaper notices I wrote a few lines saying I would answer at length, but I have not yet done so."[28]

Emil, Elly, and their three children survived World War I. Emil died in Berlin about 1929.[29] Although the Joël family was only one-quarter Jewish (Elly's paternal grandfather),[30] with the rise of Hitler in Germany, Emil's wife, Elly, and the three Joël children, Helmer, Gerhard, and Helga, immigrated to the United States. Elly arrived about 1944 via England. An article dated 14 September 1944 in the *Sausalito News* reported:

> A story as dramatic and suspense-laden as the "Seventh Cross" was brought to Sausalito this week, when Mrs. Emil Joel [*sic*] of the prominent Berlin family of musicians and scientists arrived from London for a visit at the Shoobert home. . . . The Shoobert and Joel families have been friends for decades. . . . In 1939 Mrs. Joel and her three children fled Berlin as the war loomed and the liberals were forced underground.[31]

Elly eventually moved to New York and died there by her own hand in 1955.[32]

Charles Griffes's godson, Helmer Karl (born 9 May 1910), arrived in the United States via Cuba in 1941. He was a stockbroker, accountant, and bookkeeper in Germany and from 1938 to 1941 a sight-seeing driver for American tourists in Havana.[33] He settled in the New York City area, where he drove a cab, married in 1941 (no children), and died on 16 May 1982 in Middle Village, Flushing, New York.[34] Gerhard (born 17 January 1912) came to the United States via England in 1938.[35] He was a conductor whose United States experience included one season as assistant conductor-pianist at the Metropolitan Opera (1939–40) and stints conducting touring companies of *Blossom Time* and *Oklahoma!* in 1944.[36] He enlisted in the United States Army in June 1941 and was honorably discharged on 31 October 1941.[37] He married in 1944 (no children) and died by his own hand in 1947 in New York.[38] Helga Joël (born 2 March 1916) came to the United States via Canada in 1939.[39] She was a fine athlete and for a time was an instructor of physical education at the Hockaday School in Dallas, Texas.[40] She married in 1946, had three children, and died in 1965 in Mystic, Connecticut.[41]

Charles Tomlinson Griffes left Elmira in 1903 a rather immature, naive, and self-centered boy of not quite nineteen. He returned to America in 1907 a far more sophisticated (if not worldly) and musically mature man of not quite twenty-three. Naturally, he could never again be the student whose only responsibility was to study and soak up the knowledge gained by personally savoring all the cultural and experiential opportunities open to him. But because of his curiosity and probing mind, Griffes would always be a student in the best sense of the word—always searching, always learning—only from now on he would need to earn his daily bread and take his place in the "real world." Griffes knew that when he left Berlin he was going home to new responsibilities and new unknowns, and he often looked back wistfully on those four wonderful, exciting years in Germany. But he gathered up his belongings, said his good-byes, and returned to America ready to face the future.

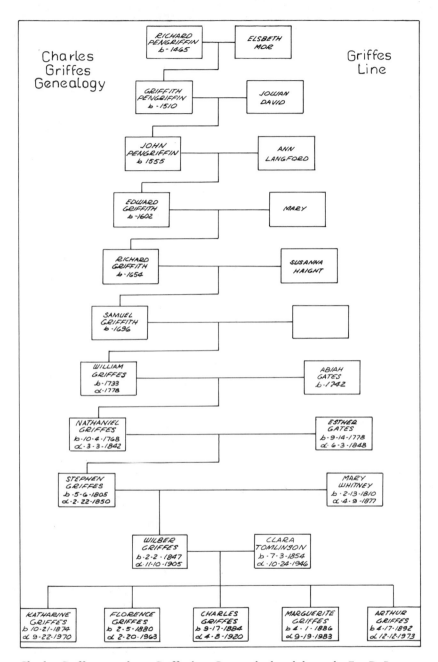

Charles Griffes genealogy: Griffes line. Researched and drawn by Fay D. Rose.

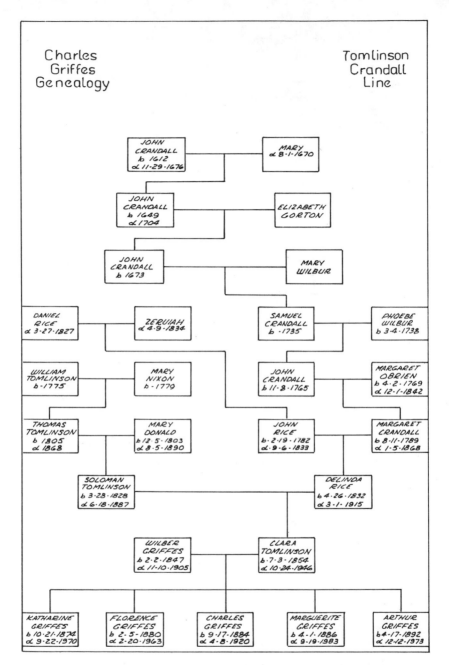

Charles Griffes genealogy: Tomlinson-Crandall line. Researched and drawn by
Fay D. Rose.

Solomon B. Tomlinson, Griffes's maternal
grandfather, an attorney in Elmira, N.Y., ca. 1853.

Delinda Rice Tomlinson, Griffes's maternal
grandmother, ca. 1853.

Wilbur Gideon Griffes, Griffes's father, shortly before his wedding to Clara Tomlinson, 1873. Photo by C. Tomlinson (no relation to the family), Elmira, N.Y.

Clara Louise Tomlinson, Griffes's mother, 18 December 1871. Photo by J. E. Larkin, Elmira, N.Y.

Clara Griffes in later life.

"Uncle Charlie," Clara's
brother Charles Tomlinson,
Griffes's uncle, an attorney
in Albany, N.Y. Photo by
Wallace & Co., Albany, N.Y.

Charles and three of his friends in costume for an Elmira theatrical
production. *Left to right:* Charles, Louis Henry, Truman Fassett, and Albert
Monroe. Photo by R. F. Snyder, Elmira, N.Y.

The Griffes family's rented home at 422 West First Street, Elmira. This is not the house where Charles was born (128 North Main Street) but is the home in which he grew up. Neither house is standing today.

Informal family portrait. *Seated, left to right:* Florence, Arthur, Clara, Marguerite, Wilber, and Charles at the piano. *Standing, left to right:* Katharine, Stephen Roake (Katharine's future husband), and May Roberts (a friend of Katharine's).

One of the Griffes family's "fancy dress parties." *Front row, left to right:* Arthur, next three persons unidentified. *Middle row, left to right:* Stephen Roake, Katharine, Charles, and Reese Pugh. *Back row, left to right:* Marguerite, Jim Aitken, Florence, unidentified.

8

Hackley School

Griffes's studies with Miss Broughton and his four years in Berlin had prepared him well for a professional career in music. After returning to the United States in July 1907, he secured a position as director of music at the Hackley School in Tarrytown, New York, succeeding John D. Hazen, who had resigned on 18 April 1907, in the middle of the spring term.[1] The position of music director was still vacant on 3 June 1907, when Headmaster Henry White Callahan wrote: "We have not as yet been able to secure our Music Teacher. I have found the man whom I would recommend if we can secure him. He is Professor George M. Chadwick, at present Professor of Music in the University of Colorado. He was at one time Director in the Conservatory of Music in Boston."[2] Callahan appears to have confused George M. Chadwick with the well-known George W. Chadwick (no relation), who was director of the New England Conservatory in Boston.[3] Fortunately for Charles Griffes, nothing came of the headmaster's attempt to secure the services of the Colorado Chadwick. Griffes obtained the Hackley position through a teachers' agency and signed on at the last minute—the Hackley 1907–8 school year began on 25 September.[4]

Situated in the beautiful Hudson River valley, about an hour's train ride to New York, Tarrytown in 1907 was a small town of slightly more than 5,000 people.[5] The area and its stately mansions had long been a favorite summer retreat for wealthy and prominent families such as the Pauldings, Goulds, Dodges, and Rockefellers.[6]

With its incorporation as a village on 9 December 1870, Tarrytown began what is known as its "golden age," 1870–1918. The village grew rapidly in services and commodities. Telephone service was installed in June 1883 and electric lights in May 1887. Tarrytown's first trolley line was established in October 1897, running until 1929 when buses replaced the trolley. The trolley ran along Benedict Avenue past Hackley to the train station and was frequently used by Griffes on his journeys to New York. Automobile manufacturing began in 1899, although horse-drawn vehicles and water transportation continued to be popular and important until after World War I. In 1907, the year Griffes arrived, Tarrytown had its first paved street, when a part of Broadway was lined with asphalt. There were also numerous places of business where one could purchase all manner of goods and services. On brick-lined Main Street alone these included a stationery store; tobacco shop; two drugstores; two dry goods stores; two bakeries; a veterinarian; a combined jewelry, optical, and watch-repair shop; an ice cream parlor; saloon; two shoe stores; a candy and toy store; barbershop; combined hardware, steamfitting, plumbing, tinsmithing, and sporting-goods store; two butcher shops and a meat market with an electric refrigeration unit; a combined luggage shop, men's clothing store, and custom tailor; a flower shop; two grocery stores; a bicycle shop; livery stable; music hall, where roller skating was the main attraction; fruit and grocery store; harness and horse-furnishing establishment; Chinese laundry; and the Far and Near Tea Room.[7] Truly, the residents of Tarrytown did not lack for much.

Tarrytown erected its first public school in 1831, replacing it in 1897 by Washington Irving High School.[8] Wealthy and upper-class children generally did not attend public schools, especially if they were preparing for college, and several private schools were established in Tarrytown between 1850 and 1900.[9] Hackley School, among the best of Tarrytown's private boys boarding schools, was founded in 1899,

> not merely as a preparatory school, though the ability to enter college is the natural result of the school routine, but as a place where everything that experience, care, and means can furnish, is given to develop all sides of a boy's life. Athletics—both in doors and out—are provided for under the care of a physical director, the physician in charge, and the masters [faculty]. . . . The social life of the boy is well provided for, and the good manners of a gentleman are expected.
>
> The religious teaching of the school, though distinctly liberal, is not controversial. It emphasizes the simple and universal truths of Christian living. Boys may attend service on Sunday morning at the Church preferred by their parents, but every boy is required to attend the school service in the Chapel Sunday afternoon, at which time visiting clergymen of different denominations give the sermon.[10]

Although guided by a Unitarian board of trustees, Hackley School was, as its catalog stated, nonsectarian.

Frances A. Hackley, the founder of the school, was born in Bethany, Pennsylvania, in 1820. Her husband, Caleb Hackley, made a fortune from mines, quarries, and property in Pennsylvania, and when he died, Mrs. Hackley inherited a considerable estate, which she used for a variety of charitable causes.[11] In 1898 Frances Hackley proposed to Colonel Carrol D. Wright, president of the

Unitarian Association, and the Reverend Samuel A. Eliot, a prominent Unitarian minister, that her summer home on Castle Ridge in Tarrytown be converted to a first-class school for boys. By October 1899 the school was in session. Soon, more room was needed, and in 1900 Mrs. Hackley purchased Waldheim, a large estate adjoining the Hackley forest, and the growth of Hackley began.[12] Frances Hackley lived at the school from 1908 until her death on 4 September 1913 at age ninety-three. Funeral services were held on 6 September in the Hackley Chapel, with Rev. Samuel A. Eliot of Boston (president of the Hackley Board of Trustees) officiating.[13]

Frances Hackley was a complex, often demanding woman.

> To most, she was a marvelous, devout old lady who cared greatly for her religion and the school that she founded and supported. To those who ran afoul of her, including Hackley's first three headmasters and some of the trustees, she was at times capricious and tyrannical. These divergent views hint at both her complex nature, and, perhaps, at the root cause of some of the trouble that was to plague Hackley in the years before her death in 1913.[14]

Mrs. Hackley was a generous benefactress to Hackley School during her lifetime and named it the principal beneficiary in her will. Griffes noted in his diary on 6 February 1914: "Mrs. Hackley's will was finally probated and the results were in the Tarrytown paper tonight. Over $1,000,000 comes to us." The *New York Times* reported the next day: "She leaves an estate of more than $1,000,000. . . . The will was changed many times during 1909, but in the last codicil Mrs. Hackley directed that the residue of the estate should go to the school that bears her name, while there are about $200,000 in bequests to relatives and institutions."[15]

Hackley's first headmaster was Rev. Theodore Chickering Williams, a well-known Unitarian minister, who resigned in 1904 to the "shock and grief" of the school.[16] Williams was replaced by Rev. James Eells, who in turn resigned suddenly, before the start of the 1906 September term. Until Dr. Henry White Callahan arrived from Boulder, Colorado, on 5 February 1907, Senior Master Seaver Buck acted as headmaster.[17] Not long after Callahan's arrival six faculty members resigned, including Griffes's predecessor, John Hazen.[18] Callahan experienced his share of trouble at Hackley from the beginning of his tenure. In addition to faculty unrest, there was friction between him and Mrs. Hackley and problems with the students.[19] Callahan resigned at the end of the 1907–8 academic year (Griffes's first year at Hackley), and Senior Master Walter Gage took over as headmaster. *The Hackley Annual* of 1909 applauded the new administration, stating: "Throughout the school improvement was emphasized—not the attainment of some arbitrary standard set indiscriminately for all. Premium was put upon effort, directed by individual and independent reasoning rather than upon unreasoning obedience to ready made rules."[20]

The early years of Hackley School were filled with turmoil, and it was not until Walter Gage became headmaster—the first noncleric to hold the job and the first to "come up from the ranks"—that things began to settle down. Nonetheless, each Hackley master, including Griffes, knew that his future ultimately lay in the powerful and sometimes arbitrary hands of Mrs. Hackley, the board of trustees, and the headmaster. Gage served as headmaster throughout Griffes's tenure at Hackley, retiring in 1939.[21]

Because of his imperious nature and insistence on strict discipline, Walter Gage was known as "The King" by both the Hackley boys and the Hackley faculty, including Griffes, who often referred to Mr. and Mrs. Gage as "the King and the Queen."[22] Griffes was always conscious of having to please Gage; sometimes he succeeded, sometimes not. For example, he noted in his diary on 28 January 1915 that "Walter jumped on the choir badly today. Says they have no ginger and that I ought to put it into them." But ten days later a proud Griffes reported, "Choir sang pretty well today, so that Walter was rather pleased and spoke of it."[23] Whatever the relationship may have been between Griffes and his headmaster, the Gages showed their concern for Charles in December 1919 when he was confined to bed at Hackley shortly before his death. The headmaster and his wife insisted that Griffes move into their house while they were away for the Christmas holiday. Marguerite Griffes recalled, "They asked my mother and me, Florence and Jim [Griffes's sister and brother-in-law] to come up there and spend Christmas, and [their cook] got a real Christmas dinner for us."[24] Gage served as an honorary pallbearer at Griffes's funeral in New York on 10 April 1920.[25]

Hackley consisted of an Upper School and a Lower School. Boys entering the Upper School for the first year had to be not less than twelve years old and not more than fourteen, except under unusual circumstances. The Lower School was preparatory to the Upper School and had a different corps of instructors. It admitted any boy beyond kindergarten or who was eight years old. Tuition and board in the Upper School when Griffes joined the faculty was $900 (equivalent to about $13,000 in 1990); in the Lower School it was $800 (equivalent to about $11,850 in 1990).[26] From the time of its founding, when it had two pupils and two masters (the year ended with an enrollment of seven boys), Hackley was an exclusive school—expensive and prestigious.[27] During the academic year 1907–8, Griffes's first at Hackley, the total enrollment was 92 boys—78 in the Upper School and 14 in the Lower School. The figure for the year 1918–19, Griffes's last complete year at Hackley, had risen to 113 boys—93 in the Upper School and 20 in the Lower School.[28]

Griffes performed a variety of duties at Hackley. They included teaching private piano (sometimes organ) in both the Upper and Lower schools, directing the choir, playing informal concerts for the faculty and students on Sunday evenings in his studio, performing in formal concerts with guest artists, playing the piano for morning chapel Monday through Saturday in Goodhue Memorial Hall, playing the organ and directing the choir for the obligatory Sunday afternoon service in King Chapel, playing for the short, after-supper informal Sunday evening hymn sing, and presiding over a table of students in the dining room for most evening meals. Wednesday was his free day—after morning chapel, of course.

The 1907–8 Hackley catalog states: "There is much to stimulate interest in music. There is a mandolin club, a small orchestra and a choir, and there are several musicales given each year by the boys, besides the concerts by outside talent."[29] Music at Hackley was an extracurricular activity. This meant that Griffes filled what can best be described as a service position. For example, he trained and directed the choir, but since choir was not a required course, he never knew what kind of a group he would have. His friend and Hackley colleague Frank Ellis ("Daddy") Bogues sang in Griffes's choir for years, helping bolster the bass section.[30] The administration, however, stressed the importance of extracurricular activities at Hackley:

> What the boy does in his idle hours, when his books are laid aside and he is free to use his time as he chooses, is of vital importance. . . . The atmosphere of the classroom invites the imposed task. Outside the classroom, freedom in the choice of real occupation quickly reveals for each individual the avocation essential to a well-rounded career. Extra-curricular activities form a considerable part of the life at School. The real Hackley boy is able to do something besides his assigned work and do it well.[31]

Although this statement comes from a Hackley publication of 1930, it no doubt applied in Griffes's day as well.

A typical day for the students at Hackley during Griffes's years there included a wake-up bell at 6:45 A.M., a five-minute warning bell at 7:05, and the final breakfast bell at 7:10. The boys had to be standing behind their chairs in the dining room at exactly 7:10 when Headmaster Gage started to say grace. It was usually a scramble between the warning bell and the final bell, with the boys staying in bed until the last possible minute. Breakfast concluded at 7:30, and the boys had a half hour before chapel, time usually spent washing up and getting organized for the day. Chapel at 8:00 in Goodhue Memorial Hall was a simple service lasting between five and ten minutes. Gage would read some homily and a prayer, and Griffes would accompany one hymn on the piano (there was no organ in Goodhue Memorial Hall). After morning chapel, classes began. At precisely 11:17 A.M. the bell rang to signal the morning snack. Classes resumed at 11:30 and continued until 1:00 P.M., at which time every-one gathered for lunch. Afternoon classes ran from about 1:30 to 3:00. Then came extracurricular activities such as athletics and music. Dinner was from 6:00 to 6:30 with a Hackley master, includ-ing Griffes, presiding over each table. Saturday was a half day and included the Saturday study period, which let out at 11:00 A.M. (unless the time was extended for a rule infraction such as being late to a meal or to morning chapel). The boys were then free until the next day, Sunday. Compulsory Sunday chapel was scheduled at 5:30 P.M. in King Chapel (also known as Sarah Goodhue King Memo-rial Chapel). On Sundays the evening meal was served at 6:30, after which the boys would sing five or six hymns in the drawing room, accompanied by Griffes on the grand piano. Almost every Sunday evening Griffes would play an informal piano concert in his studio. This was sometimes preceded by a short organ concert by Griffes, a concert by a visiting musician, or some other special event.[32]

Griffes's diaries reflect his Hackley routine, and he almost always wrote about the Sunday evening musical activities. For example, on Sunday, 17 March 1912, he accompanied a visiting violinist and played four solos in a drawing room concert, before playing the usual concert in his room. That Sunday was a fairly typical one for Griffes, and I quote in full the diary entry for that day.

Spent last night in Passaic [New Jersey, where his mother and Marguerite were living], and came up on the 9.57 from there and 11.10 from N.Y. Found the choir all sitting on the chapel steps waiting for me. The fuse was burst out so we rehearsed in my room. Mr. Simons [the guest minister] gave an amazingly strong sermon. The choir sang . . . fairly well, tho' not as well as they could. In the evening was the concert by Miss Trostwyk [Hendrika Troostwÿk] and myself. She made a great success with the boys—probably the greatest ever made here. She has a lovely violin, a beautiful silky tone and a charming finish and interpretation, especially in smaller pieces. I played my first solo, A♭ Ballade of Chopin, badly. Either I was too tired from the opera [Humperdinck's *Königskinder*, which he had heard with his mother the day before at the Metropolitan Opera— diary, 16 March 1912] or I had not "found myself" yet. Played the others, [Rameau's] "Tambourin," [Ravel's] "Jeux d'Eau" and [Liszt's] "Liebestraum" better. I have not yet learned to always be master of my moods in playing. Afterwards Miss T., Mrs. Pierce, Bogues, Newell [Lawrence "Doc" Newell, a faculty colleague] and some of the boys were up in my room. I played the Chopin Polonaise Op. 53 and Valse Op. 42 well enough to retrieve the Ballade. Mrs. Gage and Mrs. Davis in later. Spent last part of evening in Herr Schmidt's [Hugo Schmidt, a faculty colleague] room.[33]

When Griffes first went to Hackley, his living quarters and studio were in the main building. During the 1915 fall term, his studio was moved to the basement of King Chapel, but he kept his bedroom in the main building.[34] Griffes alludes to the reason for the move in a diary entry for 11 April 1915: "The question is where will they put me if they change my rooms back to infirmary." The school did take over Griffes's studio for the infirmary; his piano was moved into the new music room, and on 10 October a pleased Griffes wrote: "11 over for music. It sounds great there. I played 5 of my own pieces."[35] Griffes was delighted with having his studio in the King Chapel basement not only because the music sounded great there but also because he could work late into the night and not a sound could be heard outside. "It is complete isolation of the most agreeable sort."[36]

Griffes often felt frustrated by his duties training and directing the choir. For example, he happily noted in his diary on 28 April 1912: "Took 11.57 from Passaic. . . . [G]ot back to the school by 3.30. No choir!" On 1 May 1914 he wrote: "The choir disgusts me now. The sopranos seem more rotten all the time."

Another aspect of his Hackley duties that Griffes would just as soon have avoided was the after-supper hymn sing. On 8 February 1914 he wrote in his diary: "Walter tried letting the boys select the hymns tonight. It sounded like an auction."

And, although Griffes did not mind his "meal duty" when his tablemates were interesting, he frequently found this duty tiresome, as shown by an 8 October 1912 diary entry: "The table is very dull now. Edgar B. [Edgar Black, Hackley 1915?] is on one side and Foot [Eliot Foot, Hackley 1914] on the other. Before that I had Blaine [Isaac Blaine Stevens, Hackley 1916] and Arlo [Arlo Garnsey, Hackley 1915] beside me. I wish that could have lasted the whole year."[37]

Griffes often went to New York on Saturdays immediately after morning chapel, keeping in mind that he had to be back at Hackley on Sunday in time to rehearse the choir and then play and direct the choir for the 5:30 P.M. chapel service. On his free day (Wednesday), Griffes sometimes stayed at Hackley to practice, compose, enjoy light recreation, and so on: "Practiced 4 hours. Can play the [Liszt] 10th Rhapsody pretty well now and have begun on the 9th. Won a set of tennis from Jimmie Scudder [Hackley, sometime member, 1917] 8–6. Frank [Towsley, a colleague] was in later to have some grape-juice with me. Spent the evening correcting my song proofs [opp. 3 and 4]. Arlo in this evening."[38] However, Griffes naturally spent much of his free time during the school year as well as most school vacations in New York, promoting his music, meeting with friends, making new acquaintances, and generally enjoying the rich opportunities there.

The following diary entries demonstrate a typical week for Griffes (outside of his Hackley responsibilities) during the school year. His level of activity was staggering:

Monday, 28 February 1916: "Practiced 2 hours. Started copying out the 'Peacock' for [Toronto-born dancer] Maud Allan. Note from Mrs. Robinson. Wrote mother."[39]

Tuesday, 29 February 1916: "Practiced 3 hours."

Wednesday, 1 March 1916: "8.32 for Town. Talked with [Leo] Ornstein [Russian pianist and composer] on the 'phone. Rehearsal of the pantomime at the Lewisohn's this A.M. Met mother and Marguerite for lunch at the Rip van Winkle and then they went to Maude Adams in the 'Little Minister,' and I went up to Mrs. Elliot's [Laura Elliot, a close friend]. We went down to see [Brooklyn-born artist] Katharine [Katherine] Dreier's place 'The Ark.' It is a wonderful room with walls entirely hung in gray draperies. It was all done by Elizabeth Duncan [sister of dancer Isadora Duncan]. Tea at the Mallet-Prévost's [friends] at 4.30. I played my 'Scherzo' and 'White Peacock.' They asked me to come up and play my things to their club. At 6.30 down at Maud Allan's to take her the 'Peacock.' Various English managers there. Quite a talk with Griswold [a New York policeman]. Supper with John [Meyer]. 10.45 train back. Rode with Harrington [unknown to author]."[40]

Thursday, 2 March 1916: "Practiced 4 hours. Blaine in after dinner. He talks in a discouraged way about being able to get through and into Harvard next Fall."

Friday, 3 March 1916: "Practiced [number is crossed out] hours. Letter from Miss [Mary] Dreier that she has given up the idea of a reception for the present."[41]

Saturday, 4 March 1916 (another busy day in New York): "8.32 for Town. Rehearsal with Miss Hyland at the Lewisohn's from 10 to 12.15. Lunch alone at the Scheffelhalle. Stopped at [sculptor Onorio] Ruotolo's studio in 14th Street but found him out. Rehearsal of the pantomime again from 3 till 5 o'clock. From there went up to Mrs. Elliot's. [Then in German:] I talked on the way to the former Broadway-17th, who is now stationed at 13th-5th. He told me about an accident, which kept him in the hospital for one month. I'm going to see him again. [Then in English:] Dinner with Mrs. E. at Jack's. Went over to Codington with John [Meyer] at 9 and then back to Mrs. E's again till 11.15. Took the 11.30 back. [Then in German:] Spoke for 10 minutes with Ayres [a policeman] and arranged for him to see me sometime this spring with his car. . . . [Then in English:] Letter from [Noble] Kreider [a musician friend]. Schirmers are returning the Wilde songs for the present. Letter from Henry [Harold Henry, his friend from the Berlin days]. He arrives on Sunday and his recital is on Tuesday."

Sunday, 5 March 1916: "Sketched out two songs to poems by Blake.[42] Sullivan preached. 8 over for music. Frank [Towsley] in for tea afterward. Started [Clayton] Hamilton's 'On the Trail of Stevenson.'"

Even when Griffes allowed himself a "loaf day" (following an "agreement" he had made with his New York friend Laura Elliot), he kept busy. On Wednesday, 12 January 1916, for example, he wrote three letters, read 150 pages in *Madame Bovary,* which he found "wonderful," read some in "The Song of Hugh Glass," an epic poem written in 1915 by John G. Neihardt, went into Tarrytown in the afternoon, and then "watched our first basket-ball [sic] game."[43]

Griffes developed friendships with a few colleagues at Hackley, namely Hugo C. A. ("Herr") Schmidt, who taught German and sciences; Frank Ellis ("Daddy") Bogues, who taught English; Lawrence Whittier ("Doc") Newell, who taught French and German; Ernest Edgar Pierce, who taught Latin and Greek; Frank Hathaway Towsley, who taught mathematics and sciences; and Harry Martin Cook, who replaced Towsley as teacher of mathematics and sciences in 1917.[44] He also developed friendships with Hackley students and their families, notably Isaac Blaine Stevens (Hackley 1916) and Arlo Garnsey (Hackley 1915), as well as with other students who studied with him, such as Harvey Stevenson (Hackley 1913), W. Houston Kenyon, Jr. (Hackley 1917), and Fredrick Y. Smith (Hackley 1922). Griffes's diaries are filled with references to his Hackley colleagues and students and illustrate the warm and friendly times he shared with many of them. For example:

Spent the evening in Herr Schmidt's room; we had the windows open and listened to the sound of the rain. It is a pleasant sound! (12 March 1912)

Newell came in in the evening after lessons and staid [*sic*] till 11 o'clock. We made tea, and discussed modern French authors. (27 May 1912)

Frank in this evening for a while. After coffee we went out and sat on a bench by the chapel. It was a wonderful evening. At such times one appreciates what a beautiful place this is up here. (31 May 1915)

Played 2 sets of tennis with Kenyon, won one 7–5 and lost the other 7–5. (4 October 1915)

Over at the Garnseys for dinner. Mr. Garnsey was still over at the fair. They brought me back in the car. 8 over for music. (14 November 1915)

Down-town [*sic*] this A.M. with Walter and Mrs. G. in the car.
(3 November 1916)

Griffes's colleague Harry Cook described him as a "small-faced Charlie Chaplin." He remembered Griffes as being quite conservative in his dress, retiring and always decorous, quiet, self-sustaining, interested primarily in his music, and as having only a few friends among the students and faculty. Cook admired Griffes's "cleverly arranged" choir programs, which did a great deal to make up for the often rough quality of the singing. And, perhaps most important, Cook remembered Griffes as a kind and gentle teacher, who never discouraged even the most untalented student. He also commented that the students were impressed because Griffes's music was being performed in New York and added that many of the Hackley boys recognized Griffes's talent and admired him because he was modest about his accomplishments.[45] After the performances of *The Kairn of Koridwen* in New York in 1917, the school magazine included a short paragraph in praise of Griffes: "THE HACKLEY wishes to extend its most hearty congratulations to Mr. Griffes both on the composition of the long and difficult passages of music, and on its excellent rendition, as played by him in the orchestra of the theatre. A large delegation of fellows who went in to see the performance pronounced it perfect and complimented the music most highly."[46]

Many of Griffes's Hackley students remembered him with respect and admiration. Harvey Stevenson studied piano with Griffes from 1908 to 1913:

In all humility I believe I was then his favorite pupil, not because of any proficiency—God knows I never really progressed beyond Ethelbert Nevin . . . but because he sensed some latent sensitivity and wanted greatly to bring it to fulfillment. That of course is the essence of a Teacher, and as that too he was therefore great. . . . I try only to convey that, apart from all high musicianship, there was here an educator in the full sense of the term—which includes inspiring the pupil to analyze himself—on however barren the ground.[47]

Stevenson also fondly recalled Griffes's informal Sunday night concerts, "mainly such old stunts as playing ragtime in the manner of the great composers. And he did have humor."[48]

W. Houston Kenyon, Jr., who studied piano and organ with Griffes between 1912 and 1917, described him as a smallish man, tending to baldness, always properly dressed—in fact somewhat "stuffy" about his attire—and not given much to small talk.[49] Although Kenyon admitted to having no particular musical talent, Griffes was a patient and encouraging teacher. Kenyon also reminisced about the "vigor and swing" of Griffes's hymn playing: "I have never since heard hymns played quite so fast. This was not irreverence, but probably a distaste for maudlin sentimentality. Certainly he breathed into familiar hymns a quality of majesty and hopefulness which dawdling play misses."[50]

Fredrick Y. Smith studied piano and sang in Griffes's choir in 1919. He recalled that

> Charles T. Griffes was not an easy man to know. I felt flattered that he paid as much attention to me as he did. . . . He terrified me at first and I thought he was rather a cold, unapproachable character. Perhaps it was our mutual interest in photography that broke the barrier. I'm sure I don't really know what it was, but it wasn't long before I placed him on a pedestal all of his own.[51]

Since Griffes was an avid photographer, it was only natural that when young Smith showed Griffes his new Kodak camera, the two began to share that common interest. Griffes took numerous photographs of the scenery and activities in and around Hackley, many of which he developed himself at the school.[52]

Smith remembered an incident that occurred at one of his piano lessons. He was playing Liszt's *Liebestraum* and struck a wrong note that sounded perfect to him but that Griffes heard and corrected. Smith was astounded at the acuteness of Griffes's ear, and Griffes nonchalantly told him that he could recognize any note played on the piano, even if several were struck at the same time.

> This I doubted and told him so. With that he walked to the farthest corner of the room and with his back to the piano asked me to play any combination of notes. . . . This chance to fool him seemed simple, so I banged all ten digits down at once with some of my fingers pressing more than one key. He then named correctly EACH and EVERY note starting from the lowest— going to the highest! I just couldn't believe such a perfect sense of pitch, so this exercise was repeated several times—but he never made ONE mistake.[53]

Smith's letter makes it clear that Griffes had perfect pitch. This would account for his ability to play by ear and to learn and memorize the vast amount of piano literature he performed at his informal Sunday night concerts during the Hackley years.

Griffes's salary at Hackley was modest but far from inadequate. He was probably hired for the 1907–8 academic year at something close to the $500 his predecessor John Hazen had been earning.[54] Only two diary entries, however, comment on salary. On 24 April 1912 Griffes recorded: "Arranged definitely with Mr. Gage today that I should come back next year, but no settlement in regard to guarantee. He does not want to increase it from $1300 to $1400." From this we know that Griffes earned $1,300 for 1911–12 and probably the same for 1912–13. By the 1915–16 academic year his guarantee had increased to $1,500 (probably from $1,400 in 1914–15),[55] and, according to Edward Maisel, Griffes earned $1,600 in 1916–17 and 1917–18 and $1,700 in 1918–19.[56]

A comparison of faculty salaries indicates that Hackley, not surprisingly, hired new teachers at low salaries and rewarded faculty with longstanding tenure with steady, if not spectacular, raises. Griffes seems to have fit the pattern (if he started out at $500, his salary climbed very quickly during the first four years). The evidence, however, shows that Griffes received somewhat less than comparably experienced colleagues.[57] This is probably because, as director of music at Hackley, Griffes could supplement his guaranteed income (for directing the choir, playing hymns at the various chapel services, performing informal Sunday night concerts, and teaching an assured number of piano and organ students each term) by taking on additional private students.[58] And while Griffes would not have lost salary if he taught fewer students than promised, he would have felt the financial pinch if the number of private pupils above his guarantee dropped off.[59] Hence, his remark in October 1912: "I have only 15 pupils this year, compared to 18 last year. That means economy, I suppose."[60] Griffes's income from lessons was, of course, dependent on the number of students he had at any one time and was always an unknown. According to his extant diaries, he had between fourteen and twenty students each term between 1911 and 1917.[61]

The salary figures cited above do not represent Griffes's total earnings at Hackley, nor do they take into account that Griffes also received free room and board. In fact, the provision of free room and board was among the principal benefits enjoyed by unmarried faculty at the school, and, like Griffes, most of the teachers at Hackley during Griffes's tenure were bachelors.[62]

In 1915 Griffes began repaying Miss Broughton the money she had loaned him during his four years of study in Berlin. He noted in his diary:

> Letter from Miss Broughton. She wants a note for her $1800, which I guess is right. She always said that I needn't worry as

the debt would be canceled in case of her death. Probably that was only on account of uncertainties. Now that I have made good, it probably seems different to her. Or is it the war which has changed things? At any rate 5% interest seems to me too much. The whole thing worries me. I must begin to pay back.[63]

On 15 March 1915 Griffes wrote to Miss Broughton enclosing the note for $1,800.[64] This was a considerable amount, representing more than a year's salary for Griffes, but he apparently did finally pay off the debt.[65]

At the time she asked Griffes to begin repaying his debt, Miss Broughton was earning $950 cash plus $200 room and board at Elmira College.[66] As Griffes had suspected, she was greatly affected by the war and sent every penny she could spare to England for the war effort.[67] In 1915 she was also likely worried about her own financial situation as well as her health. She had suffered a nervous breakdown about 1913 and, as a result, eventually had to relinquish her position as head of the piano department at Elmira College. For the last few years of her life, Miss Broughton taught Spanish (and German?) at Elmira College.[68] She never recovered her health and died on 7 June 1922.[69]

On 3 March 1915 Griffes noted in his diary that he and his Hackley colleague and friend Frank Towsley had started $50 savings accounts in the Tarrytown Savings Bank and that he hoped to increase the amount before 1 April when the bank began paying interest. On 18 March 1915 Griffes deposited another $200 in the bank, and by 3 April 1916 he had accumulated $416.65.[70] Griffes's sister Marguerite recalled that Charles had $2,000 in his savings account when he died in 1920.

[T]here has always been a thing that "rankled" in all of our minds since Charles's death. In the beginning they said it was done to bring to people's attention that young composers had so much to contend with and needed help. It's the one thing I don't like in Mr. St. Aubyn's article, "he now undertook . . . to aid his family financially since he was one of five now fatherless children. He continued to do so for the rest of his life to the extent of half his salary." That is really quite silly. He sent his mother $35 a month, not nearly half his salary, although it was ridiculously small. When he came back from Germany, my sister Katharine had been married for some years and quite apart from the family. Florence graduated from College before Charles left and went immediately into teaching. I myself was working for the last four years of his life and was quite independent. My brother Arthur was in college for four of those years when C. was "struggling to support the family." Also he had $2,000 in the savings bank at the time of his death. I remember Laura Elliot saying she thought it quite remarkable—she never heard of an artist having money in the bank. Charles had enough good old American thrift not to want to start out on a project like setting up his own studio until he was sure he could make a go out of it. I'm just getting this off my chest after all these years.[71]

If Charles sent $35 a month to his mother, that would have amounted to $420 a year, far short of half his salary, as Miss Griffes pointed out.[72] It is also questionable whether Griffes would have needed to continue sending his mother support money after Uncle Charlie died in January 1917, in view of the considerable sum Mrs. Griffes had inherited from her brother.

Griffes expertly and conscientiously fulfilled his obligations at Hackley, but it was his dream to move to New York and establish his own studio so he could devote all his time and energy to composition and performance. That dream was never realized. Griffes must have been painfully aware that he would never be able to support himself completely on his publishing royalties, commissions, and public performances. During his lifetime the most he earned from royalties in a single year was $62.49 (1 August

1915 through 31 July 1916), and his total royalty earnings from 1909 (the year his first published works appeared) to August 1920 were only $307.66.[73] Griffes was a practical man. He told his sister Marguerite that he could never be the starving artist living in a garret and that if and when he moved to New York, he wanted to be financially secure and independent. "Charlie had a streak of sense that way."[74] Griffes was unwilling to risk leaving the financial security of Hackley for the financial uncertainty of New York. His own tentativeness in this regard no doubt exacerbated the frustration he often felt at Hackley. ("It is very dull and stupid to be back," he once wrote in his diary.)[75]

Nevertheless, the position at Hackley was of great importance to Griffes. He may not have found his duties as director of music intellectually or musically challenging or rewarding, but the position had its advantages. On 18 April 1912 Griffes noted in his diary: "Wrote Mr. Rogers saying I would not do anything further about the position at the Utica conservatory, about which he wrote me. The salary is better than here but I hate to leave the many other advantages here." Among those advantages were the lasting friendships he formed with colleagues and students; the beauty and tranquility of Hackley's surroundings; a considerable amount of free time that allowed him to compose, practice, and perform; a modest but steady salary coupled with room and board; and, I would venture to say, the prestige of the school itself—all of which in no small way satisfied his need for environmental and financial security. The proximity of Tarrytown to New York was another important consideration for Griffes. If he had not been able personally to pursue and promote his career in New York, quite possibly he would not have established himself as one of the leading young American composers of his generation.

What Hackley took from Griffes no amount of money could replace—his energy. He spent untold hours on the New York Central commuting between Hackley and Manhattan. When he decided to spend the day in New York, he took the earliest train possible, spent an action-packed few hours showing his musical wares, meeting with friends, and attending concerts, and then caught the late train back to Tarrytown. Once back in Tarrytown, he took the trolley up Benedict Avenue to the Hackley entrance and then had to climb up the steep hill to Hackley proper.[76] These trips, although exciting and stimulating, were exhausting for Griffes both physically and mentally. But he knew they were absolutely necessary to establish himself as a composer.

Griffes himself viewed his Hackley position as both a blessing and a burden, and he was mindful that it offered him a firm base from which he could pursue both his life and his career.

9

Building a Career

New York City, 1909–1918

When Griffes began to establish himself as a composer and pianist in New York City in the second decade of the twentieth century, this city of almost five million people was the largest in the United States, second in the world only to London.[1] New York had everything a young man like Griffes could desire: the best and most diversified array of theaters, art galleries, museums, movie houses, concert halls, opera companies, and ballet and modern dance companies in the United States; 893 newspapers and periodicals—127 of them printed in twenty foreign languages and dialects (these figures were for 1905 and no doubt included all five boroughs); the majestic New York Public Library; beautiful parks, zoos, and other recreational facilities; myriad exotic restaurants; exceptional bookstores; and a wonderfully cosmopolitan population with all the cultural and ethnic benefits such diversity lends to any city. The German population of New York in Griffes's day exceeded that of any German city except Berlin. The city had more Irish than in Dublin and well-defined Italian, Chinese, Jewish, French, Russian, Greek, Armenian, and Arab communities.[2]

In Griffes's lifetime, as today, New York was the cultural center of the United States and home to some of the most influential and powerful music critics in America. The musical life of the city was extraordinarily rich and varied, with such organizations as the Metropolitan Opera (the Manhattan Opera closed in 1910), the New York Symphony Orchestra and the New York Philharmonic Orchestra (the two orchestras merged in 1928), the Russian Symphony Orchestra, the Oratorio Society, the Modern Music Society, and the MacDowell Club. Important concert halls included Carnegie Hall and Aeolian Hall, and the city was the home of such instrumental chamber groups as the Flonzaley [String] Quartet, the Barrère Ensemble and Little Symphony, and the New York Chamber Music Society, all of which played an important role in Griffes's career. New York was also the world headquarters of G. Schirmer, Inc., the exclusive publisher of Griffes's music during his lifetime.[3]

Griffes enjoyed the personal contacts he made in New York. His association with Walter Damrosch, German-American conductor of the New York Symphony Orchestra; Georges Barrère, French-born founder and conductor of the Barrère Ensemble and Little Symphony and first flutist of the New York Symphony Orchestra; and Daniel Gregory Mason, scion of a famous family of American musicians and a member of the faculty at Columbia University, helped gain him recognition by the New York "musical establishment." His relationships with Arthur Farwell, progressive American composer, conductor, educator, and founder of the Wa-Wan Press; Edgard Varèse, avant-garde French composer; and Canadian soprano Eva Gauthier brought him into contact with new developments in music, a niche in which he felt particularly at home. His ties with Russian-born Adolf Bolm, member of the Ballets Russes and founder of the Ballet-Intime, and Tokyo-born Michio Ito, among the century's most imaginative choreographer-dancers, kept him abreast of developments in the

dance world. His close connection with the Americans Alice and
Irene Lewisohn, founders of the Neighborhood Playhouse,
brought him into contact with experimental theater and dance.
His friendship with Italian poet and labor activist Arturo Giovannitti exposed him to new trends in poetry and politics; and his
friendship with Ohio-born Laura Moore Elliot, voice coach and
physiologist, suffragette, and member of the Women's Trade
Union League, among other things, made him keenly aware of
political and social issues. Griffes's creative vision was multifaceted, and he moved as naturally and comfortably in the worlds
of dance and theater as he did in the world of music.[4]

The public gradually became aware of Griffes's music beginning in 1909, when G. Schirmer published five of his German
songs ("Auf dem Teich, dem regungslosen," "Auf geheimem Waldespfade," "Nacht liegt auf den fremden Wegen," "Der träumende See," and "Wohl lag ich einst in Gram und Schmerz"), the
first of his works to appear in print. The next year Schirmer
issued another German song, "Zwei Könige sassen auf Orkadal."
The publication of his German songs was a milestone for Griffes
and must have given him a sense of pride and accomplishment.
After all, he had been a professional musician for only two years.
However, repeated attempts between 1910 and 1915 to interest
Schirmer in publishing more of his works met with rejection, and
Griffes became frustrated and filled with self-doubt: "In a bad
humor all day because Schirmers write that they don't want my 3
piano pieces [*The Lake at Evening, The Vale of Dreams,* and *The
Night Winds*]. I don't know what to think of it. Is it Schirmer's
mercenary spirit, or was Farwell mistaken in thinking so highly of
the pieces? It takes away one's confidence. Am I on the right track
or not?"[5] In April 1912 Schirmer told Griffes that his new music
was "too shimmering" and not as "deep" as his German songs,
and in May of that year, Griffes wrote, "I wish I could get out one
or two real big successes for Schirmer and then they would take

my other things which they don't want to risk now."[6] By 1912 Griffes had already moved away from the German style and was experimenting with the more subtle, colorful, and harmonically free aspects of impressionism. Apparently, Schirmer did not like the direction his music was taking. But to Griffes's credit, he continued on his own path, undeterred by Schirmer's criticism.

On 17 July 1912 Griffes played *The Vale of Dreams* for Arthur Farwell, who found it

> too exquisite and full of beauty of an ethereal and unearthly kind. . . . He says I should, however, give up seeking after this exquisite beauty and seek for the universal and the human. . . . At the same time he considers that I am losing the sense of tonality. "Kubla Kahn" [*sic*] he thought strange and more inter-esting in every way, but impossibly "unklaviermässig" [un-pianistic]. He is right![7]

But the news from Schirmer was still unfavorable: "Had word from Schirmers today that my [German] songs had had no sales at all this year. Strange!"[8]

While in New York on Saturday, 30 November 1912, Griffes

> saw [Kurt] Schindler [at G. Schirmer] at 10 and found him very affable. Played him various songs and piano things. He thinks me still seeking to "find myself" and advises me to hear every-thing possible. But how shall I? I played him the things rejected by Schirmer and he said to hand them in again and he would try to get them through. He thought "Kubla" a remarkable piece— my best so far, and advised sending it in in its present [piano solo] form. On the whole he gave me the greatest encourage-ment, and thought I was decidedly to be reckoned with.[9]

Griffes persisted in his efforts. He visited his publisher regularly, composed steadily, producing several songs and piano pieces, and tirelessly called on other musicians, performing and sharing his works with them.

In July 1913 Griffes sent Gottfried Galston copies of his piano pieces *Barcarolle, The Pleasure-Dome of Kubla Khan, The Lake at Evening,* and *Scherzo.* He remarked in a letter accompanying the manuscripts that he had not yet submitted the *Barcarolle* and *Scherzo* to Schirmer but was sure they would be rejected because, as he put it, "[Schirmer] will probably say that the pieces are too difficult to risk it. That is always their story. Therefore, I will be very grateful for any effort on your part."[10]

On 3 April 1914 Griffes's friend from the Berlin years, Canadian pianist Leslie Hodgson, played possibly the first performance of *The Lake at Evening* at the Chamber Music Hall in Carnegie Hall. Griffes attended the concert and noted in his diary that Hodgson played "*very* well."[11] Apparently *The Lake at Evening* excited some interest because on 9 May 1914 Griffes commented: "Hodgson told me that various people had asked for my 'Lake at Evening,' including some one [*sic*] from out West. Schirmers phoned to him to find out who published it."[12] Only four days earlier a discouraged Griffes had confided to his diary: "Note from Babe and letter from mother enclosing one from Uncle Charlie, in which he speaks of me as a success in life. I wish I could feel that way about it."[13] The irony that Schirmer phoned Hodgson to find out who published *The Lake at Evening,* a work the publisher had rejected in 1912, could only have added to Griffes's dejection.

Griffes did not approach his publisher again until 21 October 1914, when he left five English song manuscripts with Mr. Schirmer himself.[14] On 7 November 1914 Gustave White of Schirmer's staff told Griffes that the songs would most likely be accepted, but Griffes, remembering past disappointments, commented, "I shall believe when I hear."[15] Two weeks later a jubilant and relieved Griffes wrote: "Word from Schirmers today that they have accepted my 5 songs for publication! I thought it would never come."[16] The five songs would be issued late in 1915 in two separate collections: *Tone-Images,* op. 3 ("La Fuite de la lune," 1912;

"Symphony in Yellow," ca. 1912; and "We'll to the Woods, and Gather May," 1914), and *Two Rondels,* op. 4 ("This Book of Hours," before May 1914; and "Come, Love, across the Sunlit Land," before May 1914).

On 30 January 1915 Griffes was back at Schirmer with some of his piano compositions.

> Spent the day [Saturday] in New York. Went to Schirmer's at 12 o'clock and played my "Barcarolle," "Scherzo," "Notturno," and "Lake at Evening" to [Kurt] Schindler. He didn't think they would have much of a popular success in spite of very fine workmanship. Schirmer himself is away now, so Schindler advised me to take the ms. [*sic*] to Busoni. . . . He said he thought I was writing too dreamily and subjectively, and needed to get out into the outer world more.[17]

Griffes immediately wrote to Busoni, went backstage after Busoni's concert on 6 March, and made an appointment to meet with him the following week.[18]

Thursday, 11 March 1915, the day of his meeting with Busoni, assumed special significance for Griffes:

> Took the 12.48 for New York and went up to see Busoni at 2.30. . . . Mrs. Busoni said at once that she remembered my face, [and] wanted to know where she had met me before. It rather surprised me as I haven't seen her since I was at their house in Berlin in 1906 or '07. Busoni asked me to play my manuscripts. To my own surprise I didn't feel at all nervous but played them fairly well. I think "Kubla Khan" interested him. He said there was very good oriental atmosphere in it, and praised the themes. But he advised me to either do it for orchestra or make it shorter for piano. I myself had thought of cutting it up into two pieces. . . . Then he sat down and wrote a letter to Schirmer recommending my pieces very highly. [Griffes couldn't help but add:] Busoni did not look especially attrac-

tive; he had on a peculiar and rather soiled collar and no tie. His hands did not look so large to me at close range. I thought Mrs. Busoni seemed much stouter.[19]

Busoni's recommendation produced immediate results. On 12 March 1915 Griffes signed a royalty agreement with G. Schirmer for the publication of six piano compositions: *Three Tone-Pictures*, op. 5 (*The Lake at Evening*, 1910; *The Vale of Dreams*, 1912; and *The Night Winds*, 1911, rev. 1915) and the three *Fantasy Pieces*, op. 6 (with no collective title indicated—*Barcarolle*, 1912; *Notturno*, 1915; and *Scherzo*, 1913, rev. 1915). The agreement also covered the five English songs for voice and piano, opp. 3 and 4, that Schirmer had accepted in November 1914.[20] This was the breakthrough for which Griffes had been waiting.

During the next five months Griffes was busy preparing the eleven manuscripts for publication. The proofs of the songs were ready by 11 May, and Griffes corrected the proofs and began adding fingering and pedal marks to the piano pieces on 14 May.[21] The next day he was in New York to discuss the markings with Mr. Pinter of Schirmer's editorial staff and to play his piano arrangement of Debussy's *Les Parfums de la nuit* (from *Ibéria*) for Pinter and Gustave White. Because of copyright restrictions, Schirmer could not publish the arrangement, but White suggested sending it to the French publisher Durand and offered to write to Debussy to facilitate the matter.[22] Nothing ever came of this, and Griffes's arrangement is no longer extant.

On 20 May 1915 Griffes was at the New York Public Library, where he found some poems to go with his *Three Tone-Pictures*. He then took the manuscripts to Schirmer. A week later he decided on prefatory texts for the *Fantasy Pieces*. On 7 June he received the second proofs of the songs and finally chose the title *The Vale of Dreams* for the second of the *Tone-Pictures*. By 14 August 1915 all the preparations were complete.[23] During all this activity, Griffes continued writing new music. On 8 June, for example, he noted that he had practically finished a new piano piece, *The White Peacock,* which he had started on 30 May, and on 14 June he began another piano piece, *Legend,* and completed it two days later.[24]

The publication of the five English songs and six piano pieces was an important step in the advancement of Griffes's career. American composer and music critic A. Walter Kramer reviewed the *Three Tone-Pictures* and *Fantasy Pieces* in the 4 December 1915 issue of *Musical America.* Kramer began by discussing the state of piano music in America, concluding that the number of piano compositions written in the United States paled in comparison with America's song output.

> And so one welcomes a newcomer in the ranks of our composers for the piano. The composer we have in mind is Charles T. Griffes. . . . Some eight years ago he published a set of songs for solo voice with piano accompaniment; but these did not bring him before the public. . . . The [piano] pieces are not obvious; they are subtle and there will always be plenty of opposition to the utterance of a man who refuses to follow beaten paths. . . . First let me warn those persons for whom music ended with Beethoven that this composer is a modern—a full-fledged one! He has no desire to write fluent, pretty pieces; he is interested in vital modern music. And I know few native creative musicians who can compare with him for proficiency in doing so. . . . There is considerable discussion as to what is American in music and what is not. I am sure I do not know. But there is a quality in this Barcarolle [op. 6, no. 1]—I should like to call it "punch"—that suggests the live character of our country. . . . They are a notable addition to our piano literature, for in them Mr. Griffes has combined the gift of having something to say with the ability to write it splendidly for the piano.[25]

The review must have been satisfying to Griffes, who had been struggling so long with Schirmer's resistance to his new style, and who had been agonizing about whether or not he was on the right track. Here was welcome affirmation that he was, indeed, on the right track. Griffes, for the first but not the last time, found himself characterized as a modern American composer. A delighted Griffes commented in his diary: "Kramer's article on my piano pieces came out in Mus. Am. It is splendidly written."[26]

The next week Kramer's review of the *Two Rondels,* op. 4, and *Tone-Images,* op. 3, appeared.

> It is pleasant indeed to note that as a song composer, Mr. Griffes is also able. . . . The rondels are perfect songs. . . . In ["This Book of Hours"] one feels a certain atmosphere akin to Ravel. . . . The second rondel ["Come, Love, across the Sunlit Land"] is a bright and cheery one, melodious in character with a swiftly moving piano accompaniment that is finely handled. The first two "Tone-Images" are remarkable songs. ["La Fuite de la lune"] is indeed a splendid piece of imagery, but in the "Symphony in Yellow" there is more than that, there is a perfect representation in tone of Oscar Wilde's curious poem. . . . The song is an impression. . . . The Henley setting, "We'll to the Woods, and Gather May," is a bright cheery concert song, not artistically in the same class as the two Wilde songs, but nevertheless worthy of being sung.[27]

These two reviews represented another milestone for Griffes because, for the first time in his career, his music was the subject of in-depth discussion by an important and respected writer in a major American periodical.

Griffes had no more works published until 1917, but he continued his high level of activity composing and promoting performances of his music. Griffes had decided to spend the summer of 1915 in New York, sharing an apartment with William Earl Brown at 12 West Forty-sixth Street.[28] Laura Elliot had an apartment at the same address, and the two met on 13 July. Griffes noted in his diary that day that he found her "interesting." Charles and Mrs. Elliot became lifelong friends—their relationship was among the most satisfying and happiest of Griffes's life. As their friendship developed, they attended many concerts, plays, ballets, and other events together. They kept up a correspondence during the school year, and Griffes generally dropped in to see Elliot on his trips to New York. From 1916 he used Mrs. Elliot's apartment as his summer residence.[29]

As an admirer of Griffes's music, Laura Elliot tried to help further his career in whatever way she could. On 1 December 1915 Griffes noted in his diary that Elliot "had talked with Farwell about me and had lots to say. She thinks I must get into pageantry or some bigger thing." Equally important, she introduced Griffes to her wide and varied circle of friends, among them the poet Arturo Giovannitti and the Lewisohn sisters, Alice and Irene, founders of the Neighborhood Playhouse, on whose staff Laura Elliot served.[30] As Griffes's circle of professional acquaintances and friends broadened, so, too, did the opportunities for having his music performed, published, and made more widely known.

The last months of 1915 were filled with Griffes's usual flurry of activity. He was working on woodwind-harp chamber arrangements of his *Three Tone-Pictures* for Georges Barrère, two songs to texts by Oscar Wilde ("Le Jardin" and "Impression du matin"), and the piano piece *De Profundis.*[31]

Griffes continued to call on fellow artists and musicians in New York. On 7 October 1915 he saw Polish-American pianist, composer, and teacher Alexander Lambert, who told Griffes that he neither liked nor understood modern music. Nonetheless, Griffes played him some of his compositions, and Lambert "admitted they were well made and far above the niveau [level] of some other Americans he mentioned. Ornstein he had refused to meet. Farwell's pieces he thought frightful. He called my 'Lake' charming. He also said: 'Do you know, you are an excellent pianist. You have a very beautiful touch.'"[32] Later that day Griffes also called on Italian pianist Paolo Martucci, "who said he played little modern music and then only of his father [Giuseppe]."[33] Griffes stood no chance of having his music performed by either of these gentlemen.

Griffes visited Arthur Farwell on 9 October, played him several of his new pieces, looked at some of Farwell's latest manuscripts, and took away two of Farwell's piano pieces "to look through to give him my opinion. I don't like them very much. . . . At least they are not pianistic."[34] On 16 October Griffes visited yet another pianist, Charles Cooper, a young Californian: "Had a most delightful long call on Charles Cooper this P.M. Found him unsympathetic toward 'impressions' and vague music, including all modern French, on the other hand very interested in Schönberg, whom he admired for simplicity of Klaviersatz [piano style] and getting away from rhythm. He is worth knowing. He said he would like to learn the 'Lake.'"[35] Cooper performed *The Lake at Evening* in a New York concert on 25 November 1916, which Griffes and Frank Towsley attended together.[36] On 25 October 1915 Griffes noted in his diary that Indiana-born composer and pianist Noble Kreider had sent him a long letter in which he said he might learn Griffes's *Scherzo* and *The Night Winds*. Griffes also noted that Lewis Isaacs, of Pelham, New York, whom he had met in March 1914, had sent him his *Peterborough Sketches*, which Griffes did not like because "they are all too much MacDowell to suit me."[37]

Griffes attended a variety of concerts during 1915, finding, among other things, Beethoven's symphonies boring, American composer Charles Martin Loeffler's *La Mort de Tintagiles* too long in spite of much beautiful work, Ravel's String Quartet exciting and stirring, Percy Grainger's *Tribute to Foster* a stunt in color technique, and Stravinsky's *Petrouchka* delightful music.[38]

During 1916 Griffes continued to promote his music actively. He met for the first time or continued his acquaintance with such people as Adolf Bolm, French conductor Pierre Monteux, Edgard

Varèse, Swiss pianist, conductor, and teacher Rudolph Ganz, No-
ble Kreider, American pianist Katherine Ruth Heyman, British-
American conductor Walter Rothwell, American composer and
pianist Arthur Whiting, Australian pianist and composer Percy
Grainger, Leo Ornstein, French cabaret singer-actress Yvette
Guilbert, and a host of others.

The year 1916 was also a busy period from a compositional
standpoint. Among the works Griffes composed were several
songs, including "Landscape," "The Old Temple among the
Mountains," "Tears," "In a Myrtle Shade," "Waikiki," "Phantoms"
(Giovannitti), "La Mer" (second version), and "Song of the Dagger." Griffes added to his piano oeuvre the Piano Piece in E Major,
Nightfall, The Fountain of the Acqua Paola, Clouds, and Dance in A
Minor. Compositions from 1916 also included "These Things Shall
Be," a labor song for unison chorus and piano written at the
request of Laura Elliot,[39] and *The Kairn of Koridwen,* a dance-
drama written for the Neighborhood Playhouse. Finally, Griffes
began composing his orchestral version of *The Pleasure-Dome of
Kubla Khan,* a process that would occupy him for more than a
year and a half.

On 23 February 1916 English pianist Winifred Christie premiered *The White Peacock* (not yet published) on her New York
recital at the Punch and Judy Theatre at 155 East Forty-ninth
Street.[40] Griffes attended Christie's recital with Laura Elliot and
his sister Marguerite but was not entirely satisfied with Christie's
performance: "She played mostly modern things. The 'Peacock'
lacked color. Mrs. E. said she played according to melodic phrases
rather than harmonically, which is quite true."[41] Because of Christie's reputation, the concert attracted much critical attention, but
only British-born Sylvester Rawling of the *Evening World* mentioned Griffes specifically: "The names of Debussy, Ravel, Frederick Jacobi, Charles Griffes and Alfredo Casella were associated
with those of Bach, Brahms and Chopin. The combination was

fascinating."[42] This was hardly a rave review for Griffes, to be sure, but Rawling was a respected critic on a major New York newspaper, and even to be thus mentioned carried some significance. Equally important, Griffes was told by Mr. Meyer at Schirmer that there had been several requests for *The White Peacock*.[43] Such requests would stand him in good stead when submitting new pieces to Schirmer for publication.

Two more New York performances took place in 1916. On 12 April singer-composer Tom Dobson premiered "Symphony in Yellow" in an afternoon recital at the Punch and Judy Theatre.[44] At least four reviews of Dobson's recital appeared, but none of them mentioned Griffes. Strangely, Griffes did not attend Dobson's concert. Instead, he had lunch with Laura Elliot and saw Charlie Chaplin's movie burlesque of *Carmen*.[45] On 19 December at the Cort Theatre on Forty-eighth Street near Broadway, the Barrère Ensemble premiered Griffes's woodwind-harp arrangements of *The Lake at Evening* (November–December 1915) and *The Vale of Dreams* (December 1915), both of which Griffes had written specifically for Barrère.[46] Several reviews appeared, one of which called Griffes's arrangements "a sort of modern musical tweedle-dee and tweedle-dum."[47]

Griffes kept up his visits to G. Schirmer during 1916, and although nothing appeared in print that year, he signed a contract for his piano pieces *Roman Sketches*, op. 7 *(The White Peacock, Nightfall, The Fountain of the Acqua Paola,* and *Clouds)*, on 11 December 1916.[48] Griffes had taken the pieces to Gustave White at Schirmer on 23 August 1916 and commented in his diary, "He was very enthusiastic and called them the last word in piano music."[49]

Percy Grainger told Griffes on 1 April 1916 that he was writing an article for the New York *World* about Griffes's compositions. Nothing came of that, but through Grainger, Griffes met Ratan Devi and her husband, Dr. Ananda Coomaraswamy.[50] Devi, an English singer who specialized in performing Indian ragas and

Kashmiri folk songs, accompanying herself on the tamboura and dressed in authentic costume, was a member of Adolf Bolm's Ballet-Intime when Griffes joined the troupe for its summer tour and New York performances in August 1917.[51]

On 6 May 1916 Griffes met Yvette Guilbert at a party. He remarked in his diary: "Yvette was great to everybody and kept the place amused. I played her 3 of my pieces and got an invitation to come and see her at the hotel. Arthur Whiting, who was there, was astonished at my mastery of the French style."[52]

A week later Griffes "called on Rudolf Ganz and had a splendid time. Played him all my stuff. He thought I was between Scriabin and the later Ravel, and said some flattering things. I shall go up again in 3 wks. At 5.45 was down at the Knickerbocker to see Yvette Guilbert. Played my stuff to her and her husband, Dr. [Max] Schiller. He proposed a scheme of concerts of American music for next year."[53] Nothing came of Dr. Schiller's "scheme," but Griffes's meeting with Ganz did yield fruit. In a *Musical America* article dated 1 July 1916, Ganz remarked: "I was looking over some compositions the other day which a young composer, Charles Griffes by name, had brought me. I found them both interesting and beautiful. He goes his own way, though in style and workmanship his pieces are somewhat along the lines of Schönberg and Ravel."[54] Later that year Griffes dedicated *The White Peacock* to Ganz.[55]

In June 1916 Griffes called on Arthur Whiting and "played him 'Kubla' and the new piano pieces. He raked me over the coals for dreaming of writing an orchestral score [*The Pleasure-Dome of Kubla Khan*] until I knew the separate instruments thoroughly. . . . We had a splendid talk. He advises Bach, rhymical [*sic*] studies, and striving for more vitality and red-blood. He lent me [Cecil] Forsyth's 'Orchestration.'"[56]

On 11 October, Griffes met Pierre Monteux: "This A.M. I went over to the Manhattan to the Ballet russes [*sic*] rehearsal. . . .

I got acquainted with Pierre Monteux, the new French conductor and had a fine talk with him. He invited me to the stage rehearsals of [Richard Strauss's] 'Till Eulenspiegel.'"[57] Just two days earlier Monteux, perhaps reflecting the anti-German sentiment sweeping America at the time, had refused to conduct the Ballets Russes performance of *Till Eulenspiegel*.[58]

Griffes called on Edgard Varèse on 19 November 1916 and noted in his diary that he "had a most interesting time. [Varèse] showed me an extraordinary score. His views are most radical. . . . We spoke German entirely. He seems well acquainted with Schönberg, Ravel, Debussy, Strawinsky, Strauss and everybody else. He was interested in my stuff and wants to hear the Pantomime [*The Kairn of Koridwen*, which Griffes had recently written for the Neighborhood Playhouse]."

One of Griffes's most important professional collaborations was with the Neighborhood Playhouse, founded in 1915 by Alice and Irene Lewisohn and located on the lower East Side of New York at 466 Grand Street. The Lewisohns founded the Playhouse "from the need to integrate media of production at a time when photographic representation dominated the commercial stage, when lyric forms expressed through the dance, or through song, were relegated to the music hall, opera bouffe, or opera ballet."[59] Experimentation brought about a desire for unity in the theater as well as in the other arts. In his book *The American Theatre*, Ethan Mordden credited Gordon Craig for spearheading the movement: "Craig recommended deposing the actor-managers and their Big Moments in favor of a more organic concept: light and sound, color and movement, all would flow together, suggesting to the spectator the most profound and universal images."[60] Little theaters like the Neighborhood Playhouse grew up all over the United States as a result of this experimentation. "[They] developed a sense of style, carrying a look and feel all their own from work to work. They alerted each other to new achievements abroad, staying young. And they cut themselves off entirely from the regular run of Broadway's prefabricated concoctions set in living rooms or police headquarters."[61]

Griffes's first professional encounter with the Neighborhood Playhouse came about in 1916 when he was engaged as one of two pianists, along with the staff pianist Lily May Hyland, to accompany a series of performances of Igor Stravinsky's ballet *Petrouchka*. The ballet was also being presented by Serge Diaghilev's Ballets Russes during their 1915–16 New York season, with orchestra, of course. The Playhouse *Petrouchka* opened on 11 March 1916. Griffes noted in his diary, "Everything was splendid." About three weeks later Griffes attended a Ballets Russes performance of *Petrouchka* with Laura Elliot and Lily Hyland and noted proudly, "The stage is more animated and brilliant at the Playhouse 'Pètrouchka [*sic*].'"[62] The Playhouse production was so popular that it was revived the next season with Griffes again engaged as pianist.[63]

Griffes's association with the Neighborhood Playhouse led to commissions for two of his most unusual works: *The Kairn of Koridwen* (1916), a dance-drama produced by the Playhouse in February, March, and April 1917, and *Salut au monde* (1919, score completed by Edmond Rickett after Griffes's death), a festival drama produced at the Playhouse in April and May 1922.

Alice and Irene Lewisohn first suggested *The Kairn* Neighborhood Playhouse project to Griffes on 22 June 1916: "At 5 o'clock down at the Lewisohn's for 2 hours discussing next year's plans. They are thinking of a fine old druid legend for which I may do the music."[64] Griffes received the commission and worked steadily on *The Kairn* during August and December 1916, sketching, orchestrating, polishing, and playing his music at various times for a variety of people.[65] At this point in his career, a success with *The Kairn* could open doors for him and help put him on the map, musically speaking, and Griffes knew it. Therefore, when *The*

Kairn of Koridwen opened on 10 February 1917 (Nikolai Sokoloff conducted members of the Barrère Ensemble with Griffes at the piano),[66] one of the reviews was of special importance to Griffes. New York–born literary and music critic Paul Rosenfeld, in a long, penetrating article for *Seven Arts,* commented that he found the mise-en-scène unusually monotonous and ineffective and the dancers lacking subtlety. But of Griffes he wrote:

> One could at least return home with the sense of having undergone an experience. That was made possible by the musical setting, the work of Mr. Charles T. Griffes. It alone lifted the little dance-drama from mediocrity into importance. For Mr. Griffes' score is something more than an able setting. It is a felicitous and often brilliant piece of work. . . . It abounds in passages of rare loveliness. It is skillful and imaginative. . . . Better than anything that occurred on the stage, it expressed the essential idea that underlay the drama. Mr. Griffes' score is significant for another reason. For in it, his talent for the first time has made a satisfactory manifestation. An idiom a little undecided, a little derivative, a personal expression a little hesitant, has become formed and individual and respectable. The music for "The Kairn of Koridwen" should bring Mr. Griffes reputation more surely than his piano music, more surely, indeed, than anything that he has hitherto composed. . . . Today, there can be no more question of Mr. Griffes' rare ability.[67]

Rosenfeld's view that *The Kairn* represented a stylistic breakthrough for Griffes was a perceptive one. The score is stylistically in a class by itself, quite unlike anything else that Griffes ever wrote, either before or after. Rosenfeld was correct in stating that Griffes's talent had here "made a satisfactory manifestation," but one could argue with the phrase "for the first time." Unfortunately, when Rosenfeld stated that *The Kairn* score should enhance Griffes's reputation more than anything he had composed up to that time, his prediction was wrong. It did not enhance Griffes's reputation to the extent it should have, primarily because *The Kairn* was neither published nor performed again during Griffes's lifetime. Even today the score remains unpublished.

The year 1917 had started out on a good note for Griffes, thanks to *The Kairn of Koridwen,* and it continued to be a good year. Publications included the *Roman Sketches,* op. 7, for piano, "These Things Shall Be," and *Five Poems of Ancient China and Japan,* op. 10, for voice and piano ("So-fei Gathering Flowers," 1917; "Landscape," 1916; "The Old Temple among the Mountains," 1916; "Tears," 1916; and "A Feast of Lanterns," 1917).[68]

Compositions completed in 1917 included several songs, among them "In the Harem" (late 1916?), "So-fei Gathering Flowers" (April), "A Feast of Lanterns" (August), and "Sorrow of Mydath" (December); the pantomime *Sho-jo* (July); a movement for string quartet; the chamber arrangements *Sakura-sakura, Noge no yama,* and *Komori uta;* and a chamber orchestra arrangement of Alexander Maloof's piano solo *A Trip to Syria.* In 1917 Griffes also began what was to be one of his greatest works, the Piano Sonata and completed what was to become his best-known orchestral work, *The Pleasure-Dome of Kubla Khan.* Griffes began trying to interest conductors in performing *The Pleasure-Dome,* and to that end he left a score with Walter Damrosch on 6 October and sent a score to Leopold Stokowski on 24 October.[69] Nothing came of these attempts, but both Stokowski and Damrosch conducted first performances of other Griffes works in 1919.

The publication of Griffes's *Roman Sketches,* op. 7, in 1917 elicited several reviews. Critics continued to comment on his "modernity." Perhaps the most insightful review was that in the *Musical Leader.*

These works are new in every sense of the word for Mr. Griffes has fearlessly and frankly championed the cause of the "ultra modern" and has evolved a style that is sincere and original. More than any other American composer has he dared to free himself from tradition without overstepping the bounds of honesty and beauty. . . . Perhaps the highest praise to be given these works is that they are absolutely pianistic, a virtue that is lacking in much of the so-called "ultra modern" piano music.[70]

New York performances of Griffes's music in 1917 were numerous. Premieres included *The Kairn of Koridwen* with the Neighborhood Players and the Barrère Ensemble (Griffes at the piano) at the Neighborhood Playhouse on 10 February; possible first performances of *The Vale of Dreams* (op. 5, no. 2) and *The Night Winds* (op. 5, no. 3) by pianist Cadance Meakle (a pupil of Eugene Heffley) at Heffley's studio in Carnegie Hall on 5 May;[71] "These Things Shall Be" by the New York Community Chorus, Harry Barnhart conducting, at the Hippodrome on 1 June;[72] *Assyrian Dance, Sakura-sakura,* and *Sho-jo* by Adolf Bolm's Ballet-Intime (Griffes at the piano), in Atlantic City on 5 August (subsequent performances in Washington, D.C., and New York);[73] and *Five Poems of Ancient China and Japan,* op. 10, featuring soprano Eva Gauthier (Griffes at the piano), in Aeolian Hall on 1 November.[74]

Griffes's connection to the world of dance was a vital one. He met Adolf Bolm, the great Russian dancer, in 1916 when the latter came to this country as a member of the Ballets Russes. During the company's second American tour, Bolm injured himself and decided to stay in the United States, forming the Ballet-Intime in New York.[75] Bolm's new company included such artists as Michio Ito and Danish dancer Tulle Lindahl,[76] both of whom starred in the 1917 performances of *Sho-jo.*

Sho-jo is among Griffes's best "oriental" compositions. In conjunction with the Ballet-Intime performances, American librettist and writer Frederick H. Martens interviewed Griffes for an article in the *New Music Review and Church Music Review.* Griffes explained to Martens that *Sho-jo* was "developed" Japanese music. He further elaborated:

> I purposely do not use the term "idealized." [Charles Wakefield] Cadman and others have taken American Indian themes and have "idealized" rather than "developed" them in Indian style. There is really nothing in them save themes; the harmonization, etc., might have come from Broadway. Modern music tends more and more toward the archaic, especially the archaism of the East. . . . There is a striving for harmonies which suggest the quarter-tones of Oriental music, and the frequent employ of the characteristic augmented second; as well as the organ point [pedal point] common to both systems. . . . And all this I have borne in mind in the development of the *Sho-Jo* music.[77]

Griffes's *Sho-jo* harmonizations omit major thirds and sixths and are all in octaves, fifths, fourths, and seconds. "The orchestration is as Japanese as possible: thin and delicate, and the muted string *points d'orgue* serve as a neutral-tinted background, like the empty spaces in a Japanese print."[78]

Among the many reviews of the New York Ballet-Intime performances was one in the *Musical Leader* that must have been especially pleasing to Griffes because it indicates how successfully he had captured the oriental idiom.

> From the musical standpoint the detail which stood out in bold relief was the orchestration supplied by Chas. T. Griffes for a pantomime done by Itow and Miss Lindahl. . . . He caught the spirit of Japan to a remarkable degree using here and there a few themes that are genuine folk tunes. . . . Throughout[,] the music and the dance as well as the staging had the delicacy and distinction of a Japanese print.[79]

The 1 November performance of his op. 10 songs with soprano Eva Gauthier was of great significance to Griffes for several reasons. First, Gauthier's reputation as a singer of avant-garde music generated considerable critical interest in the concert, which, in addition to the Griffes songs, featured the American premieres of works by Igor Stravinsky, Maurice Ravel, and Nikolai Rimsky-Korsakov. Second, the concert took place in Aeolian Hall, one of New York City's "prestige" recital halls. For Griffes this marked his New York debut as accompanist in his own songs. Gauthier and Griffes rehearsed even as the composer was correcting proofs for the publication of the songs.[80] The performance elicited at least fifteen reviews. One, by Philadelphia-born and Princeton-trained musicologist Sigmund Spaeth, must have especially pleased Griffes because it compared him favorably with Igor Stravinsky, whose *Trois poésies de la lyrique japonaise* were also premiered by Gauthier on the November program. Spaeth commented:

> But the real features of Mme. Gauthier's programme were the Chinese and Japanese inspirations of Charles T. Griffes and Igor Strawinsky. Of the two, Mr. Griffes adhered the more closely to the traditional scales of the far East, and in general made his effects the more intelligible and hence convincing. This American composer has already given many proofs of his ability to appropriate and revitalize the oriental spirit, and the five examples of his work presented last evening were in his happiest vein.[81]

The critic from the *Boston Evening Transcript* was less enthusiastic: "Mr. Griffes's five experiments with the Chinese pentatonic scale . . . suggest no little cleverness on the part of the composer. . . . The songs are sufficiently 'Chinese' in character to satisfy the most exotic imagination. But they achieve little beauty and less variety."[82]

On the night of Gauthier's concert, a new theater admissions war tax went into effect, and several reviewers noted that the tax had not reduced attendance. This new tax was a reminder that the United States was fighting in World War I. The Selective Service Act of 18 May 1917 had provided for the registration and classification for military service of all men between the ages of twenty-one and thirty. Griffes, not quite thirty-three, was exempt. However, the Man Power Act of 31 August 1918, which amended the Selective Service Act, required the registration of all men between eighteen and forty-five years.[83] Griffes, who would be thirty-four on 17 September 1918, was now subject to the draft. In an attempt to take advantage of his skill in languages, Griffes took tests in German and French hoping to secure a commission as an interpreter. He was told by the examiner that he spoke better German than most Germans.[84] On 3 November 1918 Griffes wrote to his friend Burnet Tuthill (New York–born composer) that he was a candidate for a commission in the Interpreters' Corps in France, had passed all the examinations with excellent marks, and "understood that I was accepted and would sail about this time. Now the matter seems to be held up for more references. At any rate . . . I told them they could get information from you if they cared to."[85] Fortunately, an armistice bringing an end to the hostilities was signed by President Woodrow Wilson on 11 November 1918. World War I had ended, and Griffes would not have to serve.

Griffes's Chinese and Japanese songs, op. 10, appeared in print in late 1917 or early 1918 (the copyright date is 1917) with the title *Five Poems of Ancient China and Japan.*[86] Publication reviews of the op. 10 songs were positive. Critic A. Walter Kramer found the songs "rather more tangible than the majority of his present output. . . . The modern note is far from absent; in fact, they are fully modern enough, but their modernity rings true."[87]

In 1918 G. Schirmer published several Griffes compositions: *Three Poems,* op. 9 ("In a Myrtle Shade," "Waikiki," and "Phantoms," all written in 1916);[88] *Three Poems by Fiona Macleod,* op. 11 ("The Lament of Ian the Proud," "Thy Dark Eyes to Mine," and

"The Rose of the Night," all written in 1918);[89] and three sets of piano pieces written for children under the pseudonym Arthur Tomlinson—*Six Short Pieces, Six Patriotic Songs,* and *Six Bugle-Call Pieces*—all probably written in 1918. These were the last works published during Griffes's lifetime. Griffes may also have written two additional sets of children's pieces, *Six Familiar Songs* and *Six Pieces for Treble Clef,* in 1918 or circa 1919, but these were not published until 1920.

Compositions from 1918 included some of the composer's most significant works: the Piano Sonata (December 1917–January 1918, rev. May 1919); the three songs "The Rose of the Night" (January), "The Lament of Ian the Proud" (May), and "Thy Dark Eyes to Mine" (May) in both voice and piano and voice and orchestra versions (the latter ca. 1918); "An Old Song Re-sung" (July); *Poem for Flute and Orchestra; Notturno für Orchester* (1918? probably earlier); Lento e mesto for string quartet (June; first movement of *Two Sketches for String Quartet Based on Indian Themes*); and the piano pieces for children.

The year itself had opened with an important concert for Griffes, namely, an "Evening of Compositions by Charles T. Griffes," sponsored by the MacDowell Club of New York on 26 February—the first major concert devoted exclusively to Griffes's music. The concert included *Sho-jo,* danced by Michio Ito (first performance of the version for piano and dancer); the op. 10 Chinese and Japanese songs, performed by Eva Gauthier; the premiere of the Piano Sonata; *Roman Sketches,* op. 7; and the piano pieces *Barcarolle* (op. 6, no. 1), *The Lake at Evening* (op. 5, no. 1), and *Scherzo* (op. 6, no. 3). Griffes appeared as both piano soloist and accompanist.[90]

Several reviews of the all-Griffes program on 26 February appeared. The reviewer for the *Musical Leader* commented that the *Barcarolle, The Lake at Evening,* and *Scherzo* were the work of a "thoroughly schooled musician with something to say" and that the *Roman Sketches* "sound a much freer, bolder note without sacrificing the poetic sense or temperamental quality." He was less enthusiastic about the Piano Sonata, concluding that it "breaks completely away from convention and belongs frankly to a field of endeavor that must be called experimental."[91] Sylvester Rawling pointed out, rightly so, that it was a "rather trying test" for Griffes to give an entire program of his own works. He continued: "Four piano Roman Sketches and a sonata, played by Mr. Griffes himself, were among the principal numbers. They showed originality and a close knowledge of Debussy without distinct plagiarism from the French composer. The sonata in one movement I would like to designate by some other name; but Mr. Griffes insisted to me that it was true to form."[92] New York–born music critic Herbert F. Peyser in *Musical America* commented that Griffes's "modernistic tendencies" and "impressionistic idiom" were already familiar. He remarked that "the best things heard last week were the songs, already admired for their atmosphere, and the earlier-written piano sketches. Ravel has done to far better purpose what Mr. Griffes strives for in the 'Roman Sketches' . . . while the sonata, after ten minutes' wandering in the nowhere, ends without any disclosure of musical beauty or tangible invention. Mr. Griffes played his pieces with delicacy and tenderness."[93]

Perhaps one reason most of the reviewers did not like or understand the Sonata is that it should not be played with either delicacy or tenderness. It is an overpowering work, full of anger and passion, and Griffes was probably not the ideal interpreter for his own composition in this case. His friend Marion Bauer wrote in 1943, "I was present when Griffes showed the Sonata to Harold Bauer, who was deeply impressed by the work and expressed himself as wanting to push the composer off the piano bench and to play the last pages with the élan and virtuosity demanded by the score."[94]

The reviewer for the *Christian Science Monitor* was not as intimidated by the Sonata as his peers seemed to be. "The work, though strange, perhaps, to some hearers, proves to be clear in structure, intense in feeling and refined in expression. On the whole it should have been easily intelligible to a public that has long known the music of Debussy."[95] As one might expect, pianists such as Rudolph Ganz and Harold Bauer were quicker to see the merits of the piece than were the critics. Ganz remarked in an interview in *Musical Courier* in April 1918: "Charles T. Griffes' new piano sonata, which he played recently at the MacDowell Club, is free from all foreign influences. He is going his own way. . . . These two [Griffes and Marion Bauer] reach out for new problems and don't lean upon Indian or negro theme[s] in order to make the people believe they are American."[96] Harold Bauer characterized the Piano Sonata as "a splendid piece of writing, broad and noble in outline, subtle in atmosphere."[97]

When Griffes's *Three Poems*, op. 9, for voice and piano were published by G. Schirmer in 1918, they elicited one of the most negative reviews Griffes had ever received—from the pen of A. Walter Kramer. The three songs are tonally obscure, dissonant, and experimental, and Kramer's once positive view of Griffes's songs turned decidedly sour:

> "Three Poems for Voice and Piano" Mr. Griffes calls these compositions. We are glad that he does not call them "songs." "In a Myrtle Shade"—a William Blake poem—is splendid [it is also the least obscure and intricate of the three songs]; . . . Rupert Brooke's "Wai Kiki" [*sic*] has escaped Mr. Griffes. If this be the music that he has felt from knowing this poem, then indeed is he the American Stravinsky, as he has been dubbed by his disciples in the nether regions of Greenwich Village [probably a reference to Griffes's connection with the Neighborhood Playhouse and the Greenwich Village Theatre]! . . . [O]ne feels that Mr. Griffes is more interested in ravelling and unravelling

the material of which modern music is made than saying what he has to say straightforwardly. For doctors of music, for esthetic dancers who constitute themselves authorities on modern music [probably a reference to Adolf Bolm's Ballet-Intime dancers], for self-appointed music critics whose writing is as distinct as their knowledge of their subject is not, this song and the uninspired setting of Mr. Giovannitti's "Phantom" [*sic*] will be master works before which they will prostrate themselves and about which they will wax enthusiastic. . . . Mr. Griffes writes for ["Phantoms"] an essay on the validity of the minor second as a factor of beauty in musical art.[98]

On 22 April 1918, in Aeolian Hall, soprano Eva Gauthier presented another of her unusual and daring programs. She featured premieres of songs by several composers, including Griffes's "Sorrow of Mydath" (unpublished at the time of the performance) and "Waikiki" (no. 2 of the op. 9 songs) and compositions by Leo Ornstein, Gabriel Fauré, Maurice Ravel, Eugene Goosens, and Gustave Ferrari, among others.[99] This concert seemed to anger or confuse most of the critics because of its "ultramodernity," but Griffes fared fairly well at the hands of his judges, except in one or two reviews. Herbert F. Peyser of *Musical America* considered over three-fourths of the program "ill-sounding and vacuous trash." He characterized much of the music, including Griffes's two songs, as "variously ugly, neurotic or senseless spasms" and concluded, "Over the tantrums of Messrs. Griffes . . . and the rest one prefers to draw the veil."[100] New York–born critic, editor, and writer Max Smith, writing in the *New York American,* commented that Griffes's "Sorrow of Mydath" and (to a lesser degree) "Waikiki" disclosed "genuine creative gifts."[101] Sigmund Spaeth stated that "both of the new Griffes numbers showed an advance in the direction of ultra-modernism on the part of that gifted composer."[102] Griffes must have been pleased by the words of Smith and Spaeth, and perhaps not too upset by the Herbert Peyser tirade, since he had at least been raked over the coals in good company and was not the sole target as he had been in A. Walter Kramer's caustic review of the op. 9 songs.

Griffes was active as a pianist in 1918. He appeared with Michio Ito at the Greenwich Village Theatre in a recital of dances and pantomimes given on three consecutive Sundays in April (7, 14, and 21) on which *The White Peacock,* choreographed by Ito, was performed for the first time.[103] On 8 April, Griffes performed *The Lake at Evening, The White Peacock,* and *Scherzo* at the Second American Composers' Festival at the John Wanamaker Auditorium in New York. Some of the composers who appeared in the festival besides Griffes were Charles Wakefield Cadman, Marion Bauer, A. Walter Kramer, Mana-Zucca, and Harvey Worthington Loomis.[104] On 27 June, Griffes played the same three compositions at the Thirteenth Annual Convention of the New York State Music Teachers Association, held at the Hotel Majestic in New York.[105]

In August, Griffes toured the East Coast and Washington, D.C., with Michio Ito and a company of Japanese dancers.[106] On 5 September he performed at the National American Music Festival ("The World's Greatest Week of American Music") in the Thurston Auditorium in Lockport, New York, about 390 miles northwest of New York City. On this occasion Griffes appeared as accompanist for soprano Louise Lancaster, who sang three of his songs.[107]

Other pianists were performing Griffes's music in various parts of the country as well. For example, on 23 January 1918 Anna Dazé played *The Lake at Evening* and *Scherzo* in Chicago on an "All American Program" presented by the artist pupils of Walter R. Knupfer; Leslie Hodgson performed *The Lake at Evening* at a concert at Randolph-Macon Institute in Virginia on 16 April; Cadance Meakle played *The White Peacock* at Eugene Heffley's studio in Carnegie Hall on 18 May; Emily Greenough played *The Fountain of the Acqua Paola* at Heffley's studio on 1 June (a possible first performance); and German-American pianist-composer Heinrich Gebhard performed *The Lake at Evening* and *Scherzo* in Steinert Hall, Boston, on 10 December.[108] Although these performances helped bring his name and music before the public, Griffes was aware that the works being performed were early ones, and not representative of his current style. Edward Maisel recounts a conversation Griffes had with Katherine Ruth Heyman in New York (no date given, but presumably in 1918) in which she congratulated him on the growing popularity of his works. Griffes replied, "Yes, but that's only my early work they play. Nobody understands what I'm doing now."[109]

The year 1918 had proven to be the most productive of Griffes's career thus far. He had found his musical voice and had reached a peak of artistic and technical command in his Piano Sonata, the three Fiona Macleod songs, and the *Poem for Flute and Orchestra*. Numerous performances of his works had brought his music more and more before the public, albeit with some negative reaction here and there. But that was something Griffes had surely anticipated, given the harmonic, melodic, and rhythmic advances his works now exhibited.

10

The "Big Year"

New York City, 1919

The year 1919 was among the busiest of Griffes's career and the year in which he firmly and unequivocally established himself as one of the most gifted and exciting American composers of his generation. True to form he continued to be productive as a composer, while maintaining a rigorous schedule of rehearsals, practicing, and score preparation for some of the most important performances of his career. These performances included the premiere of his op. 11 songs, a Modern Music Society concert devoted exclusively to his music, and orchestral premieres by the New York Symphony Orchestra, the Boston Symphony Orchestra, and the Philadelphia Orchestra conducted, respectively, by Walter Damrosch, Pierre Monteux, and Leopold Stokowski.

Compositions completed during 1919 included two movements for string quartet—Allegro energico ma maestoso (July) and Allegro giocoso (July; second movement of *Two Sketches for String Quartet Based on Indian Themes*); arrangements for orchestra of four of his piano pieces—*The White Peacock* (June), *Clouds* (February), *Bacchanale* (most likely 1919; from *Scherzo*, op. 6, no. 3), and

Nocturne (February; second movement of the Sonata); arrangements for double quintet (winds and strings) and piano of his op. 5 piano pieces—*The Lake at Evening, The Vale of Dreams, The Night Winds* (most likely 1919); an arrangement for voice and piano of three Javanese (Sundanese) folk songs—"Hampelas," "Kinanti," and "Djakoan"; possibly two sets of children's pieces; and his last completed works, Three Preludes (editor's title) for piano. Griffes also began composing music for the Neighborhood Playhouse production of *Salut au monde,* a three-act festival, but died before he could complete the score. He had no works published in 1919, and his royalties between 1 August 1918 and 1 August 1919 amounted to about fifty-five dollars.[1]

The year started out auspiciously for Griffes when pianist Rudolph Ganz played *The White Peacock* in New York's Aeolian Hall on 23 January. Ganz repeated the recital in Oakland, California, on 6 February and in Assembly Hall at Stanford University in Palo Alto on 7 February. Winifred Christie performed *The Fountain of the Acqua Paola* and *Nightfall* (possible premiere) in Boston's Jordan Hall on 7 February, and, billed as "Britain's Greatest Pianist," she repeated the program at Aeolian Hall on 12 February. Much later that year, on 31 October, Griffes's friend Rudolph Reuter, a New York–born pianist, included the *Scherzo* and *The Fountain of the Acqua Paola* on his Aeolian Hall concert.[2]

On 23 February 1919 Sasha Votitchenko, whom Griffes had met in 1916 at a party at the Lewisohn's,[3] presented a concert of "Old and Modern Music" at Maxine Elliott's Theatre in New York. In addition to Votitchenko (identified on the program as "Russian Composer and Virtuoso of the Tympanon"), the participants included Eva Gauthier, Count Ilya Tolstoy, and the Russian Symphony Orchestra conducted by Modest Altschuler. The concert was devoted to "Music of the Allies"—Russia, America, France, Italy, Belgium, and England. Count Tolstoy opened the program with an address entitled "The Significance of Music in

Russian Life"; the Russian Symphony Orchestra played pieces by Votitchenko and others; Gauthier performed two compositions; and Votitchenko played several of his own works on the tympanon. Griffes's contribution was his orchestration of Votitchenko's *Easter Time in Little Russia* (manuscript lost).[4]

A month later, on 22 March 1919, soprano Vera Janacopulos, born in Brazil of Greek parents, premiered the voice and piano version of Griffes's *Three Poems by Fiona Macleod,* op. 11, with Griffes at the piano in an Aeolian Hall recital.[5] The Griffes premiere shared billing with the American premiere of three songs by Russian pianist-composer Sergei Prokofiev (with Prokofiev at the piano) and the first performance of four songs by Belgian cellist-composer Maurice Dambois (with Dambois at the piano). Also in March, Memphis-born soprano Marcia van Dresser and the Philadelphia Orchestra, Thaddeus Rich conducting, premiered Griffes's voice and orchestra version of the Fiona Macleod songs at the Playhouse in Wilmington, Delaware.[6]

The Janacopulos concert elicited several reviews. Katharine Lane spoke of Griffes's "strangely delightful melodies" and also commented that Janacopulos had been well accompanied.[7] A. Walter Kramer characterized the songs as "modern in the fullest sense of the word, those of Messrs. Prokofieff and Griffes being 'ultra.'"[8] And, most complimentary to Griffes, the reviewer for the *Musical Leader* wrote, "Perhaps the deepest of the songs were those by Mr. Griffes, who writes with significant power and great reserve force."[9] Janacopulos was a singer of uncommon merit. She possessed a well-trained dramatic voice and was endowed with artistic intelligence and fine interpretive skills—an ideal singer for the Fiona Macleod songs.[10]

Shortly after the first performances of the Fiona Macleod songs, publication reviews appeared.[11] A. Walter Kramer, who had so disliked Griffes's op. 9 songs ("In a Myrtle Shade," "Waikiki," and "Phantoms") and had castigated them in his *Musical*

America review in March 1918, found much to admire in Griffes's new songs:

> A fine achievement, these three songs. Mr. Griffes has changed his course from his Rupert Brooke ["Waikiki"] and Arturo Giovannitti ["Phantoms"] songs issued last winter. He sails more directly now, with less conscious feeling and with greater spontaneity; in "The Lament of Ian the Proud" [which Kramer liked the best] and "Thy Dark Eyes to Mine" he has sounded a human note. That is the way, Mr. Griffes: don't depart from it, if you would hold our interest as you have in these three songs.[12]

Kramer, however, also stated that Griffes's music did not do justice to the poem "The Rose of the Night," since it failed to express the passion of the text.

An event of great importance to Griffes was the second New York concert devoted solely to his music, this one sponsored by the Modern Music Society of New York and presented on 2 April 1919 in the MacDowell Gallery at 108 West Fifty-fifth Street.[13] The Modern Music Society, founded in 1912 by American organist-composer Benjamin Lambord, was dedicated to the stimulation and furtherance of new music, especially American.[14] The Griffes evening was the organization's seventh concert of its seventh season and featured the Flonzaley Quartet in the first performance of Two Pieces for String Quartet (an early version of Griffes's *Two Sketches for String Quartet Based on Indian Themes*); Marcia van Dresser, who, with Griffes at the piano, sang the three Fiona Macleod songs; and Griffes himself, who played his Piano Sonata and *Roman Sketches,* op. 7. Griffes must have been pleased with the reception and press notices he received for this prestigious concert. Frances Grant in *Musical America* commented that the audience was "extremely enthusiastic throughout" but concluded that Griffes was not a forceful player and lent no dignity to the Sonata, which she characterized as a "surprisingly immature work."[15] The *Musical Leader* carried the longest review, which called the Sonata the message of an earnest, sincere musician, representing something of distinct importance even though difficult to grasp on a first hearing. The reviewer called the Fiona Macleod songs "magnificent . . . of compelling beauty and dramatic effect in ultra-modern vein."

> Mr. Griffes played his own four "Roman Sketches" with much tonal beauty and subjective poetic imagination in which the compositions abound. The two pieces for string quartet played most sympathetically by the Flonzaley Quartet came as a fitting close. . . . The audience manifested great enthusiasm and interest and many seemed to realize that in the work of Mr. Griffes there is manifestation of a school of American composition with the courage of its convictions, sincere and of high ideals.[16]

Griffes conferred with Edgard Varèse about the possible April and May premieres of two orchestral arrangements: *Nocturne* (from the second movement of the Piano Sonata) and *Clouds* (from the piano piece op. 7, no. 4). Varèse planned to include a Griffes work on the first and third of three pairs of inaugural concerts (scheduled for 11–12 April, 25–26 April, and 9–10 May) to be presented in Carnegie Hall by the New Symphony Orchestra, which had recently been established to present the most advanced contemporary music, with Varèse at its helm.[17] Neither of Griffes's works, however, received performances, and Varèse's venture was short-lived. Following the orchestra's debut, critics, orchestra musicians, and sponsors (including Mrs. Newbold Le Roy Edgar, Mrs. Charles S. Guggenheimer, and Mrs. Harry Payne Whitney)—all intimidated by or hostile to "futurist" music—forced Varèse's resignation. American music journalist, critic, and author James Gibbons Huneker of the *New York Times* reviewed the inaugural concert and commented that Varèse's orchestra sounded "like a wet hen" and that "the destiny of the new symphony orchestra is on the laps of the gods—or goddesses."[18] The goddesses apparently spoke, and Varèse left his post after the first pair of concerts, his project a failure.

Griffes had no time to nurse any disappointment the Varèse incident may have caused. His good friend Adolf Bolm was preparing a series of short ballets at the Rivoli movie theater at Broadway and Forty-ninth Street and asked Griffes to provide music for one of the programs. The man behind the series was Vienna-born Hugo Riesenfeld, director of the Rivoli, Rialto, and Criterion theaters for the Paramount organization.[19] Riesenfeld believed that by including and repeating short classical compositions on his silent film programs, audiences would become familiar with them, and this, in turn, would help popularize "the finest type of music." As Bolm pointed out in an April 1919 interview in *Musical America,* he was following in Riesenfeld's footsteps: "I am doing a series of short ballets at the Rivoli Theater with Hugo Riesenfeld's co-operation. . . . The series of ballets which I am giving are short and simple, but are meeting with much success and are acquainting the audiences with a new type of art."[20] Happily accepting Bolm's commission, Griffes orchestrated one of his most popular piano pieces, *The White Peacock* (op. 7, no. 1). Margit Leeraas, solo dancer, and the Rivoli Orchestra, led by Hungarian conductor Erno Rapee, performed the work for a week commencing on Sunday, 22 June 1919. The Rivoli program (a typical silent film potpourri) also included a performance of Schubert's *Rosamunde* Overture, a Rivoli pictorial, tenor James Harrod singing James Bland's "Carry Me Back to Old Virginny," an organ solo, a Mack Sennett comedy *(Hearts and Flowers)* and the main event, the full-length silent movie *Secret Service,* starring Robert Warwick.[21] Clive Barnes characterized this performance of the Bolm-Griffes *White Peacock* "one of the very first examples, if not the first, of American ballet music."[22]

Griffes's whirlwind activity continued as 1919 moved rapidly on. He began working on the score of *Salut au monde* for the Neighborhood Playhouse during the summer, signed an agreement with the Aeolian Company to record six compositions on the Duo-Art Pianola, attended the Coolidge Chamber Music Festival in Pittsfield, Massachusetts, in late September at the invitation of its founder, Mrs. Elizabeth Sprague Coolidge, and continued to prepare scores for three critically important orchestral concerts.[23]

One of the three orchestral concerts had received publicity as early as July 1918: "Charles T. Griffes has just finished a new composition, a 'Poem' for flute and orchestra. Mr. Barrére [*sic*], who has seen the new work, has pronounced himself enthusiastic about it, and is preparing it for next season's programs."[24] True to his word, Barrère scheduled a performance for 16 November 1919 in Aeolian Hall, with Walter Damrosch and the New York Symphony Orchestra. Exactly two months before the performance, Barrère sent Griffes a postcard saying: "I am working hard on the Poem which I will play in Aeolian hall with the N.Y. Symph. on *Sunday after. Nov. 16th*. Help!! Am back in town."[25] Fortunately, in late September, Barrère and Griffes were both in Pittsfield attending the Coolidge Festival, and the two of them took the opportunity to rehearse the *Poem*.[26]

Griffes must have been aware that the premiere of the *Poem for Flute and Orchestra* represented another milestone in his career. As the first performance of a Griffes work by a major New York orchestra led by a renowned conductor, the concert marked Griffes's entry into the New York musical establishment and hence that of the country.

The Damrosch family had been established as a musical dynasty in New York since the 1870s, when patriarch Leopold Damrosch emigrated with his family from Germany to take over the Männergesangverein Arion (a prominent New York men's chorus/society). Leopold founded the New York Symphony in 1878, and under the leadership of his son Walter, the orchestra reorganized in 1903 as the New York Symphony Orchestra.[27] The elder Damrosch died in 1885. But his two sons, Walter and Frank, both took up the baton and continued the Damrosch musical tradition. By 1919 the New York Symphony Orchestra and Walter Damrosch had long been pillars of the musical world. Some years earlier, in 1908, American pianist and inveterate letter writer Amy Fay quipped to her sister Melusina:

> We now have *five* orchestras here, the Philharmonic, Boston, Areno, Volpé, and Franko, besides. The Russian Orchestra, under Modest Altschuler, has developed tremendously, and is now admirable. I forgot Walter Damrosch, who gives concerts on Sunday afternoons, and who also has a body of picked men. He and his brother, Frank Damrosch, are always in the papers! . . . Walter and Frank are like the poor, we have them always with us![28]

The premiere of the *Poem for Flute and Orchestra* on 16 November 1919 inspired several important and laudatory reviews. Harvard-trained American music critic Richard Aldrich of the *New York Times* commented on the oriental rhythm and coloring in the orchestra and wrote:

> Mr. Griffes's name has appeared several times of late on programs of local concerts, signed to music that has shown originality, a true creative impulse, technical skill. He is an American, said to be a teacher of music in a school near New York, but he bids fair to take a more important place as an American composer. This "Poem" is a composition of real charm and individuality, written, in a truly idiomatic utterance, for the flute, which thus is felt as an inevitable interpreter of the musical thought. . . . The piece attracted great attention; Mr. Barrère played it beautifully and was repeatedly recalled.[29]

The reviewer of the *New York Tribune* commented that "if Americans can but continue to produce such works, all talk of the unrequited native composer will be speedily set at rest. Mr. Griffes is a composer who will bear watching."[30] The *New York Herald* critic called the *Poem* "among the best works produced by a native composer."[31]

The references to Griffes as an "American composer" in these and other earlier and later reviews reflect to some degree the "problem" of the American composer and the often apologetic air surrounding the music of native-born composers during Griffes's lifetime. That many contemporary works (too often American) were forgotten after only one hearing also rankled some critics.

Boston-born and Harvard-trained music critic and writer Henry T. Parker (who always signed his reviews "H. T. P.," sometimes humorously translated as "Hard To Please" or "Hell To Pay"), commented a few months after Griffes's death that

> every conductor of symphony concerts is expected in the course of a season to traverse by sample the classics . . . the established moderns . . . sundry unheard pieces by the composers of our own time and even to effect a revival or two from the ancients. . . . Mr. Griffes's tone-poem of Kubla-Khan deserve[s] repetition and would pleasure hearers. Yet how, between these other pressures, is he to find room for them? . . . The problem remains—the problem. Yet if one dared suggest less performances of classics of the second order, how the upholders of the good, the true and the beautiful—if only it be fifty or a hundred years old—would claw and scream.[32]

Two years after Griffes's death, the *Musical Courier*, inspired by the publication of the *Poem for Flute and Orchestra* (arranged by Barrère for flute and piano and edited by Hugo Kortschak for violin and piano), contended:

One of the sad things about music by American composers is that the better it is the less it is played. . . . And now Griffes is taking his turn at being neglected. It is often said that if a person is dead he may hope to get a hearing. It does not seem to be the case in the matter of the Americans. . . . The most serious obstacle with which the American composer has to contend is the failure of orchestra conductors and artists to repeat their works. . . . Giving the American a chance (in America) means to play him once and then forget all about him. Poor Griffes! Now the Poem is issued in a form that puts it within reach of all. It is a splendidly effective piece of music, and you do not have to feel that you are doing somebody a favor by playing it.[33]

American music, drama, and literary critic Lawrence Gilman addressed the questions of the American composer in an article prompted by a performance of *The Pleasure-Dome of Kubla Khan* by the New York Philharmonic in Carnegie Hall on 11 December 1924, the first performance of the work by a New York orchestra, with Willem van Hoogstraten conducting. Gilman wrote:

Probably the worst thing that can happen to an American composer is to be exploited because he is a good American rather than because he is a good composer. Philip Hale once protested, in a phrase that has become classic, against "covering mediocrity with a cloak of patriotism." But it is possible to err in the other direction: there is good American music which is ignored for no better reason, apparently, than because it is American.

For example, take the case of the late Charles T. Griffes, widely recognized before his premature death as one of the most gifted composers born in America. . . . We know of at least two eminent foreign-born conductors of American orchestras who have never given a single performance of a work by Griffes, despite the fact that his most consequential score,

"The Pleasure-Dome of Kubla Khan," has been available in published form for four years, and that other works of his have been known and available in manuscript for longer than that.[34]

Obviously these issues disturbed many musicians and writers in the early twentieth century. Certainly among the most frustrating problems Griffes faced (a problem not unique to him by any means) was that of finding a forum where his music could be heard, and then heard again. Therein lies the rub. The true value of a composition can be assessed and appreciated only through repeated performances. Few composers enjoy that luxury, and, like it or not, the music of Bach, Beethoven, Mozart, Brahms, Wagner, Debussy, and other giants of the past is preferred to the music of our own time. The motto of the public and, unfortunately, of many musicians seems to have become, *Musicos non numero nisi mortuos* ("I honor none but dead musicians"). The obstacles Griffes encountered during his lifetime—being a "modern" composer, an American, and finding himself outside the musical establishment—are those he would have to confront even today if he were alive and trying to get his music performed, repeated, and understood—with one exception. I believe that being an "American composer" would no longer be at issue.

Griffes was pleased with the reception the *Poem* had received, but he could not stop to savor his success because he was hard at work preparing scores and parts for upcoming orchestral performances of *The Pleasure-Dome of Kubla Khan, Notturno für Orchester, The White Peacock, Clouds,* and *Bacchanale.* At about $250 a score, Griffes simply could not afford to hire professional copyists.[35] And even when he did, the results were not always satisfactory. Marguerite Griffes recalled that for one piece entrusted to a copyist, "Charlie went [to New York] to get it, and he looked it over, and the copyist had left some out. So [Charles] had to do the whole thing over again."[36] To lighten his burden Griffes enlisted

the help of Marguerite and his mother, Clara. "He spread everything out on the dining room table, and my mother and I put in
the clefs, you know, and did things like that, to speed it up a little.
He was in *such* a hurry."[37] Charles's sister-in-law, Charlotte, also
helped out.

> There was a question of timing. He had to get it [*The Pleasure-
> Dome of Kubla Khan*] ready by a certain date to get up there to
> Boston. I was very embarrassed when he was getting the music
> ready for that concert. He was supposed to do all the parts.
> And he said, "Well, here Charlotte, I don't know why I'm
> trying to do all this. Get busy!" . . . And I was so slow and
> pokey. I said to Charles, "Oh, Charles, I'm just no good at this
> at all." He said, "[Why] did you go to a college of music if you
> can't write music?"[38]

The orchestral performances of the six Griffes works, all
within a short span of time (two works in November and four in
December 1919), required an enormous amount of preparation on
the part of the composer. (One should note that *Clouds* had been
prepared for the ill-fated Varèse concert in April, and *The White
Peacock* had been played at the Rivoli in June, so Griffes had
already given these two scores his attention.) The time spent
copying and correcting manuscripts, the effort, the tension knowing that deadlines were fast approaching drained Griffes of his
energy and left him prey to the illness that seized him that fall of
1919.

The next key event in Griffes's career was the performance
in Boston of *The Pleasure-Dome of Kubla Khan,* conducted by
Pierre Monteux. Monteux, whom Griffes first met in October
1916, was appointed conductor of the Boston Symphony Orchestra
in 1919, and he immediately began programming contemporary
works despite objections by both the audience and the orchestra,
who were accustomed to the German repertory. Griffes could not

have asked for a better orchestra or for a better conductor to premiere *The Pleasure-Dome*. The appreciation for his work and the critical acclaim that followed the first performance exceeded all his expectations.

Griffes traveled to Boston twice, both to sit in on rehearsals and to attend the performances in Symphony Hall on Friday afternoon and Saturday evening, 28 and 29 November 1919.[39] The trips to Boston were a terrible strain for Griffes, who was already suffering from what appeared to be a cold or flu but turned out to be a far more serious illness. As Marguerite Griffes recalled:

> Of course, he was sick then. He went up to Boston on the night train. He had been sick, you see, for a long time. Doctor Bancroft said that he probably had walking pneumonia. Charlie didn't know it. But he *knew* he was sick. On Thanksgiving Day [the day before the premiere], I guess, I don't know if that was the day the orchestra played, but anyway, he was invited to somebody's house for dinner, but he said he was so sick he couldn't do it. He just had a cup of soup.[40]

Griffes's inspiration for *The Pleasure-Dome* was Samuel Taylor Coleridge's poem "Kubla Khan." The composer provided the following explanation in the Boston Symphony Orchestra program notes:

> I have taken as a basis for my work those lines of Coleridge's poem describing the "stately pleasure-dome," the "sunny pleasure-dome with caves of ice," the "miracle of rare device." Therefore I call the work "The Pleasure-Dome of Kubla Khan" rather than "Kubla Khan." . . . As to argument, I have given my imagination free rein in the description of this strange palace as well as of the purely imaginary revelry which might take place there.[41]

All the important Boston newspapers covered *The Pleasure-Dome* premiere. Eminent American critic and writer Philip Hale, in the *Boston Herald,* paid Griffes the ultimate compliment for those days, remarking, "This composer is blessed with what is rare with American musicians, imagination." Continuing, Hale noted that, although Griffes had studied in Germany, there was no German influence in *The Pleasure-Dome.* Nor had Griffes "worshipped too devoutly in any one of the modern Parisian chapels" (a reference to Debussy and Ravel, no doubt). Rather, Hale found that, if Griffes had been influenced at all, "the influence is that of Rimsky-Korsakoff, Borodin, and the barbaric gorgeousness of the Russian ballet." Hale also made the important point that, in spite of these influences, "Mr. Griffes has decided and refreshing individuality; he has found an Oriental expression that is his own, as he has found new harmonic and orchestral colors."[42]

The *Boston Evening Transcript* ran a picture of a haunted-looking Griffes with its Henry T. Parker review.

> Throughout [*The Pleasure-Dome*] hardly a measure seems to be "filling." . . . Mr. Griffes perceives clearly the form in which he would cast his tone-poem, the design which he would unfold, the visions he would summon. . . . So to compose is to compose with a mind that discerns, sorts, controls. It is a rare, a precious possession for a composer still in relative youth. Mr. Griffes also composes with imagination.[43]

The *Boston Daily Globe* critic remarked that although *The Pleasure-Dome* was not a supreme masterpiece, it nonetheless "shows genuine originality and power of a sort that entitle its composer to be judged by the same standard as men like Ravel, Rachmaninoff and Stravinsky, not by that usually applied to orchestral works by unfamiliar Americans."[44]

Eminent American critic, lecturer, and author Olin Downes was somewhat reserved in his judgment, commenting that although Griffes had "real imagination, feeling, and above all a sense of color," he had less melodic originality, nor was his orchestration wholly original. But, as Downes remarked, "Who has real thematic invention at the age of 30?" (Griffes had reached his thirty-fifth birthday on 17 September of that year.) Downes continued:

> Mr. Griffes is a man to watch with care. He is not a mere objectivist and a man of ultra-refinement in his music, like [American composer] John Alden Carpenter, for example. Nor is he a man possessed of the broadly nationalistic ideals in the music of [American composer] Henry Gilbert. But he is a young American, full of spirit and receptivity, astonishingly progressive. . . . Hence it gives one great pleasure to think that out of a sparse harvest another important American composer is coming to maturity.[45]

Although Griffes rarely showed his emotions (a family trait), Charlotte Griffes recalled that after *The Pleasure-Dome* premiere he was so excited that he actually phoned home from Boston to tell his family how well everything had gone. And, as Charlotte said, "Of course, that was the thing he had been waiting for all his life."[46]

The excitement and the pressure were far from over. On 4 and 6 December the Boston Symphony Orchestra was scheduled to repeat *The Pleasure-Dome* in New York's Carnegie Hall. Griffes remarked to John Meyer in a letter written from Boston, "Let me announce to you now that the orchestra is going to play my work in New York at Carnegie Hall on Thursday night, Dec. 4th, and that this New York performance is the event of which I spoke to you some time ago as the greatest concert honor which can come to a composer in America (at least in my opinion)."[47]

The Carnegie Hall concert attracted widespread attention and drew critical acclaim. Over a dozen reviews appeared in New York newspapers and music magazines.

James Gibbons Huneker, writing in the *World,* commented on Griffes's art and science and imagination. Huneker heard in *The Pleasure-Dome* influences of Rimsky-Korsakov, Tchaikovsky, Liszt, Berlioz, and Richard Strauss. But, most important, "it is, all said and done, Griffes. He has individuality."[48] The critic on the *New York Tribune* called *The Pleasure-Dome* "the best piece of musical writing by an American we have heard within a year and altogether the most encouraging sign of life made by an American composer during a far longer period. . . . [Mr. Griffes] is that rare bird an American composer with imagination, the gift of expression, pronounced originality."[49]

Richard Aldrich wrote in the *New York Times* that *The Pleasure-Dome* was the most extensive work of Griffes's ever heard in New York, a piece "of a strongly Oriental character in its melodic intervals, in instrumentation, in harmonic basis." However, Aldrich believed that Griffes, who "has previously shown a predilection for this quality in music" and who "'does' it well," without slavishly following the "accepted Oriental formulas," would do better to find a style less obvious and remote. He concluded: "The music is quite free in structure, and while in certain passages the orchestration seems somewhat tentative, there is much that is successful in richness and brilliancy; and the piece achieves its pictorial purpose."[50]

Michigan-born and Harvard-trained critic and editor Pitts Sanborn wrote a perceptive review in which he recognized Griffes as

> unquestionably one of the most gifted composers this country has produced. . . . Mr. Griffes has written imaginative and personal music, and he has written it with a technic that gets it over to his hearers and with a singularly fine and engrossing skill in instrumental coloring. Mr. Griffes is still young. He seems to be now on the edge of a period of valuable produc-

tivity. Brilliantly performed, the work aroused marked enthusi-
asm, in response to which Mr. Griffes bowed many times from
a box.[51]

Griffes was already so ill at the time of the Carnegie Hall
concert that he could barely stand to acknowledge the applause
that filled the hall. He was suffering from pleurisy and laryngitis
and could barely speak.[52] Although he had planned to go back to
Bloomfield with his mother and sister that night, he was too ill to
do so. Marguerite Griffes recalled the evening: "We [Marguerite
and Clara Griffes] were in a box with the Bolms, and [Charlie] was
in another box. . . . That night we met him in the lobby, and he
had planned to go up to Bloomfield with us. . . . And he came in
in a great rush, and he said—he could hardly speak—it would be
better for him to go back to the school, where he could have a
nurse's care."[53] The performance of The Pleasure-Dome of Kubla
Khan in Carnegie Hall on 4 December was Griffes's last public
appearance. Shortly afterward he was confined to bed at Hackley.

Despite his illness Griffes found the energy to acknowledge a
letter from A. Walter Kramer, praising The Pleasure-Dome. Griffes
wrote to Kramer: "I have been feeling miserably all Fall and had
decided to give up my work here [at Hackley] before our vacation
came and go to Atlantic City for a week or two. To-day was the
day set for going, and then I had the bad luck to get pleurisy two
days ago. The doctor thinks I may be able to go by Saturday."[54]
Griffes never did make the Atlantic City trip, and Kramer never
saw him again.

Griffes also proudly wrote to Miss Broughton:

Didn't mean to wait so long before writing you but I couldn't
do otherwise. I have been so miserable the whole Fall that I
could only do the most necessary work. I haven't even given
lessons part of the time. Now again I am in bed with pleurisy
but hope to be up in a few days at most. I've had 2 extraordi-

nary successes this year which have sort of brought me fame over night [*sic*]. Especially in Boston I was the musical lion of the day. I have many long and splendid reviews to send you when I can get energy to collect them and cut them out. As soon as I am well enough I leave the school and go to Atlantic City probably. I am all run down.[55]

From his sickbed at Hackley, Griffes completed work on the four scores that Leopold Stokowski and the Philadelphia Orchestra were to perform in Philadelphia's Academy of Music on 19 and 20 December. Although Griffes longed to travel to Philadelphia for the rehearsals and performances, his doctor forbade him to do so. Deeply disappointed, he lamented: "But I've never heard the pieces played. I don't know if they will do them right!"[56]

Griffes wrote short descriptive paragraphs for each of his four compositions for the Philadelphia program notes. He described the mood and color of the *Notturno für Orchester* as "very sombre, expressing the gloom of night. After the opening there is a passage expressing a mental anguish and struggle, followed by a passionate climax. Then comes a passage expressing momentary rest, followed by a slipping back into the original mood. After a sound of distant horns the piece closes with a few somber chords." *The White Peacock* "was inspired by William Sharp's poem of the same title, from the 'Sospiri di Roma.' It pictures a wonderful garden filled with gorgeous color, where a white peacock moves about slowly 'as the soul, as the breath of all this beauty.' The music tries to evoke the thousand colors of the garden and the almost weird beauty of the peacock amid these surroundings." *Clouds* "was inspired, also, by William Sharp's poem 'Clouds,' from the 'Sospiri di Roma.' Sharp speaks of the clouds as suggesting the golden domes and towers of a city with streets of amethyst and turquoise. The music is a tone-picture striving for this same tenuous, far-off and yet colorful atmosphere." And, for *Bacchanale* he quoted from his own note to the published piano version of the piece (*Scherzo,* op. 6, no. 3): "'From the palace of Enchantment there issued into the night sounds of unearthly revelry. Troops of genii and other fantastic spirits danced grotesquely to a music now weird and mysterious, now wild and joyous.' The piece is wholly fantastic as a fairy tale, with a wild climax at the end."[57]

On 19 December Leopold Stokowski and the Philadelphia Orchestra performed the orchestral premiere of Griffes's *Notturno für Orchester, The White Peacock, Clouds,* and *Bacchanale.*[58] Once again the composer could not have asked for a better conductor or a better orchestra to perform his music. Stokowski had been appointed conductor of the Philadelphia Orchestra in 1912, and during his long tenure he elevated the orchestra and himself to world-class status. Like Monteux, this elegant, glamorous maestro championed modern music. Griffes first met Stokowski in November 1915 at G. Schirmer,[59] and in 1917, in his efforts to get *The Pleasure-Dome* performed, he sent scores to both Stokowski and Walter Damrosch. Now, performing compositions that Griffes would never hear, Stokowski introduced the music of this young American to his Philadelphia audience.

The reviews, though not wildly enthusiastic, were nevertheless sensitive and largely complimentary. The critic for the *Philadelphia Public Ledger* noted the influence of Debussy in *The White Peacock* (the piece most liked by the audience) and of Stravinsky in *Clouds.* "But he is no servile copyist. His score has piquancy and pungency, and it is one of the hopeful intimations for the future of American music."[60] The reviewer in the *Philadelphia Inquirer* commented on the apparent influence of Debussy (the *Notturno für Orchester* is decidedly Germanic in style) but also noted that the pieces were less vague and less tonally elusive than Debussy's music. Then came a statement that illustrates one of the important truths about Griffes's music: "They evince that gift of melody which only a few possess and which after all is the most precious of any composer's endowment."[61]

The wonderfully successful orchestral performances of *Poem for Flute and Orchestra, The Pleasure-Dome of Kubla Khan, Notturno für Orchester, The White Peacock, Clouds,* and *Bacchanale* thrust Griffes's name before the music public in a way undreamed of by most composers. Griffes's career had been developing slowly and steadily since 1909. Now, seemingly overnight, but in reality after a decade of struggle, Griffes found himself extravagantly acclaimed and recognized by musicians, critics, and audience alike. How thoroughly he enjoyed his successes; how gratefully he saw himself emerge as the respected, well-known, gifted young American composer. No one would deny that a brilliant future lay in store for him. Ironically and tragically, Griffes would not live to enjoy the rewards of his success or to continue the distinguished career that was now so firmly established. He was lying ill at Hackley School, fighting for his life.

11

Illness, Death, and Aftermath

After his Carnegie Hall appearance on 4 December 1919, Griffes's condition steadily worsened. He was too ill to travel home for the Christmas holiday, but at least one member of his family—Marguerite, Clara, Florence, or Florence's husband, Jim—was by his side at all times.[1] Marguerite Griffes recalled:

> Right before Christmas they called us from Hackley and said he had to stay there for Christmas and the nurse was going to stay and take care of him. There wouldn't be anyone else there [Headmaster and Mrs. Gage were going away for the holiday], so they asked my mother and me to come up and spend Christmas with him, at Hackley. . . . [We] stayed at the Gage's [Griffes had been moved from the infirmary to the Gage's front bedroom], and the little Gage boy, Paul, fixed a small Christmas tree and put it in Charlie's room.[2]

It became apparent that Griffes needed more extensive treatment than he could receive at Hackley. A tuberculosis specialist referred to Marguerite by a nurse at work went to Hackley to examine Griffes and recommended that the patient be moved to Loomis Sanatorium (specializing in the treatment of tuberculosis) in Loomis, New York, about eighty miles northwest of Tarrytown.[3] The doctor did not think Griffes had tuberculosis (he didn't) but informed the Griffes family that Charles's lungs were bad and that the air at Loomis would be beneficial. Griffes entered Loomis on 19 January 1920.[4] Marguerite Griffes remembered that the weather was terrible that day (it was the worst winter in her memory), and when they finally reached Loomis, the roads were so bad that Griffes had to be taken by bobsled up the hill to the sanatorium.[5] Clara Griffes stayed at Loomis at the main house to be near her son. According to Marguerite: "It was quite a walk over to the hospital. It was one of those winters when the snow was knee high. [Mama] couldn't get over to the hospital, so I went up and spent a week or so and went back and forth."[6] Marguerite rubbed Charles's hands because they felt weak to him, and Katharine sent him several small, handmade pillows to try and make him more comfortable.[7] Marguerite also remembered going to Loomis on one particular occasion because Charles insisted to his mother that she had been there the night before. She hadn't.[8]

Even at Loomis, Griffes attended to business. On 28 January he signed a royalty agreement with G. Schirmer for publication of the *Poem for Flute and Orchestra*—the last contract he ever signed.[9] *Salut au monde* was also very much on his mind. And during his illness performances of his music continued to take place. On 16 January 1920 Frederick Stock and the Chicago Symphony Orchestra performed *The Pleasure-Dome of Kubla Khan* for the first time in Chicago. On 25 January, shortly after Griffes had been admitted to Loomis, Nikolai Sokoloff (who had conducted the premiere of *The Kairn of Koridwen* in 1917) led the Cleveland Orchestra in the first performance of the revised, orchestral version of *Sho-jo* in Cleveland's New Masonic Hall. On

10 March 1920 Rudolph Reuter played the Piano Sonata (listed as "Sonata No. 1") from manuscript in the Ziegfeld Theatre in Chicago.[10]

Griffes's condition at Loomis did not improve. In fact, he was inexorably losing ground. Doctors determined that his only chance for survival lay in a rib resection, and Griffes said that if he had to have an operation, he wanted his friend "Dr. Fred" to perform it.[11] Dr. Frederick Bancroft, the husband of Ethel ("Pod") Shoobert, was on the staff of New York Hospital. So on 20 March 1920 Griffes was moved once again, this time to New York Hospital at 8 West Sixteenth Street, New York City.[12] The trip was fraught with tension. Because the stretcher did not fit through the train door, Griffes had to be lifted into the train through a window. And, because the seats in the coach could not accommodate his stretcher, Griffes and his nurse were compelled to ride in the baggage car.[13] The approximately one-hundred-mile trip must have been an agony for Griffes.

In spite of constant irrigation of Griffes's lungs and an operation on 5 April to resect part of his eighth and ninth ribs, there was nothing that Dr. Bancroft or anyone else could have done to save Griffes's life. He died on Thursday, 8 April 1920, in the early morning hours from empyema (abscesses of the lungs) resulting from influenza. At Griffes's insistence his mother had gone home for the night, and he died without any family at his side. He was thirty-five years old, and his professional career had lasted slightly more than twelve years.[14]

News of Griffes's death shocked his friends, colleagues, students, and acquaintances, among them Elizabeth Sprague Coolidge. After their initial meeting in January 1919, Mrs. Coolidge took an interest in Griffes. At her invitation he attended her chamber music festival in Pittsfield in late September, and she later requested that he perform his *Poem* with Georges Barrère at her home. About the latter invitation, Laura Elliot wrote to Mrs.

Coolidge at Griffes's request to explain that he was ill and could not accept her invitation for the time being.

> He asked me to do so several weeks ago but the anxiety has been so great that I left it until now. . . . Mr. Griffes has been actually at the point of death since Christmas time [1919]. . . . He, of course, does not know how small a chance the doctors thought he had of recovery. He merely wanted me to acknowledge your note and tell you of his illness. . . . [And a postscript] Please do not let him know how long I procrastinated before attending to his request.[15]

The patronage of Mrs. Coolidge, an influential and wealthy supporter of music, would have been of inestimable value to Griffes. Unfortunately, it was too late for that.

Griffes's funeral services were held at 2 P.M., 10 April 1920, in the Community Chapel of the Church of the Messiah, Thirty-fourth Street and Park Avenue, New York.[16] The Reverend John Haynes Holmes officiated, and honorary pallbearers included Adolf Bolm, Burnet Tuthill, Georges Barrère, French harpist Carlos Salzedo (a member of the Trio de Lutèce with Barrère and Paul Kéfer), Walter B. Gage of Hackley School, and Oscar G. Sonneck of G. Schirmer.[17] An article in the *Musical Leader* recounted the event:

> It had been decided to have no music, but, singularly, at the hour of two as the services were opened the Bach Trombone Choir from the parapet of the 71st Regiment Armory across the street intoned the [Martin] Luther hymn, "God is our refuge. . . ." [M]any composers, musicians, and well known literary folk attended the service. Flowers and telegrams were received from the most noted musical people of the country.[18]

On the day of Griffes's funeral, Mary Selena Broughton wrote a poem in memory of her beloved pupil and friend. It reads (in part):

Thy music, mighty Bach, that day was heard
With chorus full and giant orchestras,
With rolling drum and clashing brass,
The pomp and state of music majesty.

. . . .

And in that selfsame hour, within a quiet room
Lay one in his last sleep who loved and honoured thee.

. . . .

'Twas fitting, Bach, that in that last sad hour,

. . . .

That 'twas thy music, flung upon the air
Should be his Requiem.[19]

Griffes was buried in Bloomfield Cemetery, Bloomfield, New Jersey, where his mother and Marguerite were living, and where two of his sisters and their husbands would also eventually be laid to rest.

Following Griffes's death, there were articles lamenting his untimely demise, tributes, a memorial concert, an abortive attempt to establish a Griffes fellowship at the MacDowell Colony in Peterborough, New Hampshire, and all the typical flurry in music circles that often accompanies the death of a composer, especially one who dies so "romantically" young.

Some of the articles fostered an image of Griffes as an overworked and starving artist. *Musical America* quoted American pianist Frances Nash as saying: "I know that Griffes' music is being widely played nowadays and that his sad fate is the object of much discussion. . . . I can never, I think, dissociate Charles Griffes from the bitterness of wasted effort. The struggle was cruelly sharp for him. You couldn't meet him without realizing that. The want of bread breathed its blight on his work.[20]

A. Walter Kramer, also writing in *Musical America,* commented: "What American music needs is aid to let it express itself without the problem of how the rent is to be paid. There never was a time in any country where this loomed up as a national problem more than it does here to-day. Charles T. Griffes died at the age of thirty-five, a victim of overwork."[21] Even a decade later the Griffes legend was intact. In 1931, in response to a question about Griffes from one of his readers, Lawrence Gilman wrote that Griffes had died, "worn out by drudgery and a stupid world's misuse."[22]

Griffes's friend Noble Kreider sought to put the record straight in 1944:

> One critic has said, "Griffes is dead, worn out by drudgery and a stupid world's misuse." Knowing Griffes as I did, was to realize that "drudgery" was his pleasure, his joy. The "misuse" in no way seemed to trouble him; he desired only to be let alone to have time to write the many ideas clamoring for expression. . . . The fact that Griffes from 1907 until his death had a continuous salary seems sufficient to give the lie to the stories of his abject poverty that somehow were circulated after his death. . . . There were financial family obligations which the composer had promised to shoulder, but these were no greater burdens than those of any family man.[23]

Griffes, as a young American composer, certainly did have to struggle for recognition and acceptance. The evidence clearly indicates that he was beginning to win the battle. That, of course, did not make the struggle any less overwhelming, nor the many disappointments any less heartbreaking. But to say that Griffes died in poverty of overwork and neglect is simply not true.

On the other hand, some writers attributed to Griffes a success he never really enjoyed. For example, this excerpt from the *Musical Leader:*

> After a long, hard battle the King of Shadows struck down one
> of the most brilliant leaders of the young American school of
> composers, Charles Tomlinson Griffes. The story of his last
> days reads like a romance, for suddenly his name was on the
> lips of all music lovers in East and in West. . . . Following these
> successes [the 1919 orchestral premieres and the Chicago perfor-
> mance in 1920 of *The Pleasure-Dome*] he received during those
> early days of his illness enough requests from different sources
> for ballets, operas and works of every sort to have kept him
> busy for several years to come.[24]

This, too, is an exaggeration. At the time of his death, Griffes was
working on his one commission, *Salut au monde,* for the Neighborhood Playhouse.

Ten days after Griffes's funeral Richard Aldrich wrote a *New
York Times* article titled "Aid for American Composers," in which
he commented:

> Charles Tomlinson Griffes died a few days ago just as he was
> gaining a position as one of the most gifted of the younger
> American composers. . . . We speak with pity or scorn of a
> public that could let a Mozart or a Schubert die and think that
> those bad old days are gone, but from time to time something
> uncomfortably like them and the same sort is revealed in the
> present. Perhaps one means to help in avoiding this lamentable
> sort of thing will be the new project of the American Academy
> in Rome. This institution is to extend one field of its activities
> to include musical compositions, opening its door to women as
> well as to men.[25]

Established in 1894, the American Academy in Rome was
incorporated by the United States Congress in 1905. At the time of
Aldrich's article, it offered to students of architecture, painting
and sculpture, classical literature, and archaeology financial support to work in Rome and to travel. Fellowships in composition

were added in 1921.[26] Unfortunately, this was another opportunity that came too late for Griffes.

Among the many expressions of sympathy voiced on Griffes's death, none was more touching than the following statement, which went to Griffes's mother and to the press: "In the recent death of Charles T. Griffes, one of the most gifted of contemporary American composers, the music of America suffers a great loss. We who keenly feel this loss wish to express our sorrow while offering to the memory of the man and the composer this tribute of admiration and respect." Over forty of Griffes's friends and colleagues signed the tribute.[27]

Following Griffes's death, performances of his music seemed to be everywhere. For example, on 4 June 1920 pianist Carolyn Beebe and the New York Chamber Music Society played the premiere of *Three Tone-Pictures* in an arrangement for double quintet of winds and strings plus piano that Griffes had prepared for Beebe in 1919. The program took place at Wildwood Farm, home of Mrs. Alexander L. Dommerich, in Greenwich, Connecticut.[28] The New York City premiere followed on 16 November 1920 in Aeolian Hall. The Griffes pieces were programmed "In Memoriam."[29]

On Wednesday evening, 24 November 1920, the MacDowell Club presented a concert to honor Griffes's memory. The program opened with Marion Bauer reading a tribute to the composer by Lawrence Gilman in which he stated, among other things:

> We who knew and valued him can but enact our ritual of appreciation; remembering that here was a music-maker who spoke his own thoughts, who looked out upon the world from a hilltop that he himself had discovered, where the winds were burdened with a strange and fantastic music, bearing rumors of festivals and dances from exotic groves and legend-

ary shores. He was a fastidious craftsman, a scrupulous artist. He was neither smug nor pretentious nor accommodating. He went his own way—modestly, quietly, unswervingly.[30]

Gilman's tribute was followed by performances of the *Poem* (possible first performance for flute and piano) with Nicholas Kouloukis and Walter Golde; "Waikiki," "Sorrow of Mydath," and the op. 10 songs performed by Eva Gauthier; piano compositions from opp. 5, 6, and 7 played by Charles Cooper; and "Two Indian Sketches" (possible first performance of *Two Sketches for String Quartet Based on Indian Themes*) played by the Flonzaley Quartet. A note in the program stated that the proceeds of the concert would be used to establish a Charles T. Griffes Fellowship Fund at Peterborough (home of the MacDowell Colony in New Hampshire).[31] Unfortunately, that never materialized. The program was supposed to have closed with Margit Leeraas dancing Adolf Bolm's choreography of *The White Peacock*, accompanied by Griffes's Duo-Art recording. Leeraas, however, was ill,[32] and the program closed with the sight of an empty stage and the shimmering sounds of *The White Peacock* floating in the air and then vanishing into nothingness. It must have been a poignant moment.

In December 1920 New Orleans–born mezzo-soprano Edna Thomas, Philadelphia-born violinist Sascha Jacobinoff, and Los Angeles–born pianist Olga Steeb formed an ensemble called the Griffes Group. Their publicity flyer stated:

Independence plus ability and courage is bringing some American names eminently to the fore in contemporary art, especially musical art. Last year Charles T. Griffes died just as his genius was being recognized, just as his compositions were receiving the highest recognition they merit. . . . [Thomas, Steeb, and Jacobinoff] have banded themselves together . . . under the name of the Griffes Group, in perpetuation not only of the music of Charles T. Griffes, but of his essentially American aims and ideals and the furtherance of the aims, ideals and works of other Americans like him.[33]

The Griffes Group made its debut on 30 December 1920 in Aeolian Hall and toured extensively.[34] Soprano Lucy Gates replaced Edna Thomas in January 1924.[35]

The Boston Symphony Orchestra, conducted by Pierre Monteux, reprised *The Pleasure-Dome of Kubla Khan* in Boston on 31 December 1920 and 1 January 1921 and then in Carnegie Hall on 6 and 8 January 1921.[36] Of the New York performances, Richard Aldrich commented: "Mr. Monteux did an excellent thing in repeating the composition in his concerts this year. One of the grievances of the American composer—though Mr. Griffes is not known to have audibly voiced grievances—is that his music is played once and then shelved, even when it is found deserving. This symphonic poem is well worth keeping in the orchestral repertoire."[37]

The Pleasure-Dome was performed for the first time in Minneapolis by the Minneapolis Symphony Orchestra on 31 December 1920.[38] On 12 January 1921 American pianist-composer Harold Morris included Griffes's *White Peacock* and *The Night Winds* on his New York debut recital in Aeolian Hall.[39] Margit Leeraas danced to Griffes's Duo-Art recording of *The White Peacock* in a Tarrytown "Concert and Dance" recital sponsored by the Aeolian Company of New York and Tarrytown's Masonic Solomons Lodge on 25 January 1921.[40]

Georges Barrère and Walter Golde performed the *Poem* for flute and piano in Aeolian Hall on 15 February 1921 (most likely in Barrère's arrangement, published in 1922).[41] *Musical America* described the *Poem* as "a work of some dramatic as well as melodic appeal, but over-long."[42]

On 24 February pianist Leslie Hodgson premiered Griffes's Intermezzo at a "Griffes Memorial Evening" in the Park Church

Lecture Room, Elmira, New York. Mary Selena Broughton opened the program with a sketch of Griffes's life and works, and Mrs. Ray Herrick sang Griffes's op. 10 songs.[43] Hodgson repeated the Intermezzo in Stamford, Connecticut, in the Woman's Club Auditorium on 5 December 1923 and performed it for the first time in New York in Town Hall on 22 November 1933.[44]

Walter Damrosch and the New York Symphony Orchestra performed *The White Peacock* in Carnegie Hall on 10 and 11 March 1921 as part of a "Historical Cycle" series.[45] This particular concert featured music by American composers. In addition to Griffes's *White Peacock,* the program included works by George Chadwick, Edward MacDowell, John Alden Carpenter, Charles Martin Loeffler, John Powell (who also appeared as piano soloist), and Walter Damrosch.[46]

On 27 November 1921 eminent French pianist E. Robert Schmitz included *The Fountain of the Acqua Paola* in his Town Hall concert.[47] And so it went.

The most important of the posthumous performances of Griffes's music was the premiere of *Salut au monde* at the Neighborhood Playhouse on 22 April 1922.[48] Griffes had started work on the score for the Neighborhood Playhouse production of *Salut au monde* with Irene Lewisohn during the summer of 1919. The opening was projected for May 1920, but Griffes fell terminally ill before he could complete the large assignment (1919 had been an extremely busy year for the composer, and he was not able to devote all his energies that summer to *Salut*).[49] As he lay dying in early 1920, Griffes was frustrated and disappointed that his illness prevented him from working on *Salut.* Through his mother he asked the Lewisohns to consider postponing the projected May performances until fall; when he felt better he could complete the score. On 28 February 1920 Mrs. Griffes wrote to Irene Lewisohn from Loomis Sanatorium:

I talked with my son this afternoon in regard to "Salut au Monde" and find that he has the score completely finished but only in a rough way with pencil—and he thinks it would be difficult for anyone but himself to orchestrate it—it is such a keen disappointment to him that he cannot complete it himself. . . . He has been very ill and looks only a shadow of himself—but has shown decided improvement for the last two weeks.[50]

Less than a week later, on 4 March, Mrs. Griffes wrote again, this time to say that Charles was worse, that he couldn't possibly have the score ready by May, and that the only satisfactory thing to do was to postpone the performance. She concluded: "We realize what a disappointment this is to you. As soon as Charles is able to write you will hear from him personally."[51] That was not to be. Griffes died a month later.

The Lewisohns engaged Edmond Rickett to complete Griffes's work on *Salut.* Rickett had studied at the Royal Academy of Music in England, became a Gilbert and Sullivan specialist, and for a time was Yvette Guilbert's accompanist.[52] Alice Lewisohn Crowley later recounted the *Salut* incident:

In the midst of the development of the musical and dramatic structure, we were called to England because of a family tragedy. While crossing the ocean word reached us of Griffes's dangerous illness, and soon after our return he died. For a time it seemed as if the *Salut* would have to be abandoned; for to continue without that vital association and basic support was unthinkable. The score was in sketchlike form, the orchestration but slightly indicated. On the other hand we felt the obligation to go on; Griffes had poured his soul into the composition which, even uncompleted, held the promise of a work of rare quality, if not genius. Irene then set to work with Edmund [sic] Rickett's help to decipher the musical text, which Mr. Rickett later orchestrated.[53]

The Playhouse production of *Salut au monde* was inspired by Walt Whitman's poem of that title and modeled on the *Gesamtkunstwerk* concept of theater that had inspired the opening of the Playhouse in 1915. It combined music, drama, speech, singing, dancing, choral speech, pantomime, and special lighting and color effects, including a color organ played by Thomas Wilfred.[54] The festival pageant consisted of three acts: act 1, scene 1, "The Shaded Side of the Sphere—Chaos," depicting "terror and rapacious inhumanity"; act 1, scene 2, "The Lighted Side of the Sphere—Constructiveness," portraying the joy the builders of the world found through their understanding of the "rhythm, color and pattern of life"; act 2, scenes 1–5—Hebrew, Hindu, Greek, Mohammedan, Christian—representing "five manifestations of the divine message as revealed and interpreted through religious ritual"; act 3, "Social Orders of Civilization," depicting man's endeavor to order and direct his social destiny with a band of many races "enfolded in the banner of human Brotherhood."[55] Alice Crowley wrote in 1959:

> Our hope was to convey the vision which Whitman expressed at the end of the Civil War in a form adapted to presentation on the stage. . . . The *Salut au Monde* still holds for us the vision of unity formed out of diversity, a wholly different concept from that pressed into the rubberstamp slogan of freedom; for it involves the acceptance of that which is other, strange, even questionable.[56]

That concept must have struck a consonant chord within Griffes. Among the fascinating aspects of the production were Griffes's choral speech (in which each voice intones on its own natural pitch with exact rhythm and some articulation marks) and the use of a women's chorus as a substitute for strings, because "the tone color of strings did not lend itself to the plan."[57] Griffes's instrumentation called for flute/piccolo, clarinet, two French horns, trumpet, two trombones, two harps, piano, timpani, bass drum, cymbal, and bells.[58] During the Playhouse production, the music was performed offstage, the effect of which must have been reminiscent of the unseen presence of the Wagnerian orchestra at Bayreuth.[59]

Several of Griffes's friends participated in the *Salut* production, including Georges Barrère, who conducted the ensemble, Lily May Hyland, who played the piano, and Laura Elliot, who trained and directed the chorus.[60] After the 1922 premiere, several critics noted Griffes's contribution to *Salut au monde*. Deems Taylor remarked in the New York *World:*

> As absolute music, Griffes's score would not be of great importance, for the composer was content to subordinate his accompaniment absolutely to the action and speech of the players. In view of the small instrumental and choral forces at his command, this was probably the wisest thing he could have done, and his music fits the mood of the pageant so unobtrusively and well that even when it goes virtually unheard it is a valuable adjunct to the stage action.[61]

Taylor was right on the mark. Whereas segments of Griffes's wonderfully descriptive music for *The Kairn of Koridwen* (also written for the Neighborhood Playhouse) can be performed successfully as concert music, quite apart from the drama that inspired it, the score for *Salut* is so tightly woven into the fabric of the production that it stands alone less successfully as absolute music.

Although Griffes did not live to complete the *Salut* score, his conception was clear from the beginning. Marion Bauer recalled that the composer told her he was writing *Salut* "in a style quite different from his usual one, much more diatonic and simple."[62] The music of *Salut* is an interesting combination of counterpoint and homophony, of dissonant, tonally ambiguous passages (as, for example, appropriately in the section called "Chaos"), and of clearly diatonic sections in C major and A-flat major. The piece ends chordally in A-flat major with the chorus singing, "Salut au Monde! Salut au Monde!" ("Salutation to the world!"). The score is filled with fanfares, ostinatos, and many mood changes, all consistent with the dramatic concept underlying the production, a concept that inspired Griffes to write some of his most effective theatrical music.

Since his death in 1920, Griffes's music has maintained a modest but enduring position in the orchestral and solo repertoire of the concert hall and in the teaching studio. Numerous works have been published, and a substantial Griffes discography exists. Over the years Griffes and his music have continued to be the object of discussion in a variety of articles and reviews. What seems to have fascinated writers was Griffes's struggle as an "American composer," his modernism, his independence, and the tragedy of his untimely death.

In 1925 American musicologist-pianist-organist William Treat Upton, in an article discussing American song composers, stated:

As time passes and we study [Griffes's] songs more and more with regard to their own development and their relation to other contemporary American songs, the regret continually deepens that this great talent should have been so prematurely cut down. It seems increasingly clear that Mr. Griffes had something to give that, so far at least, no one else seems quite to possess. We see in his Op. II (Three Poems by Fiona MacLeod), for instance, not only such rich accomplishment . . . but still more such sure promise of future accomplishment, yet richer, yet more worth while, that (as in the similar case of MacDowell) it seems both a national calamity and a national disgrace that such a seemingly unnecessary loss should have been possible.[63]

American composer Frederick Jacobi wrote in 1927: "With Griffes the experimental frame of mind makes its first musical appearance in our country. This is his unique importance—the more singular because of the fact that his talent was limited perhaps and his achievement incomplete."[64]

In November 1933 editor and pianist Edward Robinson wrote a scathing article using Griffes as a scapegoat for his (Robinson's) disillusionment with the state of music in America. After correctly pointing out the falsity of some of the legends still prevalent in 1933 about Griffes's poverty, neglect, and so on, Robinson went on to say:

> Everything about his career, including the relationship with his public, was thus only proof that the American spirit, whatever else it may contain, certainly does not include the capacity for musical expression. . . . [Griffes's] music was useless, and there was really no reason why anyone should bother about it. But that was due not alone to his personal limitations; it was also the only possible outcome in a society basically impervious to his art.[65]

Robinson did grudgingly admit that although, in his view, Griffes's musical expression was completely unoriginal, "there is clear indication that he possessed a keen, sensitive temperament, coupled with a genuine creative impulse."[66] Robinson's article may have been posturing for the sake of effect and to stir some thought among his readers. In any case its negativism borders on the irrational.

American composer Aaron Copland wrote about Charles Griffes in 1952:

> Composers like Charles Martin Loeffler and Charles T. Griffes were the radicals of their day. . . . No one can say how far Griffes might have developed if his career had not been cut

short by death in his thirty-sixth year, in 1920. What he gave those of us who came after him was a sense of the adventurous in composition, of being thoroughly alive to the newest trends in world music and to the stimulus that might be derived from such contact.[67]

Copland was growing up in Brooklyn during Griffes's later years and once remarked that in 1919 Griffes was one of a handful of American composers that "stood out" for him.[68]

The bicentennial of the United States in 1976 inspired a flood of musical activity before, during, and after the actual year of celebration. This activity included many recordings and performances of American music, and Griffes came in for his fair share of recognition. Perhaps the most important of the recording projects was that of the Recorded Anthology of American Music (New World Records). Among their first ten releases was a retrospective of Griffes's music (NW 273). *New York Times* critic Peter Davis, in his review of the series, characterized Griffes as "certainly one of his generation's most sensitive and original musical spirits."[69]

The Griffes Piano Sonata has been recognized as "one of the genuinely significant piano pieces of this country's first 200 years,"[70] and "one of America's great contributions to the piano literature."[71] *New York Times* critic John Rockwell, discussing New World Records NW 273 and NW 310–11 (piano works of Griffes performed by Denver Oldham) and Musical Heritage Society MHS 824678M (a two-disk album of Griffes songs), wrote in 1983:

The laudable effort by American musical historians to rediscover our own art-music tradition has led to some remarkable exhumations, above all Charles Ives. But any nationalistically motivated search through the past can lead to the undue exaltation of dross, too. So it is a pleasure to report that the musical community and the record companies have turned their attention to a genuinely worthy American composer, Charles Tomlinson Griffes. . . . His brief maturity was marked by clearly defined stylistic periods, but in all of them he maintained an originality that suggests the possibility of a remarkable synthesis, if he had only lived longer. Even as it is, his major scores in his various styles all betray a freshness lacking in the music of his peers.[72]

Many articles written about Griffes conclude that if he had not died at such a young age, he might have become a major American composer. Griffes must be judged not on what he might have produced but on what he did produce. The evidence indicates that he had established himself as a compellingly original and important presence on the musical scene before his death in 1920. There is no question that Griffes died before he could compose a large quantity of works. However, he left about 140 compositions, a reasonable number in view of the fact that he did not begin to compose seriously until he was nineteen (when he first went to Germany to study) and that his professional career lasted just more than twelve years. But there is no massive quantity of works to give depth and breadth to Griffes's output. With Griffes quality must be the principal yardstick.

Griffes made significant contributions to our song literature (*Four Impressions* and the Fiona Macleod songs, op. 11, for example), piano literature (*Roman Sketches,* op. 7, and the Piano Sonata), chamber (stage) literature *(The Kairn of Koridwen),* and orchestral literature *(Poem for Flute and Orchestra, The Pleasure-Dome of Kubla Khan, Clouds,* and *The White Peacock).* That alone makes his achievement noteworthy. And there is something else. Griffes never lost the courage to question, to reject, and to move ahead, no matter what the odds. His music has retained its freshness and immediacy and still speaks to us convincingly across the chasm of time.

Charles T. Griffes, ca. 1903.
Photo by McFarlin, Elmira,
N.Y.

Griffes as a student in
Berlin, sporting a mustache,
1907. Photo by Hänse
Herrmann, Berlin.

Emil Joël and his family, ca. 1920. *Left to right:* Emil, Gerhard, Helga, Helmer Karl (Griffes's godson), and Elly. Courtesy of Natalie Burfoot Billing. Identifications courtesy of Gary Burfoot.

Hackley School campus, Tarrytown, N.Y. Photo by Donna K. Anderson.

Griffes at his desk, Hackley School.

Griffes's drawing of King Chapel, Hackley School, *The Hackley Annual, 1916.*

Mary Selena Broughton near Cowles Hall, Elmira College, at the end of her
life. Courtesy of Gannett-Tripp Library, Elmira College.

Charles T. Griffes, ca. 1918.

A haunted-looking Griffes about the time of the premiere of *The Pleasure-Dome of Kubla Khan*, 1919. This photo was published in the *Boston Evening Transcript*, 29 November 1919. Photo by Mishkin?

Seventh Programme

FRIDAY AFTERNOON, NOVEMBER 28, at 2.30 o'clock

SATURDAY EVENING, NOVEMBER 29, at 8 o'clock

Chausson . . . . . Symphony in B-flat major. Op 20
   I. Lent; Allegro vivo.
   II. Très lent.
   III. Animé.

Songs with Orchestra:

Beethoven . . . . . "Nature's Adoration," Op. 48, No. 4

Handel . Air, "Ombra mai fù," from the Opera "Xerxes," Act 1, Scene 1

Bach . Air, "My Heart Ever Faithful," from the Cantata, "For God so Loved the World"

Griffes . . . The Pleasure-Dome of Kubla Khan (after the Poem of S. T. Coleridge)
(First Performance)

Verdi . Aria, "O Don Fatale," from the Opera "Don Carlos," Act IV, Scene 6

Chabrier . . . Bourrée Fantasque, Piece for Pianoforte, Orchestrated by Felix Mottl

SOLOIST

LOUISE HOMER

MASON & HAMLIN PIANO USED

There will be an intermission of ten minutes after the symphony

The ladies of the audience are earnestly requested not to put on hats before the end of a number.

The doors of the hall will be closed during the performance of each number on the programme. Those who wish to leave before the end of the concert are requested to do so in an interval between the numbers.

City of Boston, Revised Regulation of August 5, 1898.—Chapter 3, relating to the covering of the head in places of public amusement

Every licensee shall not, in his place of amusement, allow any person to wear upon the head a covering which obstructs the view of the exhibition or performance in such place of any person seated in any seat therein provided for spectators, it being understood that a low head covering without projection, which does not obstruct such view, may be worn.
Attest: J. M. GALVIN, City Clerk.

433

Program from the premiere performance of *The Pleasure-Dome of Kubla Khan*,

Boston, November 1919.

Griffes's last written communication, a postcard to Marguerite written 23 February 1920 from Loomis Sanatorium, not long before his death. "Dear Marguerite, This is the first time I had a pen in my [hand] so excuse [the] poor work. Sorry I didn't see you before you left here. I hope Mama writes you everything. K[atharine] is here now, Love."

12

Stylistic Overview

Charles T. Griffes is often characterized as an American impressionist. But, although some of his best-known compositions fit that categorization (e.g., *The White Peacock*), to classify Griffes exclusively as an impressionist is to fail to understand fully the variety of styles represented in his music and to disregard his individuality.

Griffes's earliest works (ca. 1903–11), written while a student in Berlin and immediately following his return to the United States, are strongly Germanic in style. That is not surprising, since Griffes immersed himself in late nineteenth-century German romanticism and could hardly have escaped its influence. It is a measure of his talent that he mastered the language so thoroughly and made it so completely his own. Nevertheless, Griffes reportedly told A. Walter Kramer that he (Griffes) considered his early German songs published by Schirmer in 1909 and 1910 "more the result of composition study than his own musical expression."[1] Perhaps the lack of impression that those songs had made on the critics and the public prompted Griffes to seemingly devalue his early efforts. But more important, by about 1911 Griffes had abandoned the German style and had been struggling for acceptance of his new experimental, impressionistic style. He had had a very difficult time convincing Schirmer to publish his new music. When Schirmer finally issued the *Three Tone-Pictures,* op. 5, and *Fantasy Pieces,* op. 6, in 1915, Kramer wrote a favorable review for *Musical America* praising Griffes as a full-fledged modern composer.[2] It seems only natural then that Griffes would have minimized his earlier, now "old-fashioned" German works. He reiterated this sentiment in an article published in the New York *Evening Sun* in December 1919:

> "When I went to Germany," Mr. Griffes said, "I was of course ready to be swept under by the later Wagner and [Richard] Strauss; it is only logical I suppose that *when I began to write* [emphasis added] I wrote in the vein of Debussy and Stravinsky; those particular wide intervalled dissonances are the natural medium of the composer who writes to-day's music."[3]

Nevertheless, Griffes's so-called German period produced some beautiful music, including twenty-six songs for voice and piano; the Sonata in F Minor (ca. 1904), which Griffes performed (first movement only) in Berlin in 1905; and two large-scale, unpublished one-movement works for orchestra, Overture (1905) and *Symphonische Phantasie* (1907). The works from these early years are clearly tonal but are liberally sprinkled with melodic and harmonic chromaticism. They emphasize beautiful lyrical melodies, regularity of rhythm and phrasing, and clearly delineated sections.

Representative of these early works is Griffes's setting (ca. 1903–11) of Heinrich Heine's poem "Am Kreuzweg wird begraben" (see ex. 1). In each of the four phrases of his modified strophic setting, Griffes offsets the regularity of rhythm and phrasing through tonal ambiguity. In the first phrase, for example, he accomplishes this through the slow chromatic descent of the

EXAMPLE 1 "Am Kreuzweg wird begraben" (ca. 1903–11), mm. 1–9

bass line (B–A♯–A♮–G♯) supporting a third-inversion seventh chord on the tonic major in measures 1–4, a half-diminished seventh chord in measures 5–6, and a seventh chord on A in measure 7. Not until measures 8–9 does Griffes establish his tonic key with a clear cadence in C-sharp minor. In the final phrase, Griffes reverts to the tonic major on which he obliquely began the piece. The harmony colors and heightens the poignancy of the suicide's fate and the silent presence of one who loved him.

From about 1911 to about 1916, Griffes began experimenting with whole-tone scales, ostinato figures, parallelism, and other impressionistic devices. The works from this period are generally free in form, highly colored, and descriptive and pictorial. Among Griffes's piano works from this period are *Three Tone-Pictures,* op.

5 (1910–15), and *Roman Sketches,* op. 7 (1915–16). Songs from these years include the *Tone-Images,* op. 3 (1912–14), and *Four Impressions* (1912–15).

In his song "Symphony in Yellow" (op. 3, no. 2) from *Tone-Images,* Griffes blurs both tonality and rhythm by means of ostinatos in the accompaniment (see ex. 2). At the beginning he laces the tonic B-major chord first with an added second (c♯") and then an added sixth (g♯"), and he sets this chord over a gentle rhythmic ostinato in measures 1–6 that shifts metric accents with ties over the barlines. The voice, on the other hand, is clearly in B major and moves regularly in four. The effect is a languid, static quality that befits the text, "Crawls like a yellow butterfly." The G-natu-

EXAMPLE 2 "Symphony in Yellow," op. 3, no. 2 (ca. 1912), mm. 1–9

rals in measure 9 introduce another beautiful tonal color (an augmented triad, with the voice adding the ninth on a♮').

Griffes used the same harmonic and rhythmic principles in his impressionistic piano compositions. For example, *The Vale of Dreams,* op. 5, no. 2 *(Three Tone-Pictures),* opens with an unresolved, third-inversion dominant seventh chord (key of E-flat major) combined with a rhythmic ostinato in the left hand (see ex. 3). Over this unstable harmonic-rhythmic foundation, the right hand presents a melodic fragment (no longer the long, lyrical melodies of Griffes's earlier works) consisting of chromatic parallel major thirds. The rhythm of the melody is more complex and less regular than in the German works, and throughout the piece Griffes colors the tonic, ending on a I⁶₄ chord.

From late 1916 to 1917, Griffes imparted his lifelong interest in oriental culture to his music. Reflecting his "oriental" compositional style are such works as *Five Poems of Ancient China and Japan,* op. 10 (1916–17), *Sho-jo* (1917), and the imaginative and color-

EXAMPLE 3 *The Vale of Dreams,* op. 5, no. 2 (1912), mm. 1–6

ful piano and orchestral versions of *The Pleasure-Dome of Kubla Khan* (1912, rev. 1915 and 1916–17). Griffes based his op. 10 songs on non-Western five- and six-tone scales, and he avoided Western harmonizations by generating vertical sonorities that emphasize fourths and fifths instead of thirds. The dynamics used in these songs are delicate, ranging from *ppp* to *mf*. Forte is used only four times in the op. 10 songs, three times in "Tears" (no. 4) and once in "A Feast of Lanterns" (no. 5). And Griffes used an authentic Chinese melody in "So-fei Gathering Flowers" (no. 1).[4]

An example of Griffes's use of non-Western scales is the six-note scale, with added foreign tone (see ex. 4), that provides the basis for "Tears," op. 10, no. 4 (see ex. 5). Griffes introduces the foreign tone, D♮, in only one passage (mm. 14–15), resulting (in m. 14) in a B-minor triad with an added sharped seventh (A♯) that highlights the key word "tears." At this point in the song, Griffes also suspends the quarter note–half note rhythmic ostinato first established in measure 1, further underscoring the text. A meter change (from ⁶₄ to ⁴₄) and tempo change (Poco più mosso) in measure 17 increases the momentum slightly, but in measure 21 Griffes returns to his opening tempo (Tempo I° = Lento), meter, and ostinato pattern. His means are simple, but the effect is impressive.

Soprano Eva Gauthier incorrectly believed that *she* was responsible for Griffes's interest in the Orient. In a 1923 interview she remarked:

EXAMPLE 4 Six-tone scale, with added foreign tone, used in "Tears," op. 10, no. 4 (1916)

EXAMPLE 5 "Tears," op. 10, no. 4 (1916), mm. 13–24

I first met Griffes in 1917, when he was preparing a score [*Shojo*] for Ito, the Japanese dancer. He had been a pupil of Humperdinck in Germany, and up to this time he had written in the old-fashioned German style. He was unknown. I gave him the melodies which I had copied in Japan, and with them he started to develop a new style. Within a short time he gained recognition as one of the leading Americans in the modern movement. . . . To complete my observations about Orientalism in modern music and my association with it, I ought to say that all the material which I originally lent to Griffes I have given to Ravel.[5]

As noted earlier, Griffes was no longer writing in the "old-fashioned German style," nor was he "unknown," when he first met Gauthier in 1917. Furthermore, he had already written three of the five songs that make up the *Five Poems of Ancient China and Japan* by the end of 1916. Nevertheless, his collaboration with Gauthier was a significant one, and her interest in and performance of Griffes's music was of great importance to the composer.

Gauthier was just the kind of person Griffes found stimulating. During her world tours she had traveled to Europe, the Malay archipelago (including Sumatra and Java), Japan, China, Siam, Australia, New Zealand, and the Philippines. Both in Java, where she apparently lived at the palace of the sultan of Solo, and in Japan, Gauthier studied and collected native music.[6] She gave some of this original material to Griffes in 1917, and Griffes used it in *Three Javanese (Sundanese) Songs* and *Sho-jo*.[7]

In the Piano Sonata (1917–18, rev. 1919) and *Three Poems by [of] Fiona Macleod,* op. 11 (1918)—in both voice and piano and voice and orchestra versions—Griffes departed significantly from all his previous compositional styles. The Sonata, for example, is uncompromisingly dissonant and muscular. Unlike the majority of Griffes's earlier piano compositions, it has no poetic program and no descriptive title. In addition, whereas the earlier piano works are generally in one movement and free in form, the Sonata is in three (connected) movements, the first and third of which are in sonata form (albeit highly modified in the case of the third movement). It is also the first of Griffes's piano compositions to be constructed on a synthetic scale (see exx. 21–31, below). The Sonata is absolute music of great power, intensity, and drama.

The Fiona Macleod songs distinctly resemble the Sonata in their use of disjunct melodic contours, sharpness of dissonance, boldness of conception, intensity of emotion, and dramatic effect. "The Rose of the Night" (see ex. 6) provides an illustration. The song's climax comes in verse 3 (at "Kiss me, Imperishable Fire," mm. 47–50). In the span of nine measures (marked *poco a poco più mosso*), Griffes builds from **mf** (mm. 38, 39) to *f* (mm. 41, 43) to *ff* (mm. 47, 49). The piano part, elaborate throughout, almost overwhelms the voice, which soars to its highest note (a fortissimo a″) on the word "Fire." As in so many Griffes songs, the contrapuntal interplay between voice and piano is skillfully and effectively handled. "The Rose of the Night" is the most tonally ambiguous of the three Fiona Macleod songs, ending on a chord spelled (ascending) G♯–C–E–G♮–A. The listener first heard this combination of notes at the beginning of the song, and it serves, in effect, as the "tonic" chord. By contrast "The Lament of Ian the Proud" ends on a root position tonic triad (F-sharp minor), and "Thy Dark Eyes to Mine" closes on a tonic A-flat triad in second inversion.

Griffes's last completed compositions, the Three Preludes for piano (1919), reflect yet another expression of his individuality. They retain the abstract harmonic idiom of the Piano Sonata but, unlike that work, represent Griffes at the height of succinctness, writing within the confines of thirty-two measures or less.

In the second prelude, for instance (see ex. 7), Griffes reduces every musical component to its barest minimum. The texture is linear with never more than three notes sounding simultaneously. In texture and brevity Griffes's Three Preludes bear an affinity to Arnold Schoenberg's *Sechs kleine Klavierstücke,* op. 19 (1911), and Alexander Scriabin's Five Preludes, op. 74 (1914), both of which Griffes owned and performed.[8]

EXAMPLE 6   "The Rose of the Night," op. II, no. 3 (1918), mm. 43–50

EXAMPLE 7 Prelude no. 2 (from Three Preludes, 1919), mm. 1–7

Any outline of Griffes's so-called stylistic periods must be viewed with a critical eye and a healthy skepticism because such categorization at best represents only a general overview of his works. The periodization of Griffes's works into "romantic," "impressionist," "oriental," and "abstract" does not take into account, for example, that one of his best-known "oriental" works, *The Pleasure-Dome of Kubla Khan,* for orchestra (1916–17), was originally conceived in 1912 as a piano piece, which Griffes completed in 1915 during his so-called impressionistic period. *The Pleasure-Dome* does exhibit some traits of impressionism, not the least of which are its brilliant tone colors. Nor can the periodization explain such works as *Three Poems,* op. 9, for voice and piano ("In a Myrtle Shade," "Waikiki," and "Phantoms"), which Griffes composed in 1916 during his "impressionistic" period, but which stand alone, tonally (and sometimes melodically) obscure and experimental. In "Phantoms," for example, note the extensive, almost obsessive, use of major, minor, and (to a lesser extent) augmented seconds, the extensive chromaticism, rhythmic complexity, and the numerous augmented and diminished sonorities (see ex. 8).

EXAMPLE 8 "Phantoms," op. 9, no. 3 (1916), mm. 6–9

Similarly, the periodization cannot account for a work like *The Kairn of Koridwen,* also written in 1916. *The Kairn* uses a synthetic scale (see ex. 9), is "oriental" in its rejection of strings and its use of harmonies emphasizing fourths and fifths, and, like the op. 9 songs, stands in a category by itself.[9] (The fourth degree—E—of the synthetic scale is often altered—shown by parentheses in ex. 9.)

Through his use of a synthetic scale in *The Kairn,* Griffes generates an abundance of melodic and harmonic augmented

EXAMPLE 9 Synthetic scale used in *The Kairn of Koridwen* (1916)

seconds, fourths, and fifths (see ex. 10). Griffes scored *The Kairn of Koridwen* for eight solo instruments. In a letter to critic Max Smith dated 13 March 1917, he remarked on the unusual scoring of the work and "suggested that Schönberg's *Pierrot Lunaire* was probably nearest to this instrumentation."[10]

Finally the periodization outlined above does not conveniently categorize *Two Sketches for String Quartet Based on Indian Themes,* written in 1918–19. In this work Griffes used for the first and only time Native American thematic material.[11]

What a stylistic overview does accomplish is to illustrate the multifaceted quality of Griffes's creativity, his genuine originality and individuality. It also points to his ability to look beyond and ultimately move out of the German-French orbit that dominated American music before and during his lifetime—among the first American composers to do so. The constant changes in Griffes's style, his use at one time or another of exotic scales, non-Western harmonies, and melodies from his own culture as well as cultures other than his own all reveal the catholicity of his interests and his desire to express as clearly as possible what he wanted to say as an artist. Each composition was a new statement, a new expression of self, and as such deserved a fresh approach. Griffes himself put it clearly in 1919 when describing *The Pleasure-Dome of Kubla Khan:* "If I have written into my score Oriental sounds and Slavic themes it is only because those tonal combinations and melodies have said and expressed the things I wanted to say."[12] That principle can be extended to all his works.

A word about the descriptive titles and texts that Griffes attached to many of his piano works is appropriate here because

EXAMPLE 10 *The Kairn of Koridwen* (1916), scene 1, mm. 15–18. Manuscript in
NN:Mu, © 1985 by Donna K. Anderson. Used with permission. All rights
reserved.

these titles and texts have contributed to the erroneous blanket categorization of Griffes as an "American impressionist." Each of the *Three Tone-Pictures,* op. 5 (*The Lake at Evening,* 1910; *The Vale of Dreams,* 1912; and *The Night Winds,* 1911, rev. 1915) bears a descriptive title and prefatory text. For *The Lake at Evening,* Griffes drew upon William Butler Yeats's poem "The Lake Isle of Innisfree" (from *The Rose*). For *The Vale of Dreams* and *The Night Winds,* he turned to Edgar Allan Poe's poems "The Sleeper" and "The Lake: To ———," respectively. But Griffes did not select the Yeats text or the second of the two Poe texts until 1915, some years after completing his compositions. On the other hand, he probably composed *The Vale of Dreams* with Poe's "Sleeper" in mind. Diary entries confirm the process. On 20 May 1915 Griffes noted in his diary, "Went to New York today to look up some poems for the 'Tone Pictures.'" But earlier diary references to "my later piece after Poe" (28 March 1912) and "the little piece with the Poe lines as introduction" (17 July 1912) suggest that Griffes had a specific poem in mind when composing *The Vale of Dreams.* (The "little piece" could not be *The Night Winds,* which is the most virtuosic of the set, and "later piece" could only refer to *The Vale of Dreams,* since Griffes wrote this piece after *The Night Winds.*)

With respect to titles, none of the titles in *Three Tone-Pictures* corresponds to the poetic source, and in each case Griffes selected his title some time after completing the work: two years later for *The Lake at Evening,* three years later for *The Vale of Dreams,* and one year later for *The Night Winds.*[13] Some of Griffes's searching for titles and texts resulted from the impending publication of the *Three Tone-Pictures.*[14]

Griffes did not use poetic titles for his *Fantasy Pieces,* op. 6 (*Barcarolle,* 1912; *Notturno,* 1915; and *Scherzo,* 1913, rev. 1915), but did append a text to each piece. He did not add texts, however, until 1915, in preparation for publication of the pieces: "Spent an hour in the Library looking up a poem for the 'Barcarolle.' Finally found a combination from Fiona MacLeod. The 'Notturno' has verses from Paul Verlaine and the 'Scherzo' a couple prose sentences of my own. After that I took the ms[s]. over to Schirmer's to their editor."[15]

By contrast Griffes composed all four pieces from *Roman Sketches,* op. 7 (*The White Peacock,* 1915; *Nightfall,* 1916; *The Fountain of the Acqua Paola,* 1916; and *Clouds,* 1916), with specific poems from William Sharp's *Sospiri di Roma* in mind, as various diary entries make clear: "Started a piece on MacLeod's [Sharp's] 'White Peacock'" (30 May 1915); "Finished up 'Al far della notte'" (23 May 1916; Griffes used the English title *Nightfall* and Sharp's original Italian title as a subtitle); "Started another Sharp piece to the 'Fountains'" (27 May 1916); "Started 'Clouds' to Sharp's poem after I got back to the school at 11 o'clock. Worked till after 12" (24 May 1916).[16]

Although Schirmer published certain compositions together as sets with a collective title, Griffes did not necessarily conceive of the pieces that way. For example, the *Three Tone-Pictures* were at one time simply *Two Piano Pieces.*[17] In the case of *Roman Sketches,* Griffes may have intended a set of five, not four, compositions. In a diary entry dated 10 June 1916, Griffes referred to his *five* Sharp pieces, commenting, "Party at Mrs. Elliot's at 4.30. . . . I played for about 1½ hours—my 5 William Sharp pieces, 'Kubla Khan,' and Arturo's song ['Phantoms']." The fifth Sharp piece alluded to by Griffes could have been *De Profundis,* also named for a poem in Sharp's *Sospiri di Roma.* Griffes had started this work in November 1915 and finished it in December 1915, a year before signing the royalty agreement with G. Schirmer for the four compositions published in 1917 as *Roman Sketches,* op. 7.[18]

The commercial demands of publication and Schirmer's assessment of what would attract the public must have played a part in the groupings of pieces and in the use of poetic texts and descriptive titles. That is hardly surprising. It was the fashion of the day. For example, a small G. Schirmer brochure, *Twenty-one*

New Salon Pieces for Piano, includes compositions with titles such as "The Open Road" (Frederic Ayres), "Beauty's Waltz" (Homer N. Bartlett), "Danse de Panama" (M. Colas), "A Curious Story" (H. Frommel), "Dance of the Harpies" (Henry Hadley), "Menuet des nymphes" (Dominico Savino), and Griffes's *Fantasy Pieces*, op. 6.[19] Even Arnold Schoenberg was asked by his publisher to consider using descriptive titles for his atonal *Five Orchestral Pieces*. Schoenberg noted in his diary on 27 January 1912: "Letter from Peters, making an appointment with me for Wednesday in Berlin, in order to get to know me personally. Wants titles for the orchestral pieces—for publisher's reasons. Maybe I'll give in, for I've found titles that are at least possible."[20]

In any case, it is apparent that Griffes's musical imagination in the piano works opp. 5, 6, and 7 and in *De Profundis* was highly pictorial. One need only listen to *The Lake at Evening*, *The Night Winds*, *The White Peacock*, *The Fountain of the Acqua Paola*, and *Clouds*, for example, to appreciate that facet of Griffes's talent. Whether his imagination was reenforced by words *before* or *after* he completed a composition (or not at all, as in his later piano works) seems not to have had any influence on the intrinsic musical value of the piece.

Griffes maintained a lifelong interest in literature and poetry of all kinds and descriptions and once told Marion Bauer, "I get much more inspiration from reading Oriental folk tales than I do from looking at a tree!"[21] He read constantly and accumulated a large personal library of books often purchased from secondhand bookstores in New York.[22] His library included a great many biographies and autobiographies of musicians and other figures—from Marie Antoinette to Walt Whitman—as well as books on music, theater, art, psychology, the supernatural, architecture, and oriental culture, to name a few subjects.[23] Griffes was fluent in German, French, and Italian and preferred reading books in their original languages.

Griffes's wide-ranging tastes in literature are reflected in the variety of texts he chose for his songs as well as in his choice of poems or prose for his instrumental works. He wrote songs in German (twenty-six), English (thirty-five, eight of which are translations of Chinese, Japanese, or Rumanian texts), Javanese and Sundanese (three), and French (two). The texts he selected range from the visionary in William Blake's "In a Myrtle Shade" to the poignant plea for death as a release from the world's sorrows in John Masefield's "Sorrow of Mydath" to the aromatic exoticism of Rupert Brooke's "Waikiki" to the black despair of Heinrich Heine's "Wo ich bin, mich rings umdunkelt" to the hothouse world of Oscar Wilde in "La Fuite de la lune," "Symphony in Yellow," and *Four Impressions* to the sensuous mysticism of Fiona Macleod's "Rose of the Night" to the joie de vivre of William Ernest Henley's "We'll to the Woods, and Gather May," one of the few happy, upbeat songs Griffes ever wrote.

Griffes was a masterful songwriter. He possessed a wonderful melodic gift and was equally successful when writing with the utmost simplicity, as in his setting of the Rumanian folk text "Two Birds Flew into the Sunset Glow" (see ex. 11), as when writing complex, disjunct, and knotty melodies, as in "Waikiki" (see ex. 12).

Griffes understood that a great song must be a balanced partnership between voice and piano and that the text and music must serve each other. This is illustrated in "Song of the Dagger," where the interplay between voice and piano is both subtle and at times a contest of wills, as befits a text about jealousy, revenge, and murder. At the close of the penultimate verse, the piano overshadows the voice on the words "Even as the dagger thirsteth for thy blood" (see ex. 13). As the voice plunges to its lowest pitch in the song, the accompaniment in triplet chords and octaves parallels the vocal descent but then, while the voice is silent, soars upward for the final verse.

EXAMPLE 11 "Two Birds Flew into the Sunset Glow" (1914), mm. 1–16

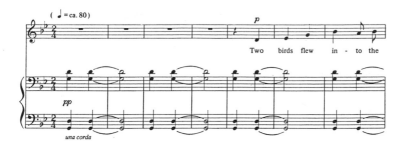

Griffes had a wonderful sensitivity to the blending of words and music. His rhythms and meters are perfectly attuned to the rhythm and meter of the text. A straightforward text often elicits a straightforward approach to rhythm and meter, as in many of his German songs and the later "Pierrot" (1912). In the first verse of "Pierrot" (see ex. 14), Griffes employs an uncomplicated rhythm and never strays from the opening $\frac{3}{8}$ meter. As the mood of the

EXAMPLE 12   "Waikiki," op. 9, no. 2 (1916), mm. 14–17

text shifts ever so slightly in subsequent verses, Griffes responds with subtle harmonic, melodic, and rhythmic changes.

More complicated texts and mood swings frequently call for changing meters and fluid rhythms (note, for instance, the alternation of $\frac{4}{4}$ and $\frac{3}{2}$ in "Phantoms," ex. 8). Or sometimes Griffes highlights a mood change, a word, or a portion of the text by obscuring the beat and creating conflicting rhythmic patterns in the voice and piano. In his setting of Oscar Wilde's "Symphony in Yellow," Griffes perfectly complements the feeling of suspension in Wilde's text by composing a fluid vocal line over block harmonies of seventh, ninth, diminished, and augmented chords in the piano part, creating a languid, static quality (see ex. 2 above). In the middle verse Griffes changes meter from $\frac{4}{4}$ to $\frac{3}{4}$ and imparts greater forward motion to the voice and piano (see ex. 15). The

EXAMPLE 13 "Song of the Dagger" (1916), mm. 108–15

voice part is clearly in triple meter, but Griffes phrases the piano part to give a feeling of duple meter. Voice and piano rejoin rhythmically on the text "And like a yellow silken scarf," where Griffes puts a gentle "brake" on the momentum with an upward leap of a minor ninth in the voice part. He precedes this gentle slowdown with a change of key from B major to B-flat major, accomplished in the piano with the utmost economy of means—an enharmonic change from E♯ to F♮, the fifth of the new tonic. The third verse returns to B major, common time, and the block harmonies of verse 1. Griffes achieves in this masterful song a

EXAMPLE 14 "Pierrot" (1912), mm. 1–11

perfect fusion of text and music, creating a haunting, evocative atmosphere in which the listener hangs suspended. Griffes's attraction to Wilde's poems no doubt stems in part from their liquid, musical quality.

Griffes also admired the works of William Sharp. Born in 1855 at Paisely, Scotland, Sharp was a leading figure in the Celtic renaissance of the late nineteenth century. Under his own name Sharp wrote essays, poetry, some novels, and biographies of Rossetti, Shelley, Heine, and Browning. He also wrote poems, plays, and other works about the mystic, primitive Celtic world under the pseudonym Fiona Macleod. Apparently, much of the Fiona literature was "written under the influence of a kind of mesmeric or spirited trance, or was the record of such trances."[24] Both sides of Sharp's literary personality interested Griffes, who composed three of his greatest songs (in settings for voice and piano and voice and orchestra) to Macleod texts: "The Lament of

EXAMPLE 15 "Symphony in Yellow," op. 3, no. 2 (ca. 1912), mm. 19–27

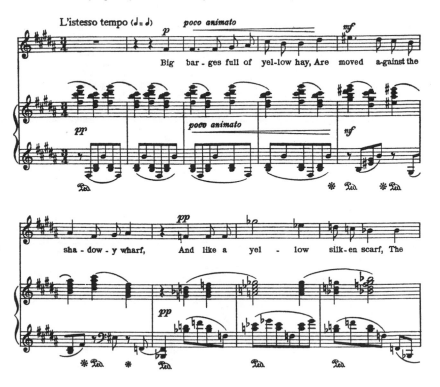

Ian the Proud," "Thy Dark Eyes to Mine," and "The Rose of the Night." Surely, one of the most exciting moments in any Griffes song comes in "The Lament of Ian the Proud" on the final line, "O blown, whirling leaf, And the old grief, And wind crying to me who am old and blind!" (see ex. 16). Although the song is in F-sharp minor, Griffes blurs the tonality at this point with harmonies that alternately suggest the tonic and the tonic major. The climax of the passage occurs in measure 44, where the voice rises to an $a\sharp''$ (its highest note in the song) on the word "wind," supported by a second-inversion tonic-major chord in the accompaniment. The sustained whole note tied to a quarter note in the voice part slows the momentum practically to a halt, as Griffes

EXAMPLE 16 "The Lament of Ian the Proud," op. 11, no. 1 (1918), mm. 40–48

works his way back to the tonic F-sharp minor in measure 47 by way of a dominant pedal point on C♯. The song concludes with a piano postlude recapitulating the material introduced by the piano at the beginning of the song. Griffes often used this type of restatement of material to achieve structural unity in his music. The piano writing in "The Lament of Ian the Proud" is essentially linear, the rhythm is varied, and, although the song clearly begins and ends in F-sharp minor, the tonality becomes more complex as the song progresses. Both the voice and piano parts are highly chromatic, and both are equally important in making Griffes's effects.

Griffes's music for piano spanned his entire career, from the Six Variations in B-flat Major (1898) to the Three Preludes (1919). Among his youthful works, the Four Preludes already exhibit Griffes's melodic gift, feeling for harmony, pianistic flair, and, in Prelude no. 2, a touch of Chopinesque melancholy (see ex. 17).

EXAMPLE 17 Prelude no. 2 (from Four Preludes, 1899–1900), mm. 1–8. Manuscript in NEE, © 1984 by Donna K. Anderson. Used with permission. All rights reserved.

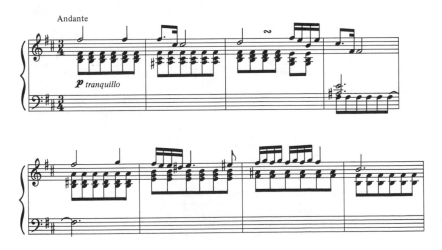

Griffes's first significant works for piano were the three pieces published in 1915 as *Three Tone-Pictures*, op. 5. With these works he began to move away from the German style to a freer, more impressionistic idiom. Instead of long, flowing melodies, we find melodic fragmentation, blurring of rhythm and tonality, and a less strict approach to structure. (See ex. 3 above.) The *Barcarolle*, op. 6, no. 1, although composed in the same year as *The Vale of Dreams*, op. 5, no. 2, is quite different in character and style. It is more clear-cut harmonically, rhythmically, and melodically and is more clearly structured. It also contains a short bitonal passage combining G-flat major and E-flat minor (see ex. 18) and some convincing contrapuntal writing (see ex. 19).

Griffes reached maturity as a piano composer in his *Roman Sketches*, op. 7, achieving a compelling structural logic and a mastery of motivic manipulation. He was now completely comfortable with whole-tone material, modality, bitonality, and nonhar-

EXAMPLE 18 *Barcarolle*, op. 6, no. 1 (1912), mm. 67–71

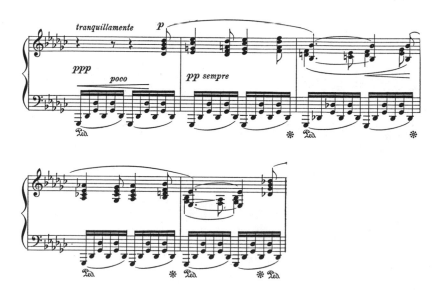

EXAMPLE 19 *Barcarolle*, op. 6, no. 1 (1912), mm. 124–27

monic chromaticism, devices he had used before, but not so extensively.

The *Roman Sketches* also contain more complex rhythmic patterns (see ex. 20) than Griffes had previously used in the *Three Tone-Pictures* and *Fantasy Pieces* and more unusual meters and frequent meter changes (see, for example, *The White Peacock,* which alternates $\frac{3}{2}$, $\frac{5}{4}$, and $\frac{7}{4}$, and *Clouds,* which includes meter signatures of $\frac{7}{4}$, $\frac{8}{4}$, and $\frac{3}{4}$).

Griffes often experimented with exotic and synthetic scales (see earlier discussion and exx. 4 and 9 above). In the case of the Piano Sonata, one of Griffes's most ambitious and complex works, musicians differ as to what the actual scale is. Gilbert Chase, in the first edition of his *America's Music: From the Pilgrims to the Present,* analyzes it as a thirteen-note scale with an augmented second between B♭ and C♯ (see ex. 21).[25] Jonathan Lee Chenette defines it as an eight-note scale with two augmented seconds (one

EXAMPLE 20 *The Fountain of the Acqua Paola*, op. 7, no. 3 (1916), mm. 29–30

EXAMPLE 21 Thirteen-note synthetic scale for the Piano Sonata (after Chase)

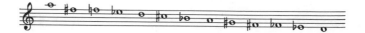

between B♭ and C♯, the other between F and G♯). The fourth
degree (E♭) is often altered (shown by parentheses in ex. 22), and
the sixth degree (F♯) is often omitted (see ex. 22).[26] Arthur Berger
offers still another interpretation, an eight-note scale comprising
two tetrachords related (intervallically) by retrograde inversion:
(counting half steps between pitches) 1–1–2–1–2–1–1 (see ex. 23).
When the pattern is repeated, an augmented second appears
between B♭ and C♯.[27] Finally, Dean Luther Arlton suggests a
seven-note scale similar to Chenette's, with augmented seconds
between F and G♯ and B♭ and C♯ (see ex. 24).[28]

EXAMPLE 22 Eight-note synthetic scale for the Piano Sonata (after Chenette)

EXAMPLE 23 Eight-note synthetic scale for the Piano Sonata (after Berger)

EXAMPLE 24 Seven-note synthetic scale for the Piano Sonata (after Arlton)

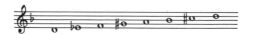

The presence of B♭ in the key signature would seem to indicate that Griffes considered this pitch important in the melodic and harmonic scheme of the Sonata. Beginning the synthetic scale on B♭ (as Chenette also does—see ex. 22), one might derive an eight-note synthetic scale as shown in example 25. This scale comprises two tetrachords related (intervallically) by retrograde inversion, with F♮ and F♯ serving as connecting (pivot) notes. The resultant intervals (counting half steps between pitches) are 3–1–1–2–1–2–1–1–3.

Despite their differences, all these scale patterns are essentially correct, illustrating the importance of the augmented second. And, because one can build fourths and fifths on almost all the degrees of the synthetic scale (for all the degrees if one considers chromatic alterations), each pattern also illustrates Griffes's harmonic scheme correctly. How one distills the scale pattern from the whole is less important than having an awareness of the melodic and harmonic configurations that generate the scale pattern or that result from it. I believe that Griffes had a certain sound in mind and that he approached the Sonata the same way he approached all his compositions—he used whatever means necessary to create the desired sound and effects. In the case of the Sonata, he turned to means largely outside of or "skirting" the major-minor system of tonality. There is, however, a strong gravitational pull to the note D throughout the Sonata, even in the second movement, which is more modal than the outer movements. While abandoning the old tonic-dominant relationship and all that it implies, Griffes did not abandon the con-

EXAMPLE 25 Alternative eight-note synthetic scale for the Piano Sonata

cept of an underlying, common area of stability. He could not have achieved the terrifying, frenzied, cumulative effect in the Sonata without that inexorable gravitational pull to D. But, of course, there is no "key" in the traditional sense—not D minor, not D major, and certainly not F major.

The first movement, Feroce–Allegretto con moto, is clearly in sonata form. Griffes himself identified the principal and secondary subjects and the development section on one of his manuscript sketches.[29] The principal theme illustrates Griffes's use of the synthetic scale and the linear writing that permeates the Sonata (see ex. 26).

Although the first movement seems as if it will end with great power and dynamism, Griffes scales down the dynamic level three measures from the end and introduces a ritardando in the penultimate measure. The movement ends on *pp* and moves without pause to the middle movement, Molto tranquillo.

The second movement is sectional in form. It has a modal flavor but derives all its material from the synthetic scale (see ex. 27). Beginning at the coda Griffes builds momentum by introducing an accelerando and *sempre accelerando*, and by increasing the dynamic level from *p* to *f*. The momentum created leads directly to the final movement, Allegro vivace, with only a short pause indicated by rests to separate the movements. Thus, although

EXAMPLE 26 Piano Sonata (1917–18; rev. 1919), first movement, principal theme, mm. 8–10

Griffes composed the Sonata in three movements, the effect is that of a "sonata in one movement" (as Griffes wished and as the piece was identified on the 26 February 1918 MacDowell Club all-Griffes program when Griffes premiered it).

The basic rhythmic pattern of the third movement—eighth note, three eighths, quarter note or some modification thereof—propels the movement forward from its opening measures (see ex. 28) to its ferocious close (see ex. 31).

Griffes wrote three different endings for the final movement (see exx. 29–31). In one manuscript sketch (ex. 29), he establishes what looks and sounds like D major in the last five measures. A fair copy version (ex. 30) similarly conveys a feeling of D major in the penultimate measure but adds an A♭ (enharmonic equivalent of G♯ from the synthetic scale) in the final measure. The final version (ex. 31) is pulled to a D-major sonority four measures from the end but closes with open fifths on D in the bass clef. The effect is well made.

The final version is superior to the first two attempts in other respects as well. Both the manuscript sketch (ex. 29) and fair

EXAMPLE 27 Piano Sonata, second movement, theme B1, mm. 22–25

EXAMPLE 28 Piano Sonata, third movement, theme A, mm. 1–10

copy (ex. 30) end in the upper register of the piano, weakening the overwhelming effect Griffes intended. His final version (ex. 31) ends in the lower register where he could achieve the necessary volume and intensity. Also, compared with both the fair copy and final version, both of which use two against three, the sketch (ex. 29) appears rather square and uninteresting rhythmically. Finally, the three extra measures in the final version add to the power of its close.[30]

Griffes often transcribed his works from one medium to another, frequently in response to an opportunity for performance. These include two arrangements of the op. 5 piano pieces, one for a chamber ensemble of woodwinds and harp, the other

EXAMPLE 29 Piano Sonata, third movement, final six measures from manuscript sketch, NN:Mu

EXAMPLE 30 Piano Sonata, third movement, final four measures from fair copy,
NEE

EXAMPLE 31 Piano Sonata, third movement, final version, mm. 216–23

for double quintet of winds and strings plus piano. He wrote only
three orchestral compositions that were not arrangements of preexisting piano works. These were the Overture, *Symphonische
Phantasie,* and *Poem for Flute and Orchestra.* The remaining nine
orchestral works—*The Pleasure-Dome of Kubla Khan, Notturno für
Orchester, Three Poems of Fiona Macleod, The White Peacock, Clouds,
Bacchanale,* and *Nocturne*—were all derived from preexisting piano
or voice and piano compositions.[31] Griffes was a superb orches-

trator, and his transformation of these works from piano to orchestra is masterly.

Example 32 shows the opening measures from Griffes's orchestral arrangement of *The Pleasure-Dome of Kubla Khan*. The scoring of the opening ("the vague, foggy beginning," as Griffes described it) suggests the sacred river Alph from Coleridge's poem "Kubla Khan."[32] Griffes achieves his effects with the divisi cellos and basses tremolo and *sul ponticello*, the "bass drum or deep gong kept in vibration by friction on the edge," the orchestral piano with both pedals in continual use, and the gradual entrance of the brass (first the trombones, then horns and trumpets), upper strings, woodwinds, celesta, and harp. The dynamics begin **ppp** and build gradually to the first climax (*f*) at letters D–E. The coloristic effects are wonderfully evocative of the sacred river running through the "caverns measureless to man down to a sunny sea."

Griffes's voice and orchestra version of the op. 11 Fiona Macleod songs is also beautifully colored, with woodwinds figuring prominently in the scheme. The motive that opens and closes "The Lament of Ian the Proud" is entrusted to the oboe, supported by sustained notes in the horns, second violins, violas, and bassoons, and with additional color provided by the harp (see ex. 33). Once the voice enters at measure 8, the dark mood and color that permeate the song have been simply but effectively established. "The Lament" closes with a recapitulation of the mournful oboe solo, but with all the other instruments silent, except strings and harp.

Griffes's orchestration in the Fiona Macleod songs skillfully complements the color of the soprano voice. Strings often "cushion" the voice, as in "Thy Dark Eyes to Mine," scored specifically for eight solo violins, second violins (not solo), two solo violas, three solo cellos, and two solo basses. In the opening measures the violas and cellos play a gentle, syncopated rhythm **pp**, the

EXAMPLE 32 *The Pleasure-Dome of Kubla Khan,* orchestral arrangement (1916–17), mm. 1–8

EXAMPLE 33 "The Lament of Ian the Proud," arrangement for voice and orchestra (ca. 1918), mm. 1–6

violins and basses are sustained, and the harps and flutes present a reiterated triplet figure. The upper solo viola plays an e♭′, the note on which the soprano enters. The effect is lovely, with the voice seeming to emerge from the body of the strings.

I suppose it is somewhat ironic that the greatest recognition accorded to Griffes during his lifetime came from the 1919 performances of one of the orchestral works he had originally written for piano, *The Pleasure-Dome of Kubla Khan.* Hearing these orchestrations, one cannot help but reflect with Kansas-born conductor

Karl Krueger, founder of the Society for the Preservation of the American Musical Heritage, who wrote, "It is as a composer for orchestra, particularly, that one might have wished that he could have been granted a few more years of development."[33]

Griffes's music is almost always elegant, exquisitely crafted, and controlled. He never overstates the obvious, nor does he allow pride of technique to enter the process. Griffes was an inward man who kept a part of himself locked away and protected from the intrusive eyes of the world. There is often an element of reserve, a "holding back," in his music, even at its most passionate. His music never jars—it persuades. Griffes owned a book of Chinese poetry that contains the following lines by Pai Ta-Shun:

> I would not paint a face
> Or rocks or streams or trees—
> Mere semblance of things—
> But something more than these.
>
> I would not play a tune
> Upon the sheng or lute,
> Which did not also sing
> Meanings that else were mute.
>
> That art is best which gives
> To the soul's range no bound;
> Something beside the form,
> Something beyond the sound.[34]

Each listener will discover his or her own "Something" in Griffes's music.

Charles Tomlinson Griffes spent his life in an incessant search for a musical language that could express his own artistic personality. He was, in the final analysis, a self-made artist. He was neither decisively shaped nor permanently influenced by any one person or by any one prevailing musical style—inspired, yes; guided, of course; but never artistically dominated. Griffes might have said with André Gide that influence creates nothing: it awakens. "An influence is like a divining rod that allows us to discover our inner wealth."[35] Griffes's artistic credo was uniquely his own—the product of his curiosity, his desire to assimilate and turn to his own use every possible experience, his vivid imagination, his driving ambition, his modesty and utter lack of pretense, his search for artistic fulfillment, his courage to follow his own path, and, finally, his unwavering devotion to his art. These traits enabled him to emerge, in the scant twelve years and seven months that separated his return from Berlin in 1907 to his death in 1920, as one of America's most significant composers. Griffes's music reveals an uncommon mind and a noble spirit.

Works List

Arranged alphabetically by medium (stage, orchestral, chamber, songs, piano, two piano, choral, and organ), the works list below provides information about dates of origin, instrumentation, arrangements, poets (for song lyrics), publication dates (abbrev. "PD"), publishers (Henmar Press, G. Schirmer, and Charles Scribner's Sons), and first performances (abbrev. "FP"). Compositions published in sets (both during and after Griffes's lifetime) appear under the collective title and before individual works. Lost and incomplete works are not listed.

STAGE

The Kairn of Koridwen (August–October 1916); fl., 2 cl., 2 hn., hp., cel., pn.—FP 10 February 1917, Neighborhood Playhouse, Barrère Ensemble, Nikolai Sokoloff (cond.), New York.

Sakura-sakura (ca. 1917); arr. of Japanese Cherry Dance for fl., cl., hp., vn. I and II, vc., db.—FP 5 August 1917, Adolf Bolm Ballet-Intime, Tulle Lindahl (dancer), New Nixon Theatre, Atlantic City.

Salut au monde (1919, completed by Edmond Rickett); fl.-picc., cl., 2 hn., tpt., 2 tbn., timp., 2 hp., pn., perc.—FP 22 April 1922, Festival Dancers of the Neighborhood Playhouse, members of the Barrère Ensemble of ww. instruments and the Little Symphony, Georges Barrère (cond.), Neighborhood Playhouse, New York.

Sho-jo (July 1917); fl., ob., cl., hp., Chinese drum, tam-tam, 2 timp., 4 muted str. (original version, lost)—FP 5 August 1917, Adolf Bolm Ballet-Intime, Tulle Lindahl, Michio Ito (dancers), New Nixon Theatre, Atlantic City. Arr. orch. (1919)—FP 25 January 1920(?), Cleveland Orchestra, Nikolai Sokoloff (cond.), New Masonic Hall, Cleveland. Arr. pn. (lost)—FP 26 February 1918, Michio Ito (dancer), Charles T. Griffes (pn.), MacDowell Club, New York.

A Trip to Syria (Assyrian Dance) (ca. 1917); arr. of A. Maloof pn. piece for fl., cl., hp., pn., timp., tam-tam, tamb., Chinese drum, str. (no va.)—FP 5 August 1917, Adolf Bolm Ballet-Intime, Adolf Bolm (dancer), New Nixon Theatre, Atlantic City.

The White Peacock (June 1919); orch. arr. of pn. piece—FP for dancer and orchestra, 22 June 1919, Adolf Bolm Ballet-Intime, Margit Leeraas (dancer), Rivoli Orchestra, Erno Rapee (cond.), Rivoli Theatre, New York. *See also* under "Orchestral."

ORCHESTRAL

Bacchanale (ca. 1919); arr. of pn. *Scherzo*—FP 19 December 1919, Philadelphia Orchestra, Leopold Stokowski (cond.), Academy of Music, Philadelphia.

Clouds (February 1919); arr. of pn. piece—FP 19 December 1919, Philadelphia Orchestra, Leopold Stokowski (cond.), Academy of Music, Philadelphia.

Nocturne (February 1919); arr. of Piano Sonata, mvt. 2.

Notturno für Orchester (1918?—probably earlier)—FP 19 December 1919, Philadelphia Orchestra, Leopold Stokowski (cond.), Academy of Music, Philadelphia. Also for pn. (n.d.; incomplete); str. orch. (n.d.); and pn. and hn. (1916; incomplete).

Overture (begun February 1905, probably completed late 1905)—FP 24 April 1961, Eastman-Rochester Orchestra, Howard Hanson (cond.), Eastman School of Music, Rochester, N.Y.

The Pleasure-Dome of Kubla Khan, op. 8 (1916–17); arr. of pn. piece—FP 28 November 1919, Boston Symphony Orchestra, Pierre Monteux (cond.), Symphony Hall, Boston.

Poem for Flute and Orchestra (1918)—PD 1951 (Schirmer); FP 16 November 1919, New York Symphony Orchestra, Walter Damrosch (cond.), Georges Barrère (fl.), Aeolian Hall, New York. Arr. fl. and pn. by Georges Barrère and vn. and pn. by Hugo Kortschak—PD 1922 (Schirmer); FP 24 November 1920(?), Nicholas Kouloukis (fl.), Walter Golde (pn.), MacDowell Club, New York. Reduction of score for fl. and pn. by Phillip Moll—PD in press (Schirmer).

Symphonische Phantasie (August 1907). *See also* under "Two Piano."

The White Peacock (June 1919); arr. of pn. piece—PD 1945 (Schirmer); FP 19 December 1919, Philadelphia Orchestra, Leopold Stokowski (cond.), Academy of Music, Philadelphia. *See also* under "Stage."

CHAMBER

Sets

Three Tone-Pictures, op. 5; arr. of pn. pieces for fl., 2 ob., 2 cl., 2 hn., 2 bsn., hp.
1. *The Lake at Evening* (November–December 1915)—FP 19 December 1916, Barrère Ensemble, Cort Theatre, New York.
2. *The Vale of Dreams* (December 1915)—FP 19 December 1916, Barrère Ensemble, Cort Theatre, New York.
3. *The Night Winds* (December 1915; rev. January 1916).

Three Tone-Pictures, op. 5; arr. of pn. pieces for dbl. qnt. of fl., ob., cl., hn., bsn., vn. I and II, va., vc., db., plus pn.
1. *The Lake at Evening* (ca. 1919)—FP 4 June 1920, New York Chamber Music Society, Carolyn Beebe (cond. and pn.), Wildwood Farm, Greenwich, Conn.
2. *The Vale of Dreams* (ca. 1919)—FP 4 June 1920, New York Chamber Music Society, Carolyn Beebe (cond. and pn.), Wildwood Farm, Greenwich, Conn.
3. *The Night Winds* (ca. 1919)—FP 4 June 1920, New York Chamber Music Society, Carolyn Beebe (cond. and pn.), Wildwood Farm, Greenwich, Conn.

Two Sketches for String Quartet Based on Indian Themes (Schirmer, 1922).
1. Lento e mesto (June 1918)—PD 1922; FP 24 November 1920(?), Flonzaley Quartet, MacDowell Club, New York. This was programmed as *Two Indian Sketches for String Quartet* and likely included the Allegro giocoso as movement 2. An early version of Lento e mesto was first performed on 2 April 1919, Flonzaley Quartet, MacDowell Gallery, New York. This was

listed as movement 1 of *Two Pieces for String Quartet* along with the Vivace [or] Allegro assai quasi presto as movement 2.

2. Allegro giocoso (July 1919)—PD 1922; FP 24 November 1920(?), Flonzaley Quartet, MacDowell Club, New York. This was programmed as *Two Indian Sketches for String Quartet* and likely included the Lento e mesto as movement 1.

Individual Works

Allegro energico ma maestoso (July 1919); str. qt.

Komori uta (ca. 1917); arr. of Japanese lullaby for fl., cl., vn. I and II, vc., db., hp.—FP 9 February 1985, Grinnell College 20th-Century Ensemble, Jonathan Chenette (cond.), Grinnell College, Grinnell, Iowa.

Noge no yama (ca. 1917); arr. of Japanese melody for fl., ob., cl., vn. I and II, vc., db., hp.—FP 9 February 1985, Grinnell College 20th-Century Ensemble, Jonathan Chenette (cond.), Grinnell College, Grinnell, Iowa.

String quartet movement in B-flat major: Minuet and Trio (October 1903).

Vivace [or] Allegro assai quasi presto (1917); str. qt.—FP 2 April 1919, Flonzaley Quartet, MacDowell Gallery, New York. This was listed as movement 2 of *Two Pieces for String Quartet* along with an early version of the Lento e mesto as movement 1.

SONGS

Sets

Five German Poems (Schirmer, 1909).
1. "Auf dem Teich, dem regungslosen" (ca. 1903–9)—N. Lenau; PD 1909; FP 15 March 1910, Mrs. Ray Herrick (sop.), Charles T. Griffes (pn.), Elmira College, Elmira, N.Y. (sung in English).
2. "Auf geheimem Waldespfade" (ca. 1903–9)—N. Lenau; PD 1909; FP 15 March 1910, Mrs. Ray Herrick (sop.), Charles T. Griffes (pn.), Elmira College, Elmira, N.Y. (sung in English).
3. "Nacht liegt auf den fremden Wegen" (ca. 1903–9; probably before 1907)—H. Heine; PD 1909.
4. "Der träumende See" (ca. 1903–9)—J. Mosen; PD 1909.

5. "Wohl lag ich einst in Gram und Schmerz" (ca. 1903–9)—E. Geibel; PD 1909; FP 15 March 1910, Mrs. Ray Herrick (sop.), Charles T. Griffes (pn.), Elmira, N.Y. (sung in English as an encore).

Five Poems of Ancient China and Japan, op. 10 (Schirmer, 1917).
1. "So-fei Gathering Flowers" (April 1917)—Wang Chang-Ling; PD 1917; FP 1 November 1917, Eva Gauthier (sop.), Charles T. Griffes (pn.), Aeolian Hall, New York.
2. "Landscape" (September 1916)—Sade-Ihe; PD 1917; FP 1 November 1917, Eva Gauthier (sop.), Charles T. Griffes (pn.), Aeolian Hall, New York.
3. "The Old Temple among the Mountains" (November 1916)—Chang Wen-Chang; PD 1917; FP 1 November 1917, Eva Gauthier (sop.), Charles T. Griffes (pn.), Aeolian Hall, New York.
4. "Tears" (November 1916)—Wang Seng-Ju; PD 1917; FP 1 November 1917, Eva Gauthier (sop.), Charles T. Griffes (pn.), Aeolian Hall, New York.
5. "A Feast of Lanterns" (August 1917)—Yuan Mei; PD 1917; FP 1 November 1917, Eva Gauthier (sop.), Charles T. Griffes (pn.), Aeolian Hall, New York.

Four German Songs (Henmar, 1970).
1. "Am Kreuzweg wird begraben" (ca. 1903–11)—H. Heine; PD 1970; FP 15 March 1965, Lois Williams (sop.), Arnold Fletcher (pn.), West Chester State College, West Chester, Pa.
2. "An den Wind" (ca. 1903–11)—N. Lenau; PD 1970; FP 15 March 1965, Lois Williams (sop.), Arnold Fletcher (pn.), West Chester State College, West Chester, Pa.
3. "Meeres stille" (ca. 1903–11)—J. W. von Goethe; PD 1970; FP 4 May 1964, Roy Samuelsen (bar.), Henry Upper (pn.), Indiana University, Bloomington.
4. "So halt' ich endlich dich umfangen" (ca. 1903–11)—E. Geibel; PD 1970; FP 15 March 1965, Lois Williams (sop.), Arnold Fletcher (pn.), West Chester State College, West Chester, Pa.

Four Impressions (Henmar, 1970).
1. "Le Jardin" (October 1915)—O. Wilde; PD 1970; FP 4 May 1964, Ronald Naldi (Rinaldo Naldi, ten.), Jack Gordon Cohan (pn.), Indiana University, Bloomington.
2. "Impression du matin" (November 1915)—O. Wilde; PD 1970; FP 4 May 1964, Ronald Naldi (Rinaldo Naldi, ten.), Jack Gordon Cohan (pn.), Indiana University, Bloomington.

3. "La Mer" (1912)—O. Wilde; PD 1970; FP 4 May 1964, Ronald Naldi (Rinaldo Naldi, ten.), Jack Gordon Cohan (pn.), Indiana University, Bloomington. Second version (1916, unpublished).

4. "Le Réveillon" (1914)—O. Wilde; PD 1970; FP 4 May 1964, Ronald Naldi (Rinaldo Naldi, ten.), Jack Gordon Cohan (pn.), Indiana University, Bloomington.

Seven [English] Songs (Henmar, 1986).

1. "Two Birds Flew into the Sunset Glow" (December 1914)—Rumanian folk text; PD 1986; FP 4 May 1964, Olive Fredricks (m.-sop.), Jack Gordon Cohan (pn.), Indiana University, Bloomington.

2. "Les Ballons" (ca. 1912; rev. 1915?)—O. Wilde; PD 1986.

3. "In the Harem" (ca. 1917, late 1916?)—Chu Ch'ing-yü; PD 1986; FP 4 May 1964, Olive Fredricks (m.-sop.), Jack Gordon Cohan (pn.), Indiana University, Bloomington.

4. "The Water-Lily" (1911)—J. B. Tabb; PD 1986; FP 7 May 1912, Gertrude Flint Frisbie (sop.), Edith Andrews (pn.), Normal School Lecture Room, Lowell, Mass.

5. "Phantoms" (ca. 1912)—J. B. Tabb; PD 1986.

6. "Pierrot" (May 1912)—S. Teasdale; PD 1986; FP 15 March 1965, Lois Williams (sop.), Arnold Fletcher (pn.), West Chester State College, West Chester, Pa. (sung as an encore).

7. "Cleopatra to the Asp" (April–May 1912)—J. B. Tabb; PD 1986; FP 29 April 1984, Lisa Cellucci (sop.), Donna K. Anderson (pn.), SUNY College at Cortland, Cortland, N.Y.

Six [German] Songs (Henmar, 1986).

1. "Mein Herz ist wie die dunkle Nacht" (ca. 1903–11)—E. Geibel; PD 1986; FP 1 April 1982, Robert Ergenbright (bass-bar.), Donna K. Anderson (pn.), SUNY College at Cortland, Cortland, N.Y.

2. "Des müden Abendlied" (ca. 1903–11)—E. Geibel; PD 1986; FP 1 April 1982, Robert Ergenbright (bass-bar.), Donna K. Anderson (pn.), SUNY College at Cortland, Cortland, N.Y.

3. "Mit schwarzen Segeln" (ca. 1903–11)—H. Heine; PD 1986; FP 4 May 1964, Olive Fredricks (m.-sop.), Jack Gordon Cohan (pn.), Indiana University, Bloomington.

4. "Das sterbende Kind" (ca. 1903–11)—E. Geibel; PD 1986; FP 1 April 1982, Robert Ergenbright (bass-bar.), Donna K. Anderson (pn.), SUNY College at Cortland, Cortland, N.Y.

5. "Das ist ein Brausen und Heulen" (ca. 1903–11)—H. Heine; PD 1986; FP 1 April 1982, Robert Ergenbright (bass-bar.), Donna K. Anderson (pn.), SUNY College at Cortland, Cortland, N.Y.

6. "Wo ich bin, mich rings umdunkelt" (ca. 1903–11)—H. Heine; PD 1986; FP 1 April 1982, Robert Ergenbright (bass-bar.), Donna K. Anderson (pn.), SUNY College at Cortland, Cortland, N.Y.

Three Javanese (Sundanese) Songs (Schirmer, in press); arr. of trad. songs.

1. "Hampelas" (1919)—PD in press; FP 26 February 1984, Joan Fuerstman (m.-sop.), Eliza Garth (pn.), Carnegie Recital Hall, New York.

2. "Kinanti" (1919)—PD in press; FP 26 February 1984, Joan Fuerstman (m.-sop.), Eliza Garth (pn.), Carnegie Recital Hall, New York.

3. "Djakoan" (1919)—PD in press; FP 26 February 1984, Joan Fuerstman (m.-sop.), Eliza Garth (pn.), Carnegie Recital Hall, New York.

Three Poems, op. 9 (Schirmer, 1918).

1. "In a Myrtle Shade" (March 1916)—W. Blake; PD 1918.

2. "Waikiki" (April 1916)—R. Brooke; PD 1918; FP 22 April 1918, Eva Gauthier (sop.), Marcel Hansotte (pn.), Aeolian Hall, New York.

3. "Phantoms" (March 1916)—A. Giovannitti; PD 1918.

Three Poems by Fiona Macleod, op. 11 (Schirmer, 1918).

1. "The Lament of Ian the Proud" (May 1918)—F. Macleod; PD 1918; FP 22 March 1919, Vera Janacopulos (sop.), Charles T. Griffes (pn.), Aeolian Hall, New York.

2. "Thy Dark Eyes to Mine" (May 1918)—F. Macleod; PD 1918; FP 22 March 1919, Vera Janacopulos (sop.), Charles T. Griffes (pn.), Aeolian Hall, New York.

3. "The Rose of the Night" (January 1918)—F. Macleod; PD 1918; FP 22 March 1919, Vera Janacopulos (sop.), Charles T. Griffes (pn.), Aeolian Hall, New York.

Three Poems of Fiona Macleod, op. 11; arr. voice and orch. (ca. 1918)—FP 24 March 1919, Philadelphia Orchestra, Thaddeus Rich (cond.), Marcia van Dresser (sop.), Playhouse, Wilmington, Del.

Tone-Images, op. 3 (Schirmer, 1915).

1. "La Fuite de la lune" (1912)—O. Wilde; PD 1915; FP 5 September 1918, Louise Lancaster (sop.), Charles T. Griffes (pn.), Thurston Auditorium, Lockport, N.Y.

2. "Symphony in Yellow" (ca. 1912)—O. Wilde; PD 1915; FP 12 April 1916, Tom Dobson (ten. and pn.), Punch and Judy Theatre, New York.

3. "We'll to the Woods, and Gather May" (1914)—W. E. Henley; PD 1915.

Tragödie (Schirmer, 1941; Schirmer, in press).
    1. "Entflieh mit mir" (ca. 1903–11)—H. Heine; PD in press; FP 4 May 1964, Marion Cawood (sop.), Jack Gordon Cohan (pn.), Indiana University, Bloomington.
    2. "Es fiel ein Reif" (ca. 1903–11)—H. Heine; PD in press; FP 4 May 1964, Marion Cawood (sop.), Jack Gordon Cohan (pn.), Indiana University, Bloomington.
    3. "Auf ihrem Grab" (ca. 1903–11)—H. Heine; PD 1941, in set in press.

Two Poems by John Masefield (Schirmer, 1920).
1. "An Old Song Re-sung" (July 1918)—J. Masefield; PD 1920.
2. "Sorrow of Mydath" (December 1917)—J. Masefield; PD 1920; FP 22 April 1918, Eva Gauthier (sop.), Marcel Hansotte (pn.), Aeolian Hall, New York.

Two Rondels, op. 4 (Schirmer, 1915).
    1. "This Book of Hours" (before May 1914)—W. Crane; PD 1915.
    2. "Come, Love, across the Sunlit Land" (before May 1914)—C. Scollard; PD 1915; FP 5 September 1918, Louise Lancaster (sop.), Charles T. Griffes (pn.), Thurston Auditorium, Lockport, N.Y.

Individual Songs

"Elfe" (ca. 1903–11)—J. von Eichendorff; PD 1941 (Schirmer).

"Evening Song" (ca. 1912; rev. July 1912)—S. Lanier; PD 1941 (Schirmer); FP 7 May 1912, Gertrude Flint Frisbie (sop.), Edith Andrews (pn.), Normal School Lecture Room, Lowell, Mass.

"The First Snowfall" (before March 1912)—J. B. Tabb; PD 1941 (Schirmer).

"Frühe" (ca. 1903–11)—J. von Eichendorff.

"Das Grab" ("Mir war als müsste ich graben") (ca. 1903–11)—F. Hebbel; FP 4 May 1964, Olive Fredricks (m.-sop.), Jack Gordon Cohan (pn.), Indiana University, Bloomington.

"The Half-ring Moon" (1912)—J. B. Tabb; PD 1941 (Schirmer).

"Ich weiss nicht, wie's geschieht" (ca. 1903–11)—E. Geibel; FP 26 February 1984, Constantine Cassolas (ten.), Walter Hilse (pn.), Carnegie Recital Hall, New York.

"Könnt' ich mit dir dort oben gehen" (ca. 1903–11)—J. Mosen; PD 1941 (Schirmer).

"La Mer" (August 1916; *Four Impressions*, no. 3, 2d version, unpublished)—O. Wilde; FP 26 February 1984, Constantine Cassolas (ten.), Walter Hilse (pn.), Carnegie Recital Hall, New York.

"Nachtlied" (1912)—E. Geibel; PD 1983 (Henmar); FP 26 February 1984, Constantine Cassolas (ten.), Walter Hilse (pn.), Carnegie Recital Hall, New York.

"Si mes vers avaient des ailes" (1901)—V. Hugo; FP 21 May 1903, Mrs. William Barron (sop.), Charles T. Griffes (pn.), Elmira College Chapel, Elmira, N.Y.

"Song of the Dagger" (1916)—Rumanian folk text; PD 1983 (Henmar); FP 4 May 1964, Roy Samuelsen (bar.), Henry Upper (pn.), Indiana University, Bloomington.

"Sur ma lyre l'autre fois" (ca. 1901)—C. A. Sainte-Beuve; FP 21 May 1903, Mrs. William Barron (sop.), Charles T. Griffes (pn.), Elmira College Chapel, Elmira, N.Y.

"The War-song of the Vikings" (1914)—F. Macleod; PD in press (Schirmer); FP 29 April 1984, Robert Ergenbright (bass-bar.), Donna K. Anderson (pn.), SUNY College at Cortland, Cortland, N.Y.

"Winternacht" (ca. 1903–11)—N. Lenau; PD in press (Schirmer); FP 29 April 1984, Lisa Cellucci (sop.), Donna K. Anderson (pn.), SUNY College at Cortland, Cortland, N.Y.

"Zwei Könige sassen auf Orkadal" (ca. 1903–10)—E. Geibel; PD 1910 (Schirmer); FP 15 March 1910, George M. McKnight (bar.), Charles T. Griffes (pn.), Elmira College, Elmira, N.Y. (sung in English).

PIANO

Sets

Fantasy Pieces, op. 6 (Schirmer, 1915).
1. *Barcarolle* (1912)—PD 1915; FP 3 November 1914, Charles T. Griffes (pn.), Colonial Hall, Lowell, Mass.
2. *Notturno* (January 1915)—PD 1915.

3. *Scherzo* (1913; rev. 1915)—PD 1915; FP 11 January 1916(?), George Clifford Vieh (pn.), Park Church Lecture Room, Elmira, N.Y.

Four Preludes, op. "40" (1899–1900).

Roman Sketches, op. 7 (Schirmer, 1917).
1. *The White Peacock* (May–June 1915)—PD 1917; FP 23 February 1916, Winifred Christie (pn.), Punch and Judy Theatre, New York. FP (dancer and pn.) 7 April 1918, Michio Ito (dancer), Charles T. Griffes (pn.), Greenwich Village Theatre, New York.
2. *Nightfall* (May 1916)—PD 1917; FP 7 February 1919(?), Winifred Christie (pn.), Jordan Hall, Boston.
3. *The Fountain of the Acqua Paola* (May–June 1916)—PD 1917; FP 1 June 1918(?), Emily Greenough (pn.), Eugene Heffley Studio, Carnegie Hall, New York.
4. *Clouds* (May 1916)—PD 1917.

Six Bugle-Call Pieces (ca. 1918; Arthur Tomlinson, pseud.)—PD 1918 (Schirmer): Reveille, Taps, Adjutant's Call, The General's March, Assembly March, To the Colors.

Six Familiar Songs (ca. 1919; Arthur Tomlinson, pseud.)—PD 1920 (Schirmer): "My Old Kentucky Home," "Old Folks at Home," "America," "Yankee Doodle," "Maryland, My Maryland," "The Old Oaken Bucket."

Six Patriotic Songs (ca. 1918; Arthur Tomlinson, pseud.)—PD 1918 (Schirmer). "America," "Yankee Doodle," "Marching through Georgia," "The Star-Spangled Banner," "The Red, White and Blue," "Dixie."

Six Pieces for Treble Clef (ca. 1919; Arthur Tomlinson, pseud.)—PD 1920 (Schirmer): the pieces are numbered, not titled.

Six Short Pieces (ca. 1918; Arthur Tomlinson, pseud.)—PD 1918 (Schirmer): March, Dance-song, Marching Song, Evening Song, Parade March, Waltz.

Three Preludes (1919)—PD 1967 (Henmar); FP 30 December 1949, John Ranck (pn.), Town Hall, New York.

Three Tone-Pictures, op. 5 (Schirmer, 1915).
1. *The Lake at Evening* (1910)—PD 1915; FP 3 April 1914, Leslie Hodgson (pn.), Chamber Music Hall, Carnegie Hall, New York.
2. *The Vale of Dreams* (1912)—PD 1915; FP 5 May 1917(?), Cadance Meakle (pn.), Eugene Heffley Studio, Carnegie Hall, New York.
3. *The Night Winds* (1911; rev. 1915)—PD 1915; FP 5 May 1917(?), Cadance Meakle (pn.), Eugene Heffley Studio, Carnegie Hall, New York.

Individual Works

"Barcarolle" (arr.) from *Les Contes d'Hoffmann,* by Jacques Offenbach (1910 or before)—FP 15 March 1910, Charles T. Griffes (pn.), Elmira College, Elmira, N.Y. (played as an encore).

Dance in A Minor (May 1916).

De Profundis (November–December 1915)—PD 1978 (Henmar); FP 4 May 1964, Henry Upper (pn.), Indiana University, Bloomington.

The Kairn of Koridwen (1916); arr. of stage work.

Legend (June 1915)—PD 1972 (Charles Scribner's Sons); FP 4 May 1964, Henry Upper (pn.), Indiana University, Bloomington.

Mazurka (1899–1900).

Piano Piece in B-flat Major (ca. 1915).

Piano Piece in D Minor (April 1915).

Piano Piece in E Major (1916).

Piano Sonata (December 1917–January 1918; rev. 1919)—PD 1921 (Schirmer); FP 26 February 1918, Charles T. Griffes (pn.), MacDowell Club, New York.

The Pleasure-Dome of Kubla Khan (1912; rev. 1915)—PD in press (Schirmer); FP 21 September 1984, James Tocco (pn.), Coolidge Auditorium, Library of Congress, Washington, D.C.

Rhapsody in B Minor (1914)—PD in press (Henmar); FP 29 April 1984, Denver Oldham (pn.), SUNY College at Cortland, Cortland, N.Y.

Six Variations in B-flat Major, op. 2 (1898).

Sonata in D-flat Major, one mvt. (ca. 1909–10)—FP 4 November 1984, Kristina Suter (pn.), Mount Vernon College, Washington, D.C.

Sonata in D-flat Major, two mvts. (ca. 1911)—FP 10 November 1984, Kristina Suter (pn.), Mansfield University, Mansfield, Pa.

Sonata in F Minor, two mvts. (ca. 1904)—FP 22 June 1905 (1st mvt. only), Charles T. Griffes (pn.), Stern Conservatory, Berlin, Germany.

Sonata in F-sharp Minor, one mvt. (ca. 1912–13)—FP 9 November 1985, Kristina Suter (pn.), University of Maryland, College Park.

A Winter Landscape (ca. 1912).

TWO PIANO

Overture to Hänsel und Gretel (1910 or before); arr. after Engelbert
Humperdinck—PD 1951 (Schirmer).

Symphonische Phantasie (1910 or before); arr. of orch. piece—FP 4 May 1964,
Donna K. Anderson, Robert Carrol Smith (2 pn.), Indiana University,
Bloomington.

CHORAL

"Dies ist der Tag" (1906); SSATB—I. Watts; FP 26 February 1984, Alliance for
American Song Vocal Ensemble, Carnegie Recital Hall, New York.

"Lobe den Herren" (1906); SSATB—J. Neander; FP 26 February 1984, Alliance for
American Song Vocal Ensemble, Carnegie Recital Hall, New York.

"Passionlied fünfstimmig, O Haupt voll Blut" (1906); SSATB—St. Bernard of
Clairvaux; FP 26 February 1984, Alliance for American Song Vocal Ensemble,
Carnegie Recital Hall, New York.

"These Things Shall Be" (1916); unison chorus and pn.—J. A. Symonds; PD 1917
(Schirmer); FP 1 June 1917, New York Community Chorus, Harry Barnhart
(cond.), Hippodrome, New York.

ORGAN

Chorale on "Allein Gott in der Höh' sei Ehr'" (1910? earlier?).

Works Chronology

1898

Six Variations in B-flat Major, op. 2 (pn.)

1899–1900

Four Preludes, op. "40" (pn.)
Mazurka (pn.)

1901

"Si mes vers avaient des ailes"
"Sur ma lyre l'autre fois" (ca. 1901)

1903

String quartet movement in B-flat major: Minuet and Trio

CA. 1903–9

"Auf dem Teich, dem regungslosen" (*Five German Poems*, no. 1)
"Auf geheimem Waldespfade" (*Five German Poems*, no. 2)
"Nacht liegt auf den fremden Wegen" (*Five German Poems*, no. 3; probably before 1907)
"Der träumende See" (*Five German Poems*, no. 4)
"Wohl lag ich einst in Gram und Schmerz" (*Five German Poems*, no. 5)

CA. 1903–10

"Zwei Könige sassen auf Orkadal"

CA. 1903–11

"Am Kreuzweg wird begraben" (*Four German Songs*, no. 1)
"An den Wind" (*Four German Songs*, no. 2)
"Auf ihrem Grab" (*Tragödie*, no. 3)
"Das ist ein Brausen und Heulen" (*Six [German] Songs*, no. 5)
"Elfe"
"Entflieh mit mir" (*Tragödie*, no. 1)
"Es fiel ein Reif" (*Tragödie*, no. 2)
"Frühe"
"Das Grab" ("Mir war als müsste ich graben")
"Ich weiss nicht, wie's geschieht"
"Könnt' ich mit dir dort oben gehen"
"Meeres stille" (*Four German Songs*, no. 3)
"Mein Herz ist wie die dunkle Nacht" (*Six [German] Songs*, no. 1)
"Mit schwarzen Segeln" (*Six [German] Songs*, no. 3)
"Des müden Abendlied" (*Six [German] Songs*, no. 2)
"So halt' ich endlich dich umfangen" (*Four German Songs*, no. 4)
"Das sterbende Kind" (*Six [German] Songs*, no. 4)
"Winternacht"
"Wo ich bin, mich rings umdunkelt" (*Six [German] Songs*, no. 6)

CA. 1904

Sonata in F Minor (pn.; two mvts.)

1905

Overture (orch.)

1906

"Dies ist der Tag" (SSATB)
"Lobe den Herren" (SSATB)
"Passionlied fünfstimmig, O Haupt voll Blut" (SSATB)

1907

Symphonische Phantasie (orch.)

CA. 1909–10

Sonata in D-flat Major (pn.; one mvt.)

1910

"Barcarolle" (arr. for pn.) from *Les Contes d'Hoffmann* (1910 or before)
Chorale on "Allein Gott in der Höh' sei Ehr'" (organ; 1910? earlier?)
The Lake at Evening (pn., *Three Tone-Pictures*, op. 5, no. 1)
Overture to Hänsel und Gretel (arr. for 2 pn.) after Humperdinck (1910 or before)
Symphonische Phantasie (2 pn. arr. of orch. piece; 1910 or before)

1911

The Night Winds (pn., *Three Tone-Pictures*, op. 5, no. 3; rev. 1915)
Sonata in D-flat Major (pn.; two mvts.; ca. 1911)
"The Water-Lily" (*Seven [English] Songs*, no. 4)

1912

"Les Ballons" (*Seven [English] Songs*, no. 2; ca. 1912, rev. 1915?)
Barcarolle (pn., *Fantasy Pieces*, op. 6, no. 1)
"Cleopatra to the Asp" (*Seven [English] Songs*, no. 7)
"Evening Song" (ca. 1912, rev. July 1912)
"The First Snowfall" (before March 1912)
"La Fuite de la lune" (*Tone-Images*, op. 3, no. 1)
"The Half-ring Moon"
"La Mer" (*Four Impressions*, no. 3, 1st version)
"Nachtlied"
"Phantoms" (*Seven [English] Songs*, no. 5; ca. 1912)
"Pierrot" (*Seven [English] Songs*, no. 6)
The Pleasure-Dome of Kubla Khan (pn.; rev. 1915)
"Symphony in Yellow" (*Tone-Images*, op. 3, no. 2; ca. 1912)
The Vale of Dreams (pn., *Three Tone-Pictures*, op. 5, no. 2)
A Winter Landscape (pn.; ca. 1912)

CA. 1912–13

Sonata in F-sharp Minor (pn.; one mvt.)

1913

Scherzo (pn., *Fantasy Pieces*, op. 6, no. 3; rev. 1915)

1914

"Come, Love, across the Sunlit Land" (*Two Rondels*, op. 4, no. 2; before May
    1914)
"Le Réveillon" (*Four Impressions*, no. 4)

Rhapsody in B Minor (pn.)

"This Book of Hours" (*Two Rondels*, op. 4, no. 1; before May 1914)

"Two Birds Flew into the Sunset Glow" (*Seven [English] Songs*, no. 1)

"The War-song of the Vikings"

"We'll to the Woods, and Gather May" (*Tone-Images*, op. 3, no. 3)

1915

De Profundis (pn.)

"Impression du matin" (*Four Impressions*, no. 2)

"Le Jardin" (*Four Impressions*, no. 1)

The Lake at Evening (ww. and hp. arr. of pn. piece)

Legend (pn.)

The Night Winds (ww. and hp. arr. of pn. piece; rev. January 1916)

Notturno (pn., *Fantasy Pieces*, op. 6, no. 2)

Piano Piece in B-flat Major (ca. 1915)

Piano Piece in D Minor

The Vale of Dreams (ww. and hp. arr. of pn. piece)

The White Peacock (pn., *Roman Sketches*, op. 7, no. 1)

1916

Clouds (pn., *Roman Sketches*, op. 7, no. 4)

Dance in A Minor (pn.)

The Fountain of the Acqua Paola (pn., *Roman Sketches*, op. 7, no. 3)

"In a Myrtle Shade" (*Three Poems*, op. 9, no. 1)

The Kairn of Koridwen (pn. arr. of stage work)

The Kairn of Koridwen (stage work)

"Landscape" (*Five Poems of Ancient China and Japan*, op. 10, no. 2)

"La Mer" (*Four Impressions*, no. 3, 2d version, unpublished)

Nightfall (pn., *Roman Sketches*, op. 7, no. 2)

"The Old Temple among the Mountains" (*Five Poems of Ancient China and Japan*, op. 10, no. 3)

"Phantoms" (*Three Poems*, op. 9, no. 3)

Piano Piece in E Major

"Song of the Dagger"

"Tears" (*Five Poems of Ancient China and Japan*, op. 10, no. 4)

"These Things Shall Be" (unison chorus and pn.)

"Waikiki" (*Three Poems*, op. 9, no. 2)

1917

"A Feast of Lanterns" (*Five Poems of Ancient China and Japan*, op. 10, no. 5)

"In the Harem" (*Seven [English] Songs*, no. 3.; ca. 1917, late 1916?)

Komori uta (chamber piece; ca. 1917)

Noge no yama (chamber piece; ca. 1917)

The Pleasure-Dome of Kubla Khan, op. 8 (orch. arr. of pn. piece; begun 1916)

Sakura-sakura (stage work; ca. 1917)

Sho-jo (stage work; arr. orch. 1919)

"So-fei Gathering Flowers" (*Five Poems of Ancient China and Japan*, op. 10, no. 1)

"Sorrow of Mydath" (*Two Poems by John Masefield*, no. 2)

A Trip to Syria (Assyrian Dance) (stage work; ca. 1917)

Vivace [or] Allegro assai quasi presto (str. qt.)

1917–18

Piano Sonata (rev. 1919)

1918

"The Lament of Ian the Proud" (*Three Poems by Fiona Macleod*, op. 11, no. 1)

"The Lament of Ian the Proud" (voice and orch. arr. of voice and pn. song,
  Three Poems of Fiona Macleod, op. 11, no. 1; ca. 1918)

Lento e mesto (*Two Sketches for String Quartet Based on Indian Themes*, no. 1)

Notturno für Orchester (1918?—probably earlier)

"An Old Song Re-sung" (*Two Poems by John Masefield*, no. 1)

Poem for Flute and Orchestra

"The Rose of the Night" (*Three Poems by Fiona Macleod*, op. 11, no. 3)

"The Rose of the Night" (voice and orch. arr. of voice and pn. song, *Three
  Poems of Fiona Macleod*, op. 11, no. 3; ca. 1918)

Six Bugle-Call Pieces (pn.; ca. 1918)

Six Patriotic Songs (pn.; ca. 1918)

Six Short Pieces (pn.; ca. 1918)

"Thy Dark Eyes to Mine" (*Three Poems by Fiona Macleod*, op. 11, no. 2)

"Thy Dark Eyes to Mine" (voice and orch. arr. of voice and pn. song, *Three
  Poems of Fiona Macleod*, op. 11, no. 2; ca. 1918)

1919

Allegro energico ma maestoso (str. qt.)

Allegro giocoso (*Two Sketches for String Quartet Based on Indian Themes*, no. 2)

Bacchanale (orch. arr. of pn. *Scherzo*; ca. 1919)

Clouds (orch. arr. of pn. piece)

"Djakoan" (*Three Javanese [Sundanese] Songs,* no. 3)

"Hampelas" (*Three Javanese [Sundanese] Songs,* no. 1)

"Kinanti" (*Three Javanese [Sundanese] Songs,* no. 2)

The Lake at Evening (dbl. qnt. plus pn. arr. of pn. piece; ca. 1919)

The Night Winds (dbl. qnt. plus pn. arr. of pn. piece; ca. 1919)

Nocturne (orch. arr. of Piano Sonata, 2d mvt.)

Salut au monde (stage work)

Six Familiar Songs (pn.; ca. 1919)

Six Pieces for Treble Clef (pn.; ca. 1919)

Three Preludes (pn.)

The Vale of Dreams (dbl. qnt. plus pn. arr. of pn. piece; ca. 1919)

The White Peacock (orch. arr. of pn. piece)

Discography

Appendix C lists all known commercial recordings of Griffes's works—as of July 1992—listed alphabetically by title of composition. All recordings are 33⅓ rpm and 12″ unless otherwise noted (i.e., 78, 45, 10″, CD, cassette).

For an overview of Griffes's songs, see Musical Heritage Society MHS 824678M *(The Songs of Charles T. Griffes),* the most comprehensive collection of English and German songs available on a single album; and Teldec 9031-72168-2 *(Ives-Griffes-MacDowell Lieder),* containing the largest number of German songs available on one album. Several collections containing all or most of Griffes's published piano music exist, among them Nonesuch 71409 *(Piano Music of Charles Tomlinson Griffes);* Musical Heritage Society MHS 3695 *(Charles Tomlinson Griffes: Piano Music);* Musical Heritage Society MHS 513043K *(Charles T. Griffes: Complete Piano Music);* Gasparo GSCD 231-34 *(MacDowell & Griffes),* which also includes the first recording of the Rhapsody and the original version of *The Pleasure-Dome of Kubla Khan;* and New World Records NW 310-11 *(Collected Works for Piano: Charles Tomlinson Griffes),* which includes unpublished as well as published works. For a representative collection of songs, orchestral compositions, and chamber arrangements, see New World Records NW 273 and NW 273-2 CD *(Charles Tomlinson Griffes),* and for orchestral compositions and chamber arrangements, see Delos DE 3099 (CD) *(The Musical Fantasies of Charles Griffes and Deems Taylor).*

"Am Kreuzweg wird begraben." Sherrill Milnes, bar.; Jon Spong, pn. New
World Records NW 273 and NW 273-2 CD: *Charles Tomlinson Griffes*, with
notes by Donna K. Anderson.

———. Thomas Hampson, bar.; Armen Guzelimian, pn. Teldec 9031-72168-2
(CD): *Ives-Griffes-MacDowell Lieder*, with notes by Paul Schiavo.

"An den Wind." Jan Opalach, bar.; Jeffrey Goldberg, pn. Musical Heritage Society MHS 824678M: *The Songs of Charles T. Griffes*, 2 discs, with notes by Edward Maisel.

———. Sherrill Milnes, bar.; Jon Spong, pn. New World Records NW 273
and NW 273-2 CD: *Charles Tomlinson Griffes*, with notes by Donna K.
Anderson.

———. Thomas Hampson, bar.; Armen Guzelimian, pn. Teldec 9031-72168-2
(CD): *Ives-Griffes-MacDowell Lieder*, with notes by Paul Schiavo.

"Auf dem Teich, dem regungslosen." Irene Gubrud, sop.; Margo Garrett, pn.
Musical Heritage Society MHS 824678M: *The Songs of Charles T. Griffes*, 2
discs, with notes by Edward Maisel.

"Auf geheimem Waldespfade." Irene Gubrud, sop.; Margo Garrett, pn. Musical
Heritage Society MHS 824678M: *The Songs of Charles T. Griffes*, 2 discs, with
notes by Edward Maisel.

———. Norman Myrvik, ten.; Emanuel Levenson, pn. EMS 501: *Survey of the Art
Song*, with notes by Emanuel Levenson.

———. Sherrill Milnes, bar.; Jon Spong, pn. New World Records NW 273
and NW 273-2 CD: *Charles Tomlinson Griffes*, with notes by Donna K.
Anderson.

———. Thomas Hampson, bar.; Armen Guzelimian, pn. Teldec 9031-72168-2
(CD): *Ives-Griffes-MacDowell Lieder*, with notes by Paul Schiavo.

——— (issued as "By a Lonely Forest Pathway"). Alexander Kisselburgh, bar.;
pianist anon. Columbia C 189M (78, 10″). Also issued on Columbia C 2041D
(78, 10″).

——— (issued as "By a Lonely Forest Pathway"). Eleanor Steber, sop.; James
Quillian, pn. Victor 10-1071A (8, 10″). Also issued on New World Records NW
247: *When I Have Sung My Songs: The American Art Song, 1900–1940*, with
notes by Philip L. Miller.

——— (issued as "By a Lonely Forest Pathway"). Elisabeth Rethberg, sop.; Fred
Persson, pn. Brunswick (USA) AMB 15146 (78, 10″). Also issued on British
Brunswick BA 62651 (78, 10″).

——— (issued as "By a Lonely Forest Pathway"). Glenn Darwin, bar.; Elsa
Fiedler, pn. Victor 36224 (78).

—— (issued as "By a Lonely Forest Pathway"). John Kennedy Hanks, ten.; Ruth Friedberg, pn. Duke University Press DWR 6417-18: *The Art Song in America,* 2 discs, with notes by John Kennedy Hanks and Ruth Friedberg.

"Auf ihrem Grab." Lucy Shelton, sop.; Margo Garrett, pn. Musical Heritage Society MHS 824678M: *The Songs of Charles T. Griffes,* 2 discs, with notes by Edward Maisel.

——. Paul Sperry, ten.; Irma Vallecillo, pn. Gregg Smith Singers Productions GSS 109: *Paul Sperry Sings Songs of an Innocent Age: Music from Victorian America,* American Songs Series, vol. 3, with notes by Paul Sperry. Also issued on Albany Records TROY CD 034-2: *Paul Sperry Sings Songs of an Innocent Age: Music from Turn of the Century America.*

——. Thomas Hampson, bar.; Armen Guzelimian, pn. Teldec 9031-72168-2 (CD): *Ives-Griffes-MacDowell Lieder,* with notes by Paul Schiavo.

Bacchanale (arr. orch.; see also *Fantasy Pieces,* op. 6). Eastman-Rochester Orchestra, Howard Hanson, cond. Mercury MG 50422 (mono) and SR 90422 (stereo): *Great Music by American Composers,* with notes by David Hall.

——. Eastman-Rochester Symphony Orchestra, Howard Hanson, cond. Mercury MG 50085: American Music Festival Series, vol. 13, with notes (anon.). Also issued on Mercury SRI 75090 (Golden Imports); British Mercury MRL 2544; and Mercury MG 40012 (Golden Lyre Series).

——. Seattle Symphony, Gerard Schwarz, cond. Delos DE 3099 (CD): *The Musical Fantasies of Charles Griffes and Deems Taylor,* with notes by Donna K. Anderson. Also issued on Delos DE 3508 (CD): *Made in the U.S.A.: A Showcase of American Symphonic Music,* with notes by Steven C. Smith.

"Les Ballons." Lucy Shelton, sop.; Margo Garrett, pn. Musical Heritage Society MHS 824678M: *The Songs of Charles T. Griffes,* 2 discs, with notes by Edward Maisel.

Barcarolle. See *Fantasy Pieces,* op. 6.

"By a Lonely Forest Pathway." *See* "Auf geheimem Waldespfade."

Clouds (arr. orch.). Eastman-Rochester Symphony Orchestra, Howard Hanson, cond. Mercury MG 50085: American Music Festival Series, vol. 13, with notes (anon.). Also issued on Mercury SRI 75090 (Golden Imports); British Mercury MRL 2544; and Mercury MG 40012 (Golden Lyre Series).

Clouds (pn.). See *Roman Sketches,* op. 7.

"Come, Love, across the Sunlit Land." See *Two Rondels,* op. 4.

Dance in A Minor. Denver Oldham, pn. New World Records NW 310-11: *Collected Works for Piano: Charles Tomlinson Griffes,* 2 discs, with notes by Edward Maisel.

"Das ist ein Brausen und Heulen." Thomas Hampson, bar.; Armen Guzelimian, pn. Teldec 9031-72168-2 (CD): *Ives-Griffes-MacDowell Lieder,* with notes by Paul Schiavo.

———. William Parker, bar.; William Huckaby, pn. New World Records NW 305, with notes by Philip L. Miller.

De Profundis. Denver Oldham, pn. New World Records NW 310-11: *Collected Works for Piano: Charles Tomlinson Griffes,* 2 discs, with notes by Edward Maisel.

———. Horatio Miller, pn. Cabrére Records 1000: *Horatio Miller: A Poet at the Piano,* with notes (anon.).

———. James Tocco, pn. Gasparo GSCD 233: *MacDowell & Griffes,* vol. 3, with notes by Allan Kozinn.

———. Joseph Smith, pn. Musical Heritage Society MHS 513043K (CD): *Charles T. Griffes: Complete Piano Music,* with notes by Joseph Smith.

"Early Morning in London." *See* "Impression du matin."

"Elfe." Lucy Shelton, sop.; Margo Garrett, pn. Musical Heritage Society MHS 824678M: *The Songs of Charles T. Griffes,* 2 discs, with notes by Edward Maisel.

———. Norman Myrvik, ten.; Emanuel Levenson, pn. EMS 501: *Survey of the Art Song,* with notes by Emanuel Levenson.

———. Thomas Hampson, bar.; Armen Guzelimian, pn. Teldec 9031-72168-2 (CD): *Ives-Griffes-MacDowell Lieder,* with notes by Paul Schiavo.

"Evening Song." Alexandra Hunt, sop.; Regis Benoit, pn. Orion ORS 77272: *Songs by Carpenter, Griffes & MacDowell,* with notes by Edwin McArthur.

———. Jan Opalach, bar.; Jeffrey Goldberg, pn. Musical Heritage Society MHS 824678M: *The Songs of Charles T. Griffes,* 2 discs, with notes by Edward Maisel.

———. Norman Myrvik, ten.; Emanuel Levenson, pn. EMS 501: *Survey of the Art Song,* with notes by Emanuel Levenson.

———. Yolanda Marcoulescou-Stern, sop.; Katja Phillabaum, pn. Gasparo GSCD-287: *Art Songs by American Composers.*

Fantasy Pieces, op. 6 (see also *Notturno* and *Scherzo*). Aldo Mancinelli, pn. Musical Heritage Society MHS 3695: *Charles Tomlinson Griffes: Piano Music,* with notes by David A. Reed.

———. Denver Oldham, pn. New World Records NW 310-11: *Collected Works for Piano: Charles Tomlinson Griffes,* 2 discs, with notes by Edward Maisel.

———. Garah Landes, pn. Koch International Classics CD 3-7045-2HI (LC6644): *The Lake at Evening: American Romantic Piano Music,* with notes by Raymond J. Osnato.

——. James Tocco, pn. Gasparo GSCD 232: *MacDowell & Griffes*, vol. 2, with notes by Allan Kozinn.

——. Joseph Smith, pn. Musical Heritage Society MHS 513043K (CD): *Charles T. Griffes: Complete Piano Music*, with notes by Joseph Smith.

——. Lenore Engdahl, pn. MGM E 3225: *Charles Tomlinson Griffes*, with notes by Edward Cole.

——. Noël Lee, pn. Nonesuch 71409: *Piano Music of Charles Tomlinson Griffes*, with notes by Donna K. Anderson.

"A Feast of Lanterns." See *Five Poems of Ancient China and Japan*, op. 10.

"The First Snowfall." Faith Esham, sop.; Thomas Muraco, pn. Musical Heritage Society MHS 824678M: *The Songs of Charles T. Griffes*, 2 discs, with notes by Edward Maisel.

——. William Parker, bar.; William Huckaby, pn. New World Records NW 305, with notes by Philip L. Miller.

Five Poems of Ancient China and Japan, op. 10. Irene Gubrud, sop.; Margo Garrett, pn. Musical Heritage Society MHS 824678M: *The Songs of Charles T. Griffes*, 2 discs, with notes by Edward Maisel.

The Fountain of the Acqua Paola (see also *Roman Sketches*, op. 7). Carol Rosenberger, pn. Delos D 3006 CD: *"Water Music" of the Impressionists*, with notes by Carol Rosenberger. Also issued on Delos DPC 2008.

——. Constance Keene, pn. Protone Records PR 155: *Constance Keene Plays American Music*, with notes (anon.).

——. David Dubal, pn. Musical Heritage Society MHS 3808: *The Piano in America*, with notes by David Dubal and Stanley Waldoff.

——. Roger Shields, pn. Vox SVBX 5303: *Piano Music in America*, vol. 2, *1900–1945*, 3 discs, with notes by Lejaren Hiller.

——. Rudolf Gruen, pn. Roycroft (USA) 171 (78, 10″).

Four Impressions (*see also* "Impression du matin" and "La Mer"). Lucy Shelton, sop.; Margo Garrett, pn. Musical Heritage Society MHS 824678M: *The Songs of Charles T. Griffes*, 2 discs, with notes by Edward Maisel. Includes 1916 version of "La Mer" instead of 1912 version.

——. Olivia Stapp, m.-sop.; Diane Richardson, pn. New World Records NW 273 and NW 273-2 CD: *Charles Tomlinson Griffes*, with notes by Donna K. Anderson.

"La Fuite de la lune," op. 3, no. 1. Jan Opalach, bar.; Jeffrey Goldberg, pn. Musical Heritage Society MHS 824678M: *The Songs of Charles T. Griffes*, 2 discs, with notes by Edward Maisel.

"The Half-ring Moon." Lucy Shelton, sop.; Margo Garrett, pn. Musical Heritage Society MHS 824678M: *The Songs of Charles T. Griffes*, 2 discs, with notes by Edward Maisel.

"Impression du matin" (issued as "Early Morning in London"; see also *Four Impressions*). Elizabeth Suderburg, sop.; Robert Suderburg, pn. University of Washington Press Oly 104: *American Sampler*, 2 discs, with notes by Naomi B. Pascal.

"In a Myrtle Shade," op. 9, no. 1. Alexandra Hunt, sop.; Regis Benoit, pn. Orion ORS 77272: *Songs by Carpenter, Griffes & MacDowell*, with notes by Edwin McArthur.

———. Faith Esham, sop.; Thomas Muraco, pn. Musical Heritage Society MHS 824678M: *The Songs of Charles T. Griffes*, 2 discs, with notes by Edward Maisel.

———. Yolanda Marcoulescou-Stern, sop.; Katja Phillabaum, pn. Gasparo GSCD-287: *Art Songs by American Composers*.

"In the Harem." Irene Gubrud, sop.; Margo Garrett, pn. Musical Heritage Society MHS 824678M: *The Songs of Charles T. Griffes*, 2 discs, with notes by Edward Maisel.

"Le Jardin." See *Four Impressions*.

"Könnt' ich mit dir dort oben gehen." Lucy Shelton, sop.; Margo Garrett, pn. Musical Heritage Society MHS 824678M: *The Songs of Charles T. Griffes*, 2 discs, with notes by Edward Maisel.

The Lake at Evening. See *Three Tone-Pictures*, op. 5.

"The Lament of Ian the Proud" (see also *Three Poems by Fiona Macleod*, op. 11). Dale Moore, bar.; Betty Ruth Tomfohrde, pn. Cambridge CRS 2715: *On the Road to Mandalay & Other Favorite American Concert Songs from 1900 to 1950*, with notes by Dale Moore.

———. Elizabeth Suderburg, sop.; Robert Suderburg, pn. University of Washington Press Oly 104: *American Sampler*, 2 discs, with notes by Naomi B. Pascal.

———. John Kennedy Hanks, ten.; Ruth Friedberg, pn. Duke University Press DWR 6417-18: *The Art Song in America*, 2 discs, with notes by John Kennedy Hanks and Ruth Friedberg.

———. William Hain, ten.; Jerome Bohm, pn. Friends of Recorded Music FRM 5 (78).

"Landscape." See *Five Poems of Ancient China and Japan*, op. 10.

Legend. Denver Oldham, pn. New World Records NW 310-11: *Collected Works for Piano: Charles Tomlinson Griffes*, 2 discs, with notes by Edward Maisel.

———. James Tocco, pn. Gasparo GSCD 234: *MacDowell & Griffes*, vol. 4, with notes by Allan Kozinn.

———. Joseph Smith, pn. Musical Heritage Society MHS 513043K (CD): *Charles T. Griffes: Complete Piano Music*, with notes by Joseph Smith.

"Meeres stille." Sherrill Milnes, bar.; Jon Spong, pn. New World Records NW 273 and NW 273-2 CD: *Charles Tomlinson Griffes*, with notes by Donna K. Anderson.

———. Thomas Hampson, bar.; Armen Guzelimian, pn. Teldec 9031-72168-2 (CD): *Ives-Griffes-MacDowell Lieder*, with notes by Paul Schiavo.

"Mein Herz ist wie die dunkle Nacht." Thomas Hampson, bar.; Armen Guzelimian, pn. Teldec 9031-72168-2 (CD): *Ives-Griffes-MacDowell Lieder*, with notes by Paul Schiavo.

"La Mer" (1912; see also *Four Impressions*). Faith Esham, sop.; Thomas Muraco, pn. Musical Heritage Society MHS 824678M: *The Songs of Charles T. Griffes*, 2 discs, with notes by Edward Maisel.

"Mit schwarzen Segeln." Thomas Hampson, bar.; Armen Guzelimian, pn. Teldec 9031-72168-2 (CD): *Ives-Griffes-MacDowell Lieder*, with notes by Paul Schiavo.

"Des müden Abendlied." Thomas Hampson, bar.; Armen Guzelimian, pn. Teldec 9031-72168-2 (CD): *Ives-Griffes-MacDowell Lieder*, with notes by Paul Schiavo.

———. William Parker, bar.; William Huckaby, pn. New World Records NW 305, with notes by Philip L. Miller.

"Nachtlied." Irene Gubrud, sop.; Margo Garrett, pn. Musical Heritage Society MHS 824678M: *The Songs of Charles T. Griffes*, 2 discs, with notes by Edward Maisel.

———. Thomas Hampson, bar.; Armen Guzelimian, pn. Teldec 9031-72168-2 (CD): *Ives-Griffes-MacDowell Lieder*, with notes by Paul Schiavo.

"Nacht liegt auf den fremden Wegen." Jan Opalach, bar.; Jeffrey Goldberg, pn. Musical Heritage Society MHS 824678M: *The Songs of Charles T. Griffes*, 2 discs, with notes by Edward Maisel.

Nightfall. See *Roman Sketches*, op. 7.

The Night Winds (see also *Three Tone-Pictures*, op. 5). Howard Wells, pn. Educo 3012: Bach to Bartok Series.

Nocturne (arr. orch. of Piano Sonata, mvt. 2). American Arts Orchestra, Karl Krueger, cond. The Society for the Preservation of the American Musical Heritage, Music in America MIA 104, with notes by Karl Krueger.

Notturno (see also *Fantasy Pieces*, op. 6). Carol Rosenberger, pn. Delos D 3030 CD: *Night Moods*, with notes by Carol Rosenberger.

Notturno für Orchester. American Arts Orchestra, Karl Krueger, cond. The Society for the Preservation of the American Musical Heritage, Music in America MIA 104, with notes by Karl Krueger.

"An Old Song Re-sung" (see also *Two Poems by John Masefield*). Donald Stenberg, bar.; Joann Crossman, pn. Educo 4006: *Album of American Art Songs,* with notes by Joseph Biskind (not included in later releases).

——. John Kennedy Hanks, ten.; Ruth Friedberg, pn. Duke University Press DWR 6417-18: *The Art Song in America,* 2 discs, with notes by John Kennedy Hanks and Ruth Friedberg.

——. Leonard Warren, bar.; Willard Sektberg, pn. RCA LM 2266: *Leonard Warren on Tour in Russia,* with notes by Irving R. Levine. Also issued on RCA 7807-2-RG (CD).

——. Norman Myrvik, ten.; Emanuel Levenson, pn. EMS 501: *Survey of the Art Song,* with notes by Emanuel Levenson.

——. Thomas Hampson, bar.; Armen Guzelimian, pn. EMI CDC 7 54012: *An Old Song Re-Sung: American Concert Songs,* with notes by Thomas Hampson.

——. William Parker, bar.; William Huckaby, pn. New World Records NW 305, with notes by Philip L. Miller.

"The Old Temple among the Mountains." See *Five Poems of Ancient China and Japan,* op. 10.

"Phantoms." Jan Opalach, bar.; Jeffrey Goldberg, pn. Musical Heritage Society MHS 824678M: *The Songs of Charles T. Griffes,* 2 discs, with notes by Edward Maisel.

"Phantoms," op. 9, no. 3. Jan Opalach, bar.; Jeffrey Goldberg, pn. Musical Heritage Society MHS 824678M: *The Songs of Charles T. Griffes,* 2 discs, with notes by Edward Maisel.

Piano Piece in B-flat Major. Denver Oldham, pn. New World Records NW 310-11: *Collected Works for Piano: Charles Tomlinson Griffes,* 2 discs, with notes by Edward Maisel.

Piano Piece in D Minor. Denver Oldham, pn. New World Records NW 310-11: *Collected Works for Piano: Charles Tomlinson Griffes,* 2 discs, with notes by Edward Maisel.

Piano Piece in E Major. Denver Oldham, pn. New World Records NW 310-11: *Collected Works for Piano: Charles Tomlinson Griffes,* 2 discs, with notes by Edward Maisel.

Piano Sonata. Abraham Stokman, pn. Centaur CRC 2082 (CD), with notes by Abraham Stokman.

——. Aldo Mancinelli, pn. Musical Heritage Society MHS 3695: *Charles Tomlinson Griffes: Piano Music*, with notes by David A. Reed.

——. Carol Honigberg, pn. Musical Heritage Society MHS 4474: *Carol Honigberg Plays 20th-Century Music*, with notes by Myrna Nachman.

——. Clive Lythgoe, pn. Philips 9500 096, with notes by Clive Lythgoe.

——. Constance Keene, pn. Protone Records PR 155: *Constance Keene Plays American Music*, with notes (anon.).

——. Del Purves, pn. Music Library Recordings MLR 7021.

——. Denver Oldham, pn. New World Records NW 310-11: *Collected Works for Piano: Charles Tomlinson Griffes*, 2 discs, with notes by Edward Maisel.

——. Garah Landes, pn. Koch International Classics CD 3-7045-2HI (LC6644): *The Lake at Evening: American Romantic Piano Music*, with notes by Raymond J. Osnato.

——. Harrison Potter, pn. Friends of Recorded Music FRM 10-11 (78), 2 discs.

——. James Tocco, pn. Gasparo GSCD 233: *MacDowell & Griffes*, vol. 3, with notes by Allan Kozinn.

——. Jeanne Behrend, pn. Allegro ALG 3024: American Piano Music Series, vol. 1, with notes by Jeanne Behrend. Also issued on Concord 3017: American Anthology, vol. 2.

——. Joseph Smith, pn. Musical Heritage Society MHS 513043K (CD): *Charles T. Griffes: Complete Piano Music*, with notes by Joseph Smith.

——. Leonid Hambro, pn. Walden W 100, with notes by Edward Jablonski and Edith Garson. Also issued on Lyrichord LL 105 (mono) and LLST 7105 (stereo).

——. Noël Lee, pn. Nonesuch 71409: *Piano Music of Charles Tomlinson Griffes*, with notes by Donna K. Anderson.

——. Susan Starr, pn. Orion ORS 77270, with notes by William Smith.

——. William Masselos, pn. MGM E 3556.

"Pierrot." Lucy Shelton, sop.; Margo Garrett, pn. Musical Heritage Society MHS 824678M: *The Songs of Charles T. Griffes*, 2 discs, with notes by Edward Maisel.

The Pleasure-Dome of Kubla Khan. James Tocco, pn. Gasparo GSCD 234: *MacDowell & Griffes*, vol. 4, with notes by Allan Kozinn.

The Pleasure-Dome of Kubla Khan, op. 8 (arr. orch.). Andre Kostelanetz Orchestra, Andre Kostelanetz, cond. Columbia MG 33728: *Andre Kostelanetz: Spirit of '76*, 2 discs, with notes by Bill Zakariasen.

——. Boston Symphony Orchestra, Seiji Ozawa, cond. New World Records NW 273 and NW 273-2 CD: *Charles Tomlinson Griffes*, with notes by Donna K. Anderson.

———. Eastman-Rochester Orchestra, Howard Hanson, cond. Mercury MG 50422 (mono) and SR 90422 (stereo): *Great Music by American Composers,* with notes by David Hall.

———. Eastman-Rochester Symphony Orchestra, Howard Hanson, cond. Mercury MG 50085: American Music Festival Series, vol. 13, with notes (anon.). Also issued on Mercury SRI 75090 (Golden Imports); British Mercury MRL 2544; and Mercury MG 40012 (Golden Lyre Series).

———. Minneapolis Symphony Orchestra, Eugene Ormandy, cond. Victor 7957 (78; slightly shortened version).

———. National Philharmonic Orchestra of London, Charles Gerhardt, cond. RCA GL 25021, with notes (anon.).

———. Seattle Symphony, Gerard Schwarz, cond. Delos DE 3099 (CD): *The Musical Fantasies of Charles Griffes and Deems Taylor,* with notes by Donna K. Anderson.

Poem for Flute and Orchestra. Alexa Still, fl.; New Zealand Chamber Orchestra, Nicholas Braithwaite, cond. Koch International Classics CD 3-7063-2, with notes (anon.)

———. Barbara Geiser-Laborier, fl.; Orchestre Symphonique de Radio-Tele Luxembourg, Jeannot A. Welter, cond. Disque 861, with notes by Jeannot A. Welter.

———. Camille Wanausek, fl.; American Recording Society Orchestra, Walter Hendl, cond. American Recording Society ARS 22 (10″), with notes (anon.). Also issued on Desto DST 424 (mono) and DST 6424 (stereo): The American Composers Series.

———. Joseph Mariano, fl.; Eastman-Rochester Orchestra, Howard Hanson, cond. Mercury MG 50379 (mono) and SR 90379 (stereo), with notes (anon.). Also issued on Mercury SRI 175020 (Golden Imports), with notes by James Ringo. See also Victor 11-8349.

———. Joseph Mariano, fl.; Eastman-Rochester Orchestra, Howard Hanson, cond. Mercury MG 50422 (mono) and SR 90422 (stereo): *Great Music by American Composers,* with notes by David Hall.

———. Joseph Mariano, fl.; Eastman-Rochester Orchestra, Howard Hanson, cond. Victor 11-8349 (78).

———. Julius Baker, fl.; chamber orchestra, Daniel Saidenberg, cond. Decca DL 4013 (10″, Gold Label Series). Also issued on British Brunswick BAXL 2015 (10″).

———. Kathleen Rudolph, fl.; CBC Vancouver Orchestra, Mario Bernardi, cond. CBC Enterprises SM 5050-2 and SMCD 5050-2: *Entre amis: Canadian and American Music for Chamber Orchestra,* with notes by Susan Mertens.

———. Keith Bryan, fl.; Radio Bratislava Symphony Orchestra, Zuohuang Chen, cond. Opus 9310 2050 (stereo), with notes by Egon Krák, trans. Selma Steinerová and Jaroslava Perlakiová.

———. Maurice Sharp, fl.; Cleveland Sinfonietta, Louis Lane, cond. Epic LC 3754 (mono) and BC 1116 (stereo): *Music for a Golden Flute,* with notes by Louis Lane. Also issued on British Columbia 33SX 1682 (mono) and SCX 3539 (stereo).

———. Scott Goff, fl.; Seattle Symphony, Gerard Schwarz, cond. Delos DE 3099 (CD): *The Musical Fantasies of Charles Griffes and Deems Taylor,* with notes by Donna K. Anderson.

———. William Kincaid, fl.; Philadelphia Orchestra, Eugene Ormandy, cond. Columbia ML 4629 (91A-02003): *The Philadelphia Orchestra First Chair,* with notes (anon.).

Poem for Flute and Orchestra (arr. fl. and pn. by Georges Barrère). Carol Wincenc, fl.; Samuel Sanders, pn. Nonesuch 79114-1 (LP) and 79114-2 (CD), and 364190 (CD and cassette): *Carol Wincenc: American Music for Flute,* with notes by Ara [Armen?] Guzelimian.

———. Gary Woodward, fl.; Brooks Smith, pn. Stereophile LP STPH 001 and CD STPH 001-2, with notes by Denis Stevens.

———. Stephanie Jutt, fl.; Randall Hodgkinson, pn. GM Records 2026-CD, with notes by Richard Dyer.

"Le Réveillon." See *Four Impressions.*

Rhapsody in B Minor. James Tocco, pn. Gasparo GSCD 232: *MacDowell & Griffes,* vol. 2, with notes by Allan Kozinn.

Roman Sketches, op. 7 (see also *The White Peacock* and *The Fountain of the Acqua Paola*). Aldo Mancinelli, pn. Musical Heritage Society MHS 3695: *Charles Tomlinson Griffes: Piano Music,* with notes by David A. Reed.

———. Denver Oldham, pn. New World Records NW 310-11: *Collected Works for Piano: Charles Tomlinson Griffes,* 2 discs, with notes by Edward Maisel.

———. Duncan Stearns, pn. Orion ORS 79352, with notes by Romulus Franceschini.

———. James Tocco, pn. Gasparo GSCD 231: *MacDowell & Griffes,* vol. 1, with notes by Allan Kozinn.

———. Joseph Smith, pn. Musical Heritage Society MHS 513043K (CD): *Charles T. Griffes: Complete Piano Music,* with notes by Joseph Smith.

———. Lenore Engdahl, pn. MGM E 3225: *Charles Tomlinson Griffes,* with notes by Edward Cole.

———. Leonid Hambro, pn. Walden W 100, with notes by Edward Jablonski and Edith Garson. Also issued on Lyrichord LL 105 (mono) and LLST 7105 (stereo).

————. Noël Lee, pn. Nonesuch 71409: *Piano Music of Charles Tomlinson Griffes,* with notes by Donna K. Anderson.

————. Veronica Jochum, pn. Golden Crest CRS 4168: *Veronica Jochum Plays MacDowell-Griffes,* with notes (anon.).

"The Rose of the Night." See *Three Poems by (of) Fiona Macleod,* op. 11.

Scherzo (see also *Fantasy Pieces,* op. 6). Rudolph Reuter, pn. Duo-Art Piano Roll 70308.

"So-fei Gathering Flowers." See *Five Poems of Ancient China and Japan,* op. 10.

"So halt' ich endlich dich umfangen." Thomas Hampson, bar.; Armen Guzelimian, pn. Teldec 9031-72168-2 (CD): *Ives-Griffes-MacDowell Lieder,* with notes by Paul Schiavo.

Sonata. *See* Piano Sonata.

"Song of the Dagger." Jan Opalach, bar.; Jeffrey Goldberg, pn. Musical Heritage Society MHS 824678M: *The Songs of Charles T. Griffes,* 2 discs, with notes by Edward Maisel.

————. Sherrill Milnes, bar.; Jon Spong, pn. New World Records NW 273 and NW 273-2 CD: *Charles Tomlinson Griffes,* with notes by Donna K. Anderson.

"Sorrow of Mydath." See *Two Poems by John Masefield.*

"Das sterbende Kind." Thomas Hampson, bar.; Armen Guzelimian, pn. Teldec 9031-72168-2 (CD): *Ives-Griffes-MacDowell Lieder,* with notes by Paul Schiavo.

Symphonische Phantasie (issued as *Symphonic Fantasy*). Royal Philharmonic Orchestra (London), Karl Krueger, cond. The Society for the Preservation of the American Musical Heritage, Music in America MIA 129, with notes by Karl Krueger.

"Symphony in Yellow," op. 3, no. 2. Jan Opalach, bar.; Jeffrey Goldberg, pn. Musical Heritage Society MHS 824678M: *The Songs of Charles T. Griffes,* 2 discs, with notes by Edward Maisel.

————. John Kennedy Hanks, ten.; Ruth Friedberg, pn. Duke University Press DWR 6417-18: *The Art Song in America,* 2 discs, with notes by John Kennedy Hanks and Ruth Friedberg.

————. Norman Myrvik, ten.; Emanuel Levenson, pn. EMS 501: *Survey of the Art Song,* with notes by Emanuel Levenson.

"Tears." See *Five Poems of Ancient China and Japan,* op. 10.

"This Book of Hours." See *Two Rondels,* op. 4.

Three Poems, op. 9. *See* "In a Myrtle Shade," "Waikiki," and "Phantoms," op. 9, no. 3.

Three Poems by Fiona Macleod, op. 11 (*see also* "The Lament of Ian the Proud" and "Thy Dark Eyes to Mine"). Faith Esham, sop.; Thomas Muraco, pn. Musical Heritage Society MHS 824678M: *The Songs of Charles T. Griffes,* 2 discs, with notes by Edward Maisel.

——. Norman Myrvik, ten.; Emanuel Levenson, pn. EMS 501: *Survey of the Art Song,* with notes by Emanuel Levenson.

Three Poems of Fiona Macleod, op. 11 (arr. voice and orch.). Phyllis Bryn-Julson, sop.; Boston Symphony Orchestra, Seiji Ozawa, cond. New World Records NW 273 and NW 273-2 CD: *Charles Tomlinson Griffes,* with notes by Donna K. Anderson.

Three Preludes. Alan Mandel, pn. Desto DC 6445-47: *An Anthology of American Piano Music, 1780–1970,* 3 discs, with notes by Alan Mandel.

——. Denver Oldham, pn. New World Records NW 310-11: *Collected Works for Piano: Charles Tomlinson Griffes,* 2 discs, with notes by Edward Maisel.

——. James Tocco, pn. Gasparo GSCD 231: *MacDowell & Griffes,* vol. 1, with notes by Allan Kozinn.

——. John Ranck, pn. Zodiac Z 1002: *Zodiac Piano Series,* with notes (anon.). Also issued on International Piano Archives IPAM 2002.

——. Joseph Smith, pn. Musical Heritage Society MHS 513043K (CD): *Charles T. Griffes: Complete Piano Music,* with notes by Joseph Smith.

——. Veronica Jochum, pn. Golden Crest CRS 4168: *Veronica Jochum Plays MacDowell-Griffes,* with notes (anon.).

Three Tone-Pictures, op. 5 (arr. double quintet of winds, strings, and pn.). American Arts Orchestra, Karl Krueger, cond. The Society for the Preservation of the American Musical Heritage, Music in America MIA 104, with notes by Karl Krueger.

——. New World Chamber Ensemble. New World Records NW 273 and NW 273-2 CD: *Charles Tomlinson Griffes,* with notes by Donna K. Anderson.

——. Victoria Bogdashevskaya, pn.; members of the Seattle Symphony, Gerard Schwarz, cond. Delos DE 3099 (CD): *The Musical Fantasies of Charles Griffes and Deems Taylor,* with notes by Donna K. Anderson.

Three Tone-Pictures, op. 5 (see also *The Vale of Dreams* and *The Night Winds*). Aldo Mancinelli, pn. Musical Heritage Society MHS 3695: *Charles Tomlinson Griffes: Piano Music,* with notes by David A. Reed.

——. Denver Oldham, pn. New World Records NW 310-11: *Collected Works for Piano: Charles Tomlinson Griffes,* 2 discs, with notes by Edward Maisel.

——. Garah Landes, pn. Koch International Classics CD 3-7045-2HI (LC6644): *The Lake at Evening: American Romantic Piano Music,* with notes by Raymond J. Osnato.

——. James Tocco, pn. Gasparo GSCD 234: *MacDowell & Griffes,* vol. 4, with notes by Allan Kozinn.

————. Joseph Smith, pn. Musical Heritage Society MHS 513043K (CD): *Charles T. Griffes: Complete Piano Music,* with notes by Joseph Smith.

————. Lenore Engdahl, pn. MGM E 3225: *Charles Tomlinson Griffes,* with notes by Edward Cole.

————. Noël Lee, pn. Nonesuch 71409: *Piano Music of Charles Tomlinson Griffes,* with notes by Donna K. Anderson.

————. Susan Starr, pn. Orion ORS 77270, with notes by William Smith.

————. Veronica Jochum, pn. Golden Crest CRS 4168: *Veronica Jochum Plays MacDowell-Griffes,* with notes (anon.).

"Thy Dark Eyes to Mine," op. 11, no. 2 (see also *Three Poems by Fiona Macleod,* op. 11). Alexandra Hunt, sop.; Regis Benoit, pn. Orion ORS 77272: *Songs by Carpenter, Griffes & MacDowell,* with notes by Edwin McArthur.

"Time Was When I in Anguish Lay." *See* "Wohl lag ich einst in Gram und Schmerz."

Tone-Images, op. 3. *See* "La Fuite de la lune," "Symphony in Yellow," and "We'll to the Woods, and Gather May."

"Der träumende See." Faith Esham, sop.; Thomas Muraco, pn. Musical Heritage Society MHS 824678M: *The Songs of Charles T. Griffes,* 2 discs, with notes by Edward Maisel.

————. Thomas Hampson, bar.; Armen Guzelimian, pn. Teldec 9031-72168-2 (CD): *Ives-Griffes-MacDowell Lieder,* with notes by Paul Schiavo.

"Two Birds Flew into the Sunset Glow." Lucy Shelton, sop.; Margo Garrett, pn. Musical Heritage Society MHS 824678M: *The Songs of Charles T. Griffes,* 2 discs, with notes by Edward Maisel.

Two Poems by John Masefield (see also "An Old Song Re-sung"). Jan Opalach, bar.; Jeffrey Goldberg, pn. Musical Heritage Society MHS 824678M: *The Songs of Charles T. Griffes,* 2 discs, with notes by Edward Maisel.

Two Rondels, op. 4. Irene Gubrud, sop.; Margo Garrett, pn. Musical Heritage Society MHS 824678M: *The Songs of Charles T. Griffes,* 2 discs, with notes by Edward Maisel.

Two Sketches for String Quartet Based on Indian Themes. Coolidge Quartet. Victor Set M 558 (78), 2 discs (Victor 15416-17).

————. Delme String Quartet. The Society for the Preservation of the American Musical Heritage, Music in America MIA 117, with notes by Karl Krueger.

————. Kohon Quartet. Vox SVBX 5301: *The Early String Quartet in the U.S.A.,* 3 discs, with notes by Robert D. Darrell.

———— (movement 1, Lento e mesto). Kreiner Quartet. Friends of Recorded Music FRM 5 (78).

—— (movement 2, Allegro giocoso). Coolidge Quartet. Japanese Victor SD 3067 in Set JAS 236 (78).

The Vale of Dreams (arr. orch., not by Griffes). Philharmonia Orchestra (Hamburg), Richard Korn, cond. Allegro-Elite 3150: *A Panorama of American Orchestral Music*, vol. 3. Also issued on Concord 3007: *American Anthology*, vol. 1, with notes by John Tasker Howard.

"Waikiki," op. 9, no. 2. Alexandra Hunt, sop.; Regis Benoit, pn. Orion ORS 77272: *Songs by Carpenter, Griffes & MacDowell*, with notes by Edwin McArthur.

——. Eleanor Steber, sop.; Edwin Biltcliffe, pn. St/And SLP 411-12 (mono) and SLS 7411-12 (stereo): *Songs of American Composers*, 2 discs, with notes by Jack Beeson. Also issued on Desto DST 411-12 (mono) and DST 6411-12 (stereo), 2 discs.

——. Lucy Shelton, sop.; Margo Garrett, pn. Musical Heritage Society MHS 824678M: *The Songs of Charles T. Griffes*, 2 discs, with notes by Edward Maisel.

"The Water-Lily." Irene Gubrud, sop.; Margo Garrett, pn. Musical Heritage Society MHS 824678M: *The Songs of Charles T. Griffes*, 2 discs, with notes by Edward Maisel.

"We'll to the Woods, and Gather May," op. 3, no. 3. Faith Esham, sop.; Thomas Muraco, pn. Musical Heritage Society MHS 824678M: *The Songs of Charles T. Griffes*, 2 discs, with notes by Edward Maisel.

——. Yolanda Marcoulescou-Stern, sop.; Katja Phillabaum, pn. Gasparo GSCD-287: *Art Songs by American Composers*.

The White Peacock, op. 7, no. 1 (arr. orch.). Andre Kostelanetz Orchestra, Andre Kostelanetz, cond. Columbia MG 33728: *Andre Kostelanetz: Spirit of '76*, 2 discs, with notes by Bill Zakariasen.

——. Columbia Broadcasting Symphony, Howard Barlow, cond. Columbia 17140D (78, 10″).

——. Eastman-Rochester Orchestra, Howard Hanson, cond. Mercury MG 50422 (mono) and SR 90422 (stereo): *Great Music by American Composers*, with notes by David Hall.

——. Eastman-Rochester Orchestra, Howard Hanson, cond. Victor 15659 in set M 608 (78). Also issued on Victor 12-0155-58 in set DM 608 (78), 4 discs; and Rochester Philharmonic Orchestra, LP DS-002, with notes by Linda Chiavaroli.

——. Eastman-Rochester Symphony Orchestra, Howard Hanson, cond. Mercury MG 50085: American Music Festival Series, vol. 13, with notes (anon.). Also issued on Mercury SRI 75090 (Golden Imports); British Mercury MRL 2544; and Mercury MG 40012 (Golden Lyre Series).

————. Moscow Philharmonic Orchestra, Dmitri Kitayenko, cond. Sheffield Lab TLP-27 and CD-27: *The Moscow Sessions,* with notes by Peter Mose.

————. National Philharmonic Orchestra of London, Charles Gerhardt, cond. RCA GL 25021, with notes (anon.).

————. National Symphony Orchestra, Howard Mitchell, cond. Victor LE 1009 (mono) and LES 1009 (stereo): *Children's Adventures in Music, Grade 6,* vol. 1.

————. Orchestra unidentified, Mishel Piastro, cond. Decca DL 8573.

————. Philharmonic-Symphony Orchestra of New York, Leopold Stokowski, cond. Columbia 19012D (78, 10″). Also issued on Columbia AmC A 1516 (45, 7″); Columbia ML 2167 (10″), with notes (anon.); and Columbia LP3-117 (78, 7″).

————. Royal Philharmonic Orchestra (London), Karl Krueger, cond. The Society for the Preservation of the American Musical Heritage, Music in America MIA 129, with notes by Karl Krueger.

————. Seattle Symphony, Gerard Schwarz, cond. Delos DE 3099 (CD): *The Musical Fantasies of Charles Griffes and Deems Taylor,* with notes by Donna K. Anderson.

The White Peacock, op. 7, no. 1 (pn.; see also *Roman Sketches,* op. 7). Ampara Iturbi, pn. Victor 12-3273 (78).

————. Barry Snyder, pn. Golden Crest RE 7063: *Recital Series: Barry Snyder Plays the Music of American Composers,* with notes by Jerald C. Graue.

————. Constance Keene, pn. Protone Records PR 155: *Constance Keene Plays American Music,* with notes (anon.).

————. Charles T. Griffes, pn. Duo-Art Piano Roll 64930. Also included on New World Records NW 310-11: *Collected Works for Piano: Charles Tomlinson Griffes,* 2 discs, with notes by Edward Maisel.

————. Howard Wells, pn. Educo 3012: Bach to Bartok Series.

————. Menahem Pressler, pn. MGM E 3129: *Encores in a Quiet Mood,* with notes by Edward Cole.

————. Myra Hess, pn. Columbia 9072M (78, 10″). Also issued on Columbia 50149D (78, 10″).

————. Olga Samaroff, pn. Victor 7384 (78).

————. Roger Shields, pn. Vox SVBX 5303: *Piano Music in America,* vol. 2, *1900–1945,* 3 discs, with notes by Lejaren Hiller.

The White Peacock, op. 7 (two pn. arr. by Whittemore and Lowe). Arthur Whittemore and Jack Lowe, pn. Capitol P 8550 (mono) and SP 8550 (stereo): *Exotique.*

"Wohl lag ich einst in Gram und Schmerz." Faith Esham, sop.; Thomas Muraco, pn. Musical Heritage Society MHS 824678M: *The Songs of Charles T.
Griffes,* 2 discs, with notes by Edward Maisel.

———. Paul Sperry, ten.; Irma Vallecillo, pn. Gregg Smith Singers Productions
GSS 109: *Paul Sperry Sings Songs of an Innocent Age: Music from Victorian Amer-
ica,* American Songs Series, vol. 3, with notes by Paul Sperry. Also issued on
Albany Records TROY CD 034-2: *Paul Sperry Sings Songs of an Innocent Age:
Music from Turn of the Century America.*

———. Thomas Hampson, bar.; Armen Guzelimian, pn. Teldec 9031-72168-2
(CD): *Ives-Griffes-MacDowell Lieder,* with notes by Paul Schiavo.

——— (issued as "Time Was When I in Anguish Lay"). Nancy Tatum, sop.;
Geoffrey Parsons, pn. London 26053: *Recital of American Songs.* Also issued on
British Decca LXT (mono) and SXL 6336 (stereo), with notes by Gerald
Fitzgerald.

"Wo ich bin, mich rings umdunkelt." Thomas Hampson, bar.; Armen Guzelimian, pn. Teldec 9031-72168-2 (CD): *Ives-Griffes-MacDowell Lieder,* with notes by
Paul Schiavo.

———. William Parker, bar.; William Huckaby, pn. New World Records NW
305, with notes by Philip L. Miller.

"Zwei Könige sassen auf Orkadal." Thomas Hampson, bar.; Armen Guzelimian, pn. Teldec 9031-72168-2 (CD): *Ives-Griffes-MacDowell Lieder,* with notes by
Paul Schiavo.

———. William Parker, bar.; William Huckaby, pn. New World Records NW
305, with notes by Philip L. Miller.

Notes

DLC   Library of Congress, Music Division, Washington, D.C.

Griffes diary   Material from Griffes's five extant diaries—1912, 1914, 1915, 1916, 1917—in author's collection.

NEE   Gannett-Tripp Library, Elmira College, Elmira, N.Y.

NN:Da   New York Public Library for the Performing Arts, Dance Collection, New York.

NN:Mu   New York Public Library for the Performing Arts, Music Division, New York.

NN:Th   New York Public Library for the Performing Arts, Billy Rose Theatre Collection, New York.

PI   Typed transcript of personal (taped) interviews with the author, the majority with Griffes's sister Marguerite, 1969–83. The interviews are further identified by transcript volume (1–18) and page number (e.g., "PI 1:23").

TD   Trip diary notebook of personal (untaped) interviews with the author, all with Marguerite Griffes. The interviews are further identified by page number (e.g., "TD, 23").

CHAPTER 1. Birth in Late Nineteenth-Century Elmira

1. Timothy Decker, Chemung County Historical Society, Elmira, N.Y., telephone interview with author, 14 July 1988. Population figures from *Chemung County . . . Its History* (Elmira, N.Y.: Chemung County Historical Society, 1961), 68. On Elmira's motto, see Marguerite Griffes, interview with author, 13 June 1982 (PI 16:36).

2. Marguerite Griffes, interview with author, 23 May 1981 (PI 10:9–10). On the prison camp, see J. Michael Horigan, "Elmira's Prison Camp—a Second Opinion," *Chemung Historical Journal* 30, no. 3 (March 1985): 3449, 3451, 3457.

3. Thomas E. Byrne, *Chemung County, 1890–1975* (Elmira, N.Y.: Chemung County Historical Society, 1976), 330; *Chemung County . . . Its History*, 13, 14.

4. *Chemung County . . . Its History*, 61; Michelle L. Cotton, *Mark Twain's Elmira, 1870–1910* (Elmira, N.Y.: Chemung County Historical Society, 1985), 12, 13.

5. On the Delaware, Lackawanna & Western Railroad, see *Chemung County . . . Its History*, 23.

6. Byrne, *Chemung County*, 262, 263.

7. Marguerite Griffes, interview with author, 13 June 1982 (PI 16:36).

8. Ibid., 24 July 1969 (PI 3:27). Byrne, *Chemung County*, 12; Floyd S. Carey, "Our 1900 Trip to Waverly in Father's 3-Wheel Knox," *Chemung Historical Journal* 3, no. 1 (September 1957): 364.

9. Byrne, *Chemung County*, 395.

10. I was unable to find Griffes's grade school records. According to the Chemung County Health Department, Bureau of Vital Statistics, the earliest birth date for any child on record is 1897. Griffes, however, must have entered school when he was six or seven, most likely seven. His high school record at Elmira Free Academy states, "Entered from No. 2."

11. See Byrne, *Chemung County*, 390 (picture caption) and 391 (description of No. 2 School). *Elmira City Directory, 1884–5*, comp. Boyd Cousins (Elmira, N.Y.: Elmira Advertiser Association, 1884), 33. For reasons of practicality, I have used shortened titles for all city directories.

12. W. Charles Barber, "EFA's 100 Years, *Chemung Historical Journal* 5, no. 1 (September 1959): 637.

13. Albert B. Helmkamp, "The Elmira Academy, 1836–1859: Private Venture in Education," *Chemung Historical Journal* 1, no. 2 (December 1955): 70, 71.

14. *The New Encyclopaedia Britannica,* 15th ed., s.v. "Education, History of." On the private academy movement that flourished from the 1770s to the 1860s before yielding prominence to the public high school, see Theodore R. Sizer, *The Age of the Academies* (New York: Bureau of Publications, Teachers College, Columbia University, 1964), 1, 4.

15. Byrne, *Chemung County,* 368. See also Ausburn Towner, *Our County and Its People: A History of the Valley and County of Chemung from the Closing Years of the Eighteenth Century* (Syracuse: D. Mason & Co., 1892), 304.

16. *Elmira City, Elmira Heights and Horseheads Directory, 1903* (Elmira, N.Y.: George Hanford, 1903), 34.

17. Marguerite Griffes, interview with author, 20 January 1982 (PI 13:16).

18. Information on courses from Griffes's Elmira Free Academy record for 1901–2 and 1902–3 and a handwritten list kept by Griffes (in author's collection). The card record system was not introduced at Elmira Free Academy until September 1901.

19. *Register of the Alumni of the Elmira Free Academy, 1859–1909* (Elmira, N.Y.: [Printed by the Elmira Free Academy Alumni Association, 1909]), anniversary book, Chemung County Historical Society, Elmira, N.Y. Florence does not appear in the *Register,* nor does her EFA record provide specific information as to when she entered and when she graduated. Marguerite confirmed that all the Griffes children except Arthur graduated from the academy. Marguerite Griffes, interview with author, 14 September 1973 (PI 7:4).

20. Russell Lynes, *The Lively Audience: A Social History of the Visual and Performing Arts in America, 1890–1950* (New York: Harper & Row, 1985), 2.

21. W. Charles Barber, *Elmira College: The First Hundred Years* (New York: McGraw-Hill Book Co., 1955), 130.

22. *The Seventeenth Annual Catalogue and Circular of the Elmira Female College, 1871–1872* (Elmira, N.Y.: Advertiser Association Steam Job Printing House, 1872), 15, 25. See also *The Sixteenth Annual Catalogue and Circular of the Elmira Female College, 1870–1871* (Elmira, N.Y.: Daily Advertiser Book and Job Printing Association, 1871), 14; and *The Fifteenth Annual Catalogue and Circular of the Elmira Female College, 1869–70* (Elmira, N.Y.: Daily Advertiser Book and Job Printing House, 1870), 13, 21.

23. *The Nineteenth Annual Catalogue and Circular of the Elmira Female College, 1873–1874* (Elmira, N.Y.: Advertiser Association Steam Job Printing House, 1874), 15, 16; *The Twentieth Annual Catalogue and Circular of the Elmira Female College, 1874–1875* (Elmira, N.Y.: Advertiser Association Book and Job Printing House, 1875), 17; *The Twenty-first Annual Catalogue and Cir-*

cular of the Elmira Female College, 1875–1876 (Elmira, N.Y.: Advertiser Association Book and Job Printing House, 1876), 16.

24. Graduation cards in NEE archives. *Catalogue Elmira College Fifty-first Year, 1905–1906* (n.p., n.d.), 75.

25. Information on Miss Broughton's life from "Death Claims Miss Broughton, Member of Faculty at College," *Elmira Star-Gazette*, 7 June 1922, 5.

26. *Thirty-seventh Annual Catalogue and Circular of Elmira College, 1891–1892* (Elmira, N.Y.: Advertiser Association Print, 1892), 5, 25, lists Miss Broughton as "Lena Broughton, Professor of Piano Playing."

27. *Fortieth Annual Catalogue of Elmira College, 1894–1895* (Elmira, N.Y.: Gazette Company, Book and Job Printers, 1895), 4; *Catalogue Elmira College Forty-ninth Year, 1903–1904* (Elmira, N.Y.: Advertiser Association, 1904), 60; *Catalogue Elmira College Fiftieth Year, 1904–1905* (Elmira, N.Y.: Advertiser Association, 1905), 61. The last of these catalogs does not list Miss Broughton as teaching music history. The course does not appear again until 1909–10, by which time Miss Broughton is no longer listed as head of the piano department.

28. Elmira College, general catalog, sixty-third year (1917–18), faculty page, in *Elmira College Bulletin* 8, no. 2 (November 1917).

29. See, for example, Elmira College, general catalog, sixty-seventh year (1921–22), faculty page, in *Elmira College Bulletin* 12, no. 11 [*sic*] (January 1922). Miss Broughton's bachelor of music degree is first listed in the *Catalogue* of 1904–5, officers of administration and instruction page; her master of arts degree is first listed in the *Elmira College Bulletin* 5, no. 4 (January 1915), catalog (1914–15), officers of administration, officers of instruction page.

30. Marguerite Griffes, interview with author, 23 May 1981 (PI 10:1–2).

31. Ibid., 18 January 1982 (PI 11:37).

32. Ibid., 22 July 1969 (PI 1:1).

33. Katharine first appears as piano teacher in the *Forty-fourth Annual Catalogue of the Officers and Students of Elmira College, 1898–1899* (Elmira, N.Y.: Advertiser Association, 1899), faculty page and p. 37. She last appears in the *Forty-sixth Annual Catalogue of the Officers and Students of Elmira College, 1900–1901* (Elmira, N.Y.: Advertiser Press, [1901]), faculty page and p. 43. On the date of her marriage to Stephen Roake, see Griffes family Bible.

34. Marguerite Griffes, interview with author, 22 July 1969 (PI 1:11).

35. Ibid., 13 September 1973 (PI 5:41).

36. Charles Griffes to Clara Griffes, 12 February 1905, NN:Mu.

37. Autograph manuscripts in NEE.

38. Marguerite Griffes, interview with author, 18 January 1982 (PI 11:37).

39. Griffes, for example, wrote to Miss Broughton from Berlin that he was not offended when she offered corrections. Charles Griffes to Miss Broughton, 14 February 1904, NEE.

40. Ibid., 4 January 1904, NEE.

41. See Charles Griffes to Miss Broughton, 13 December 1919, NN:Mu. Griffes signed his letter "Charles."

42. Miss Broughton to Clara Griffes, 17 November 1920, NN:Mu.

43. Woodlawn Cemetery card, Elmira, N.Y.; and "Death Claims Miss Broughton," 5.

44. Information in this paragraph from Byrne, *Chemung County*, 479–83, and *Chemung County . . . Its History*, 40–41.

45. Marguerite Griffes, interview with author, 13 September 1973 (PI 5:33).

46. See, for example, *Chemung County . . . Its History*, 44.

47. "Woman's Musical Club: A Pleased and Enthusiastic Audience Listened to Yesterday's Program," *Elmira [Daily] Advertiser*, 15 February 1901, 6.

48. On Clara's piano, see Marguerite Griffes, interview with author, 13 September 1973 (PI 5:28), and 13 June 1982 (PI 16:25). On Katharine's piano, see Marguerite Griffes, untaped interview with author, 4 June 1983 (TD, 71).

49. Marguerite Griffes, interview with author, 23 July 1969 (PI 2:2).

50. Ibid., 5 June 1975 (PI 8:8).

51. Griffes diary, 5 July 1912.

52. Marguerite Griffes, interview with author, 18 January 1982 (PI 11:12–13).

53. Ibid., 23 May 1981 (PI 9:37).

54. Original program in author's collection.

55. Griffes diary, 4 August 1916.

56. *Chemung County . . . Its History*, 40.

57. Edward Maisel, *Charles T. Griffes: The Life of an American Composer*, rev. ed. (New York: Alfred A. Knopf, 1984), 23.

58. Marguerite Griffes, interview with author, 18 January 1982 (PI 11:42).

59. Ibid., 13 September 1973 (PI 5:34).

60. Ibid.

61. Ibid., 18 January 1982 (PI 11:36).

62. Lynes, *The Lively Audience*, 4.

63. Marguerite Griffes, interview with author, 20 January 1982 (PI 13:16).

64. Ibid., 18 January 1982 (PI 11:21), and 20 January 1982 (PI 13:16).

65. Ibid., 23 May 1981 (PI 10:7).

66. Ibid., 18 June 1982 (PI 11:36), and 13 September 1973 (PI 5:36).

67. Ibid., 13 September 1973 (PI 5:35).

68. Ibid., 23 May 1981 (PI 9:48); and Marguerite Griffes, untaped interview with author, 20 January 1982 (TD, 53).

69. Marguerite Griffes, interview with author, 18 January 1982 (PI 11:46).

70. Pugh's first name from *Hanford's Elmira City and Elmira Heights Directory, 1902* (Elmira, N.Y.: George Hanford, 1902), 352. His last name from Marguerite Griffes, interview with author, 18 January 1982 (PI 11:46).

71. Marguerite Griffes, interview with author, 24 July 1969 (PI 3:27).

72. Ibid., 13 September 1973 (PI 5:36); and Maisel, *Charles T. Griffes*, 321.

CHAPTER 2. Ancestry

1. Information on Charles Griffes's ancestry from Mildred Griffith Peets, "Griffith Family History in Wales, 1485–1635, in America, from 1635," typescript (1971), 3, 5, photocopy in Huntington Historical Society, Huntington, N.Y.; Samuel Orcutt, *Henry Tomlinson and His Descendants in America, with a Few Additional Branches of Tomlinsons, Later from England* (New Haven, Conn.: Press of Price, Lee & Adkins Co., 1891), 202; and John Cortland Crandall, "Elder John Crandall of Rhode Island and His Descendants," typescript (New Woodstock, N.Y., 1949), 1.

2. Peets, "Griffith Family History," 1, 11.

3. "[Rice] Family Record" (n.d.), photocopy in author's collection. The place of Margaret's death is from Woodlawn Cemetery card, Elmira, N.Y.

4. A document confirming John Rice as executor of Daniel's last will and testament is dated 27 March 1827. Otsego County Surrogate's Court, Cooperstown, N.Y. Daniel must have died shortly before that date.

5. Information on John Crandall and Margaret O'Brien from Crandall, "Elder John Crandall," 177. Margaret O'Brien's death date from her tombstone in the Middlefield Cemetery.

6. Crandall, "Elder John Crandall," 177.

7. "[Rice] Family Record" and Tomlinson family Bible. Melissa's death date from Woodlawn Cemetery card, Elmira, N.Y.

8. I have been unable to determine the date of Margaret's and Elisha's marriage, but since Lathrop's first wife, Mary (Polly), died on 10 April 1845, Margaret and Elisha could not have been married until shortly after that.

9. Information from "Family Record of Elisha Lathrop" (n.d.), photocopy sent to author by Martha W. Jackson, 5 June 1989. Shirley B. Goerlich,

author of *At Rest in Unadilla* (Sidney, N.Y.: RSG Publishing, 1987), discovered the Lathrop monument in a farm field near Sidney, N.Y. The tombstone has Elisha's birth date as 2 February (not 7 February) 1865. Shirley Goerlich to author, 27 May 1989.

10. Elisha Lathrop, last will and testament, 12 March 1862, Otsego County Surrogate's Court, Cooperstown, N.Y.

11. Woodlawn Cemetery card, Elmira, N.Y.

12. Marguerite Griffes, interview with author, 23 May 1981 (PI 9:43). I have been unable to determine when Delinda left home, nor could I establish when or if she lived in Unadilla with her mother and Elisha Lathrop. The *United States Federal Census, Town of Unadilla, Otsego County, State of New York, 1850* does not list her with the Lathrop family. It does list her brother Adrian, however, identified as insane. Unfortunately, census reports before 1850 list only the head of the household by name, followed by the number of males or females in particular age groups.

13. Marguerite Griffes, interview with author, 29 July 1969 (PI 4:1). I have been unable to trace the Miss Rockwell's Academy in Unadilla reported in Edward Maisel, *Charles T. Griffes: The Life of an American Composer,* rev. ed. (New York: Alfred A. Knopf, 1984), 8. On Daniel Owen Rice, see "Deaths and Funerals: Daniel Owen Rice," unidentified newspaper clipping, scrapbook 38, 525, Chemung County Historical Society, Elmira, N.Y.

14. Marguerite Griffes, interview with author, 22 May 1981 (PI 9:1).

15. Maisel, *Charles T. Griffes,* 8. Maisel does not say how old Delinda was when she attended the Thurston school.

16. Herbert A. Wisbey, Jr., "Clarissa Thurston's Ladies Seminary," *Chemung Historical Journal* 34, no. 4 (June 1989): 3857.

17. *Annual Catalogue of Officers and Pupils of the Elmira Seminary, Chemung County, N.Y., for the Year Ending September 30, 1851* (New York: Baker, Godwin & Co., 1851), 13.

18. Ibid., 14, 15.

19. Information on Delinda Rice from Marguerite Griffes, interview with author, 23 May 1981 (PI 9:43), and 29 July 1969 (PI 4:1).

20. Tomlinson family Bible.

21. Information on the Tomlinsons from Orcutt, *Henry Tomlinson,* 202, and family group record prepared by Myrtle Molyneux Clark, copy in author's collection.

22. Orcutt, *Henry Tomlinson,* 202, and Clark, family group record.

23. "Death of a Veteran Lawyer," *Elmira [Daily] Advertiser,* 20 June 1887, 5. Ausburn Towner, *Our County and Its People: A History of the Valley and*

County of Chemung from the Closing Years of the Eighteenth Century (Syracuse: D. Mason & Co., 1892), 381, identifies Lowe's first name. Solomon was associated with Lowe as "Tomlinson & Lowe" between 1875 and 1877. See *Boyds' Elmira City Directory, 1875–1876* (Elmira, N.Y.: Boyd Cousins, 1875), 247; *Boyds' Elmira City Directory, 1876–1877* (Elmira, N.Y.: Boyd Cousins, 1876), 220.

24. Towner, *Our County and Its People*, 381 (district attorney and county clerk), 354–55 (alderman).

25. "Death of a Veteran Lawyer," 5. See Solomon B. Tomlinson, death record, Chemung County Health Department, Registrar of Vital Statistics, Elmira, N.Y.

26. Tomlinson family Bible.

27. Ibid.

28. Marguerite Griffes, interview with author, 5 June 1975 (PI 8:6). See also ibid., 24 July 1969 (PI 3:21); and Marguerite Griffes, untaped interview with author, 4 June 1983 (TD, 70).

29. Marguerite Griffes, untaped interview with author, 21 May 1981 (TD, 26); and Marguerite Griffes, interview with author, 23 May 1981 (PI 9:43).

30. Marguerite Griffes, interview with author, 24 July 1969 (PI 3:22), 18 January 1982 (PI 12:19), and 23 May 1981 (PI 9:43–44).

31. Ibid., 18 January 1982 (PI 12:35); and Marguerite Griffes, untaped interview with author, 13 June 1980 (TD, 22).

32. I have examined a sample of thirteen indentures (dating from 1855 to 1866), all but one of which were signed by both Solomon and Delinda. Indentures from the County Clerk's Office, Elmira, N.Y.

33. Marguerite Griffes, interview with author, 23 May 1981 (PI 9:42).

34. Marguerite Griffes, untaped interview with author, 12 June 1980 (TD, 23).

35. Barbara Welter, "The Cult of True Womanhood: 1820–1860," *American Quarterly* 18, no. 2, pt. 1 (Summer 1966): 152.

36. *The New Encyclopaedia Britannica*, s.v. "Education, History of."

37. Marguerite Griffes, interview with author, 23 May 1981 (PI 9:43).

38. Ibid. (PI 9:46, 47).

39. Ibid. (PI 9:45–46).

40. Richard M. Heath, interim director, Binghamton Psychiatric Center, Binghamton, N.Y., to Marjorie Griffes, 3 June 1988. Letter in author's collection.

41. Griffes diary, 3 March 1915.

42. *Chemung County . . . Its History* (Elmira, N.Y.: Chemung County Historical Society, 1961), 32.

43. "Young Ladies' Seminary," *Elmira Republican*, 3 July 1854, 4.

44. Ibid.

45. Photocopy of the Galatian certificate in author's collection.

46. Marguerite Griffes, interview with author, 13 June 1982 (PI 16:25–26).

47. Marguerite Griffes, untaped interview with author, 11 June 1980 (TD, 23).

48. "Deaths and Funerals: Charles H. Tomlinson," unidentified newspaper clipping, scrapbook 46, 229, Chemung County Historical Society, Elmira, N.Y. Charles Henry (Uncle Charlie) appears as "student" in *Boyds' Elmira City Directory, 1876–1877*, 220—which gives (pp. 118, 220) the address of the Tomlinsons and Griffeses as North Main, corner of Fourth Street (which must have been 614 North Main). He appears as "law student" in *Boyds' Elmira City Directory, 1878–1879* (Elmira, N.Y.: Boyd Cousins, 1878), 244—which records (pp. 130, 244) the address of the Griffeses and Tomlinsons as 614 North Main Street. Two years later *Boyds' Elmira City Directory, 1880–1882* (Elmira, N.Y.: Boyds' Cousin [*sic*], 1880), 266, lists Charles Henry as "lawyer" and gives the address of the Griffeses and Tomlinsons as 854 North Main Street (pp. 136, 266).

49. Marguerite Griffes, interview with author, 18 January 1982 (PI 12:24).

50. Marguerite Griffes, untaped interview with author, 8 January 1983 (TD, 58).

51. Charles H. Tomlinson, last will and testament, 9 January 1906, Albany County Surrogate's Court, Albany, N.Y. The "Report of Appraiser of the Estate of Charles H. Tomlinson," 27 March 1917, Albany County Surrogate's Court, Albany, N.Y., appraised the estate at $19,920.63. Subtracting $1,184.44 in debts, the value of the estate came to $18,736.19. All money conversions in this book are based on the October 1990 Consumer Price Index, using the formula in Gary A. Greene's article "Understanding Past Currency in Modern Times," *Sonneck Society Bulletin* 13, no. 2 (Summer 1987): 48.

52. Marguerite Griffes, interview with author, 22 July 1969 (PI 1:14).

53. For example, "Uncle Charlie's money came on the 9th and I wrote him in answer the next day, the 10th, so be at rest on the subject." Charles Griffes to Clara Griffes, 1 August 1904, NN:Mu.

54. Marguerite Griffes, interview with author, 10 June 1982 (PI 15:15).

55. Ibid., 23 July 1969 (PI 2:18).

56. Ibid.

57. Charles H. Tomlinson, "Standard Certificate of Death," New York State Department of Health, Bureau of Vital Statistics.

58. "Deaths and Funerals: Charles H. Tomlinson," scrapbook 46, 229.

59. *Records of the First Church in Huntington, Long Island, 1723–1779, Being the Record Kept by the Rev. Ebenezer Prime, the Pastor during Those Years* (Huntington, N.Y.: Printed for Moses L. Scudder, 1899), 91. William Griffes's birth date is not known, but Rev. Prime baptized him on 6 June 1836 (see ibid., 31). William Griffes's death date is from a family history by Julia Griffes, William's granddaughter. Photocopy and transcription in author's collection. Abiah Gates's birth date is also unknown. Her baptism took place on 16 February 1842 (*Records of the First Church in Huntington*, 37).

60. Peets, "Griffith Family History," 10.

61. Birth and death dates of Nathaniel's and Stephen's families from the Nathaniel Griffes family Bible. Wilber Griffes's place of birth from Marguerite Griffes, untaped interview with author, 8 January 1983 (TD, 54).

62. Petition and trust document, filed 14 October 1843, Schenectady County Surrogate's Court, Schenectady, N.Y. The title of this document reads, "In the matter of the application for the Sale of the Real Estate of *Nathaniel Griffes* late of the Town of Niskayuna in Said County deceased. On the application of Stephen N. Waterbury sole executor of the estate of the Said deceased."

63. "Nathaniel Griffis agt William W. Griffis, James A. Griffis, Elmira [Almira] Griffis, Wilbur Griffis, and Julia Griffis [sister of Stephen]," Supreme Court, Schenectady County, Schenectady, N.Y., dated 21 January 1856.

64. Mary Griffes first appears in the 1856 Schenectady city directory. *The Schenectady City Directory, Containing the Names of the Citizens; Also, a Business Directory, 1857* [sic] (Schenectady, N.Y.: William H. Boyd, 1856), 58.

65. All wedding dates from Nathaniel Griffes family Bible. William Whitney Griffes first appears in the 1860 Schenectady city directory— *Schenectady City and County Directory, Containing the Names of Residents of the City of Schenectady, 1860–61* (Schenectady, N.Y.: W. M. Colburne, 1860), 45. James first appears in the 1867 listing—*Schenectady City Directory for the Year 1867–8* (Schenectady, N.Y.: Bradt & Truax, 1867), 27. The latter directory identifies James as a carpenter ("Pearse and Griffes") and William and Wilber (the latter appearing for the first time in the Schenectady directory) as "W. W. Griffes & Bro. Dealers in Pictures, Oval Frames, [Books,]" etc.

66. See Maisel, *Charles T. Griffes*, 5.

67. Marguerite Griffes, untaped interview with author, 4 June 1983 (TD, 74–75).

68. *Schenectady City Directory . . . 1867–8*, 27.

69. Nathaniel Griffes family Bible. Wilber's presence in Elmira is first recorded in the *History of Elmira, Horseheads and the Chemung Valley . . . Also Directory & Business Advertiser for 1868* (Elmira, N.Y.: A. B. Galatian & Co., 1868), 187.

70. *Gazetteer and Business Directory of Chemung and Schuyler Counties, N.Y., for 1868–9* (Syracuse: Hamilton Child, 1868), 143.

71. Information from various Elmira city directories. Waldron & Griffes last appear in *Boyds' Elmira City Directory, 1878–1879*, 251, listed as "shirt manufrs, 135 E Water."

72. Michelle L. Cotton, *Mark Twain's Elmira, 1870–1910* (Elmira, N.Y.: Chemung County Historical Society, 1985), 7.

73. Nathaniel Griffes family Bible.

74. Mary Griffes ("widow Stephen") first appears in the 1871–72 Elmira city directory. *Boyd's [sic] Elmira Directory, 1871–1872* (Elmira, N.Y.: Andrew Boyd, W. Harry Boyd, n.d.), 112. On Julia Griffes, see Nathaniel Griffes family Bible and *Boyds' Elmira City Directory, 1875–1876*, 139. The *Elmira Directory for 1869, Also a Business Directory* (New York: Fitzgerald and Dillon, 1869), 66, lists Wilber as boarding with the Waldrons at 7 Columbia. The Waldrons moved to 31 College Avenue and then to 511 East Union. *Boyds' Elmira City Directory, 1875–1876*, 139, records Wilber as boarding at 614 N. Main, with Solomon and Delinda.

75. "Married," *Elmira [Daily] Advertiser*, 18 September 1873, 4.

76. Marguerite Griffes, interview with author, 23 May 1981 (PI 9:46–47).

77. Birth dates for the Griffes children from Nathaniel Griffes family Bible.

78. Ibid.

79. Julia Griffes to Henry ("Harry") Boyd Waldron, n.d., photocopy in author's collection.

80. The names of several Griffes family members are contained in the "Records of the Protestant Reformed Dutch Church of Niskayuna in the Town of Niskayuna, Schenectady County, N.Y.," ed. Royden Woodward Vosburgh, trans. New York Genealogical and Biographical Society (New York, 1919), passim. Marguerite Griffes, untaped interview with author, 22 June 1977 (TD, 9).

81. Mrs. Willard B. Oakes, assistant church clerk, First Baptist Church, Elmira, N.Y., to author, 26 July 1988; Marguerite Griffes, interview with author, 13 September 1973 (PI 5:1).

82. David Waldron is listed as a traveling salesman in the *Elmira City Directory, 1884–5* (Elmira, N.Y.: Elmira Advertiser Association, 1884), 339. This listing is the last time Waldron appears in the city directory.

83. *Boyds' Elmira City Directory, 1880–1882*, 136, lists Wilber as a shirt manufacturer located at 121 Baldwin. The same directory (p. 115) records Fairlee's men's furnishing goods, hats, and caps at 135 East Water, the address of the defunct Waldron & Griffes. In the *Elmira City Directory, 1882–4* (Elmira, N.Y.: Elmira Advertiser Association, 1882), 147, Wilber appears as a salesman at 135 East Water, having gone to work for Fairlee. The *Elmira City Directory, 1884–5*, 61, shows John Cushing as gents' furnishing goods, 135 East Water, and lists Fairlee's wife, Julia, as "widow" (p. 171) and Wilber as cutter, 135 East Water (p. 193). Cushing moved his business in 1899 to 309 East Water (*Hanford's Elmira City Directory—1899* [Elmira, N.Y.: George Hanford, 1899], 177), where Wilber worked as a shirt cutter (*Hanford's Elmira City Directory—1899*, 207). The business appears as Edward H. Colburn & Co., custom shirts, hats, caps and mens' furnishings, at the 309 East Water address in *Hanford's Elmira City and Elmira Heights Directory, 1902* (Elmira, N.Y.: George Hanford, 1902), 121.

84. Marguerite Griffes, interview with author, 13 September 1973 (PI 5:35). See also ibid., 19 January 1982 (PI 13:13–14); and "Wilber G. Griffes," *Elmira Gazette and Free Press*, 13 November 1905, 7. Conversion figures for Wilber's salary based on an average of $100 per month with the 1900 CPI as the divider.

85. Marguerite Griffes, untaped interview with author, 8 January 1983 (TD, 54).

86. Marguerite Griffes, interview with author, 13 June 1982 (PI 16:21–22), and 23 May 1981 (PI 9:29).

87. Ibid., 23 May 1981 (PI 9:31).

88. Ibid. (PI 9:47).

89. Marguerite Griffes, untaped interview with author, 4 June 1983 (TD, 73).

90. Marguerite Griffes, interview with author, 18 January 1982 (PI 12:30).

91. Ibid., 10 January 1983 (PI 17:3).

92. Wilber G. Griffes, death record, Chemung County Health Department, Registrar of Vital Statistics, Elmira, N.Y.

93. Marguerite Griffes, interview with author, 18 January 1982 (PI 12:23).

CHAPTER 3. Personality: A Perspective

1. Marguerite Griffes, interview with author, 22 July 1969 (PI 1:10).

2. Ibid., 18 January 1982 (PI 11:12).

3. Charles Griffes to Clara Griffes, 23 August 1903, NN:Mu.

4. Griffes diary, 12 June 1912.

5. Edward Maisel, *Charles T. Griffes: The Life of an American Composer,* rev. ed. (New York: Alfred A. Knopf, 1984), 11.

6. Ibid.

7. Wilber Roake, interview with author, 23 May 1981 (PI 10:17–18), and 19 January 1982 (PI 13:1–3).

8. Charlotte Griffes, interview with author, 28 May 1975 (PI 18:3).

9. Marguerite Griffes, interview with author, 10 June 1982 (PI 15:25, 26).

10. Ibid., 22 July 1969 (PI 1:11–12).

11. Ibid., 13 September 1973 (PI 5:32).

12. Ibid., 18 January 1982 (PI 12:38–40).

13. Ibid. (PI 12:39).

14. Ibid. (PI 11:35).

15. Charles Griffes to Clara Griffes, 25 January 1904, NN:Mu.

16. Ibid., 11 January 1904, NN:Mu.

17. Ibid., 1 October 1905, NN:Mu. According to the *Elmira College Bulletin* 41, no. 9 (September 1950)—"Directory of Students, 1855–1950"—Roberts graduated with the class of 1897. She is listed as a teacher at Elmira Free Academy in *Hanford's Elmira City and Elmira Heights Directory—1900* (Elmira, N.Y.: George Hanford, 1900), 33, and is still so listed in the *Elmira City, Elmira Heights and Horseheads Directory, 1903* (Elmira, N.Y.: George Hanford, 1903), 34. Charles Griffes must have been one of her students.

18. Charles Griffes to Marguerite Griffes, 22 November 1903, NN:Mu.

19. Marguerite Griffes, interview with author, 23 July 1969 (PI 2:22), and 24 May 1981 (PI 10:39).

20. Thomas E. Byrne, *Chemung County, 1890–1975* (Elmira, N.Y.: Chemung County Historical Society, 1976), 489. Marguerite Griffes, interview with author, 13 September 1973 (PI 5:23).

21. Marguerite Griffes, interview with author, 13 September 1973 (PI 5:24–25). On Elmira's Lutheran churches, see Byrne, *Chemung County,* 413.

22. Marguerite Griffes, interview with author, 18 January 1982 (PI 11:16). The church in question was probably the Centenary Methodist Episcopal Church, located about a mile or two south of the Chemung River at South Main and Pennsylvania Avenue. See *Elmira City, Elmira Heights and Horse-*

heads Directory, 1903, 40. The directory lists eight Methodist churches. See also Maisel, *Charles T. Griffes,* 30.

23. Marguerite Griffes, interview with author, 18 January 1982 (PI 11:16).

24. Ibid., 13 September 1973 (PI 6:5).

25. Ibid., 29 July 1969 (PI 3:41).

26. Lansdale last appears as general secretary of the YMCA in *Hanford's Elmira City, Elmira Heights and Horseheads Directory, 1901* (Elmira, N.Y.: George Hanford, 1901), 277. Hansen first appears as general secretary in *Hanford's Elmira City and Elmira Heights Directory, 1902* (Elmira, N.Y.: George Hanford, 1902), 215.

27. Marguerite Griffes, interview with author, 29 July 1969 (PI 3:40).

28. Ibid., 22 July 1969 (PI 1:10).

29. Ibid., 23 May 1981 (PI 10:7).

30. Charles Griffes to Clara Griffes, 24 January 1904, NN:Mu.

31. Wilber Roake, interview with author, 20 January 1982 (PI 13:2), and 23 May 1981 (PI 10:17).

32. Harvey Stevenson to author, 27 March 1967.

33. Griffes diary, 19 December 1912.

34. Ibid., 2 October 1912. Although Griffes's statement that "after all that is the most powerful remedy" may be taken to mean the sex act, in this case it was not. Maisel, *Charles T. Griffes,* 371 n. for line 29 (p. 242), states that Griffes never sought the "ultimate" with the student to whom the 2 October 1912 diary entry refers.

35. Griffes diary, 24 May 1914.

36. Addresses from George Chauncey, Jr., to author, postcard, 28 March 1989.

37. Griffes diary, 25 July 1914 (original in German).

38. Marguerite Griffes, interview with author, 13 September 1973 (PI 6:21).

39. On a list of personal property that Griffes drew up in January 1918, he indicated certain items that were to go to John C. Meyer of 128 Forty-first Street, Corona, Long Island. Notebook in author's collection. Meyer was born on 18 March 1877. He and Charles celebrated John's thirty-ninth birthday (a day early) on 17 March 1916. See Griffes diary, 17 March 1916. Maisel, *Charles T. Griffes,* calls John Meyer "Dan Martin."

40. Griffes diary, 2 June 1915.

41. Ibid., 7 June 1915.

42. Ibid., 17 July 1915 (in English).

43. Ibid., 20 June 1915.

44. Ibid., 22 June, 24 June 1915.

45. Ibid., 21 August 1915.

46. Ibid., 16 November 1912.

47. Ibid., 22 December 1912.

48. Marguerite Griffes, interview with author, 13 September 1973 (PI 6:26).

49. Ibid., 29 July 1969 (PI 3:36).

50. Marguerite Griffes, untaped interview with author, 8 January 1983 (TD, 56). On the letter to Carpenter, see Maisel, *Charles T. Griffes*, 25, 340 n. for line 19 (p. 25).

51. Marguerite Griffes, interview with author, 23 May 1981 (PI 10:8).

CHAPTER 4. Graduation from High School and on to Berlin

1. Miss Broughton promised to lend Griffes the money needed for his musical studies, expecting that he would eventually repay her. Griffes noted in his diary on 19 January 1915: "Letter from Miss Broughton. She wants a note for the $1800. . . ."

2. Marguerite Griffes, interview with author, 22 July 1969 (PI 1:14).

3. Unless otherwise indicated, dates of composition are based on autograph manuscripts, diary entries, or both. See Donna K. Anderson, *The Works of Charles T. Griffes: A Descriptive Catalogue* (Ann Arbor: UMI Research Press, 1983), for a full discussion of dates of origin.

4. Original program in author's collection.

5. "An Artistic Event. It Was at the College, and before a Cultured Audience," *Elmira Telegram*, 24 May 1903, 5.

6. Charles and Florence most likely took the 12:50 P.M. train, scheduled to arrive in Hoboken in the early evening. "Lackawanna Route—Summer Time Table, in Effect June 14," *Elmira [Sunday] Telegram*, 9 August 1903, 6. On the price of a one-way ticket, see *Elmira City, Elmira Heights and Horseheads Directory, 1903* (Elmira, N.Y.: George Hanford, 1903), 19.

7. Charles Griffes to Clara Griffes, postcard, 11 August 1903, NN:Mu.

8. Charles Griffes to Clara Griffes, 12 August 1903, NN:Mu.

9. Ibid., 13 August 1903, NN:Mu.

10. Ibid., 14 August 1903, NN:Mu. Griffes often included comments written over several days in a single letter. For example, his remarks from Friday, 14 August, are added to his letter of 13 August. The New York Public Library, Music Division, catalogs each letter by its first date. Comments

within can be traced by checking adjacent first dates. Thus, there is no cataloged letter for 14 August, only letters from 13 August and 23 August. The letter of 14 August, therefore, will be part of the 13 August letter.

11. Charles Griffes to Clara Griffes, 16 August 1903, NN:Mu.

12. Ibid., 19 August 1903, NN:Mu.

13. Ibid., 23 August 1903, NN:Mu.

14. Ibid., 26 August 1903, NN:Mu.

15. *The World Book Encyclopedia,* 1990 ed., s.v. "Berlin"; *The Encyclopaedia Britannica,* 11th ed., s.v. "Berlin."

16. *The Encyclopaedia Britannica,* 11th ed., s.v. "Berlin."

17. Ibid.

18. Ibid. On Berlin's music conservatories, see *The New Grove Dictionary of Music and Musicians* [hereafter *New Grove*], ed. Stanley Sadie (London: Macmillan Publishers, 1980), s.v. "Berlin." Unless otherwise indicated, biographical information on musicians is taken from *New Grove; The New Grove Dictionary of American Music,* ed. H. Wiley Hitchcock and Stanley Sadie (London: Macmillan Press, 1986); *Baker's Biographical Dictionary of Musicians,* 7th ed., rev. Nicolas Slonimsky (New York: Schirmer Books, 1984); and *The International Cyclopedia of Music and Musicians,* ed. Oscar Thompson (New York: Dodd Mead & Co., 1938).

19. *New Grove,* s.v. "Berlin."

20. See Charles Griffes to Clara Griffes, 2 September 1903, NN:Mu.

21. Ibid., 27 August 1903, NN:Mu.

22. Ibid., 30 August 1903, NN:Mu.

23. Ibid., 1 September 1903, NN:Mu.

24. Ibid., 2 September 1903, NN:Mu.

25. Ibid., 6 September 1903, NEE.

26. Charles Griffes to Miss Broughton, 18 September 1903, NEE.

27. Charles Griffes to Clara Griffes, 6 September 1903, NEE.

28. Ibid.

29. Ibid., 12 December 1903, NN:Mu.

30. Ibid., 6 September 1903, NEE; and 9 October 1903, NN:Mu.

31. Ibid., 9 September 1903, NN:Mu.

32. Ibid., 10 September 1903, NN:Mu.

33. Charles Griffes to Marguerite Griffes, 13 September 1903, NN:Mu.

34. Charles Griffes to Clara Griffes, 30 August 1903, NN:Mu.

35. See, for example, ibid., 29 November, 4 October, and 12 December 1903, NN:Mu.

36. Ibid., 15 October 1905, NN:Mu.

37. Ibid., 20 September 1903, NN:Mu; and Charles Griffes to Miss Broughton, 18 September 1903, NEE.

38. Charles Griffes to Clara Griffes, 4 October 1903, NN:Mu.

39. Ibid.

40. Ibid., 16 October 1903, NN:Mu.

41. Ibid., 28 December 1903, NN:Mu. *Lovey Mary* is a book by Alice H. Rice that Charles and the two Shoobert girls were reading.

42. Charles Griffes to Clara Griffes, 17 April 1904, NN:Mu.

43. Ibid., 5 July 1905, NN:Mu.

44. Marguerite Griffes, interview with author, 23 July 1969 (PI 2:21). Marguerite's memory is confirmed by an entry in Charles's diary on 7 November 1914. Charles and Babe had had dinner with the Bancrofts and then went to the theater. Griffes wrote: "After the theatre we walked home and had a very confidential talk. We told each other many things we hadn't told before."

CHAPTER 5. The Berlin Years: Spring 1904–Spring 1905

1. See Edward Maisel, *Charles T. Griffes: The Life of an American Composer,* rev. ed. (New York: Alfred A. Knopf, 1984), 54–66, for his view on the subject. (Maisel calls Emil Joël "Konrad Wölcke.") Since Charles and Emil both lived in pensions (similar to what we call in this country room and board accommodations)—Charles in one room and Emil with his mother in two or three rooms—they could not have had much privacy except on excursions or outings together.

2. Charles Griffes to Clara Griffes, 8 July 1908, NN:Mu.

3. Ibid., 27 August 1908, NN:Mu.

4. Ibid., 20 August 1910, NN:Mu.

5. Ibid., 28 February 1905, NN:Mu.

6. Ibid., 2 May 1905, NN:Mu.

7. Ibid., 13 December 1903, NN:Mu.

8. Ibid., 6 March 1904, NN:Mu.

9. Charles Griffes to Miss Broughton, 18 September 1903, 18 October 1903, 25 April 1904, 21 December 1903, 6 and 7 December 1903, 14 February 1904, 18 November 1903, and 4 January 1904, NEE.

10. Original program in NN:Mu.

11. Charles Griffes to Clara Griffes, 13 June 1904, NN:Mu.

12. Ibid., 19 June 1904, NN:Mu.

13. Ibid., 7 August 1904, NEE.

14. Ibid., 2 July, 21 August 1904, NN:Mu.

15. Ibid., 26 September 1904, NN:Mu.

16. Miss Broughton to Clara Griffes, 2 July 1904, NN:Mu.

17. Charles Griffes to Miss Broughton, 26 September 1904, NEE.

18. Ibid., 26 September, 19 October, and 20 November 1904; 19 March, 22 May 1905; and 21 January 1906, NEE.

19. Charles Griffes to Clara Griffes, 18 October 1904, NN:Mu.

20. Ibid., 10 September, 20 September 1903, NN:Mu.

21. Ibid., 20 September 1903, NN:Mu.

22. Ibid., 24 September 1903, NN:Mu.

23. Charles Griffes to Miss Broughton, 6 December 1903, NEE.

24. Only one complete string quartet movement, Allegretto scherzando in B-flat major, and an unfinished string quartet movement in E major survive from Griffes's student years in Berlin. The string quartet did not figure prominently in Griffes's output, his only major work in that genre being the *Two Sketches for String Quartet Based on Indian Themes* (June 1918–July 1919) published posthumously in 1922.

25. Charles Griffes to Clara Griffes, 23 May 1904, NN:Mu.

26. Ibid., 21 August 1904, NEE. On the Klavier-Schule Klindworth, see *The New Grove Dictionary of Music and Musicians*, ed. Stanley Sadie (London: Macmillan Publishers, 1980), s.v. "Berlin, 5. Music Education." Charles did not have the opportunity to play for Busoni and continued his piano studies with Gottfried Galston at the Stern Conservatory.

27. Charles Griffes to Clara Griffes, 29 January 1905, NN:Mu.

28. Charles Griffes to Miss Broughton, 15 March 1905, NEE.

29. Charles Griffes to Clara Griffes, 29 March 1905, NN:Mu.

30. Charles Griffes to Miss Broughton, 20 June 1905, NEE. See also Charles Griffes to Clara Griffes, 1 May, 26 June 1905, NN:Mu. An original program for the 22 June concert is in NN:Mu.

31. Charles Griffes to Clara Griffes, 13 June 1905, NN:Mu.

32. Howard Hanson and the Eastman-Rochester Symphony Orchestra presented the work at the Eastman School of Music in Rochester, N.Y., on 24 April 1961. Original program in author's collection.

33. Charles Griffes to Clara Griffes, 15 February 1904, NN:Mu.

34. Charles Griffes to Miss Broughton, 6 December 1903, NEE.

35. Charles Griffes to Clara Griffes, 31 January 1904, NN:Mu.

36. Ibid., 4 October, 24 October 1904, NN:Mu.

37. Charles Griffes to Marguerite Griffes, 23 January 1905, NN:Mu.

38. Charles Griffes to Clara Griffes, 1 May 1905, NN:Mu.

39. Charles Griffes to Miss Broughton, 5 January 1905, NEE.

40. Charles Griffes to Clara Griffes, 22 March 1905, NN:Mu.

41. Charles Griffes to Miss Broughton, 5 January 1905, NEE.

42. Ibid.

43. Charles Griffes to Clara Griffes, 12 February 1905, NEE.

44. Charles Griffes to Miss Broughton, 22 May 1905, NEE.

45. Charles Griffes to Clara Griffes, 6 March 1905, NN:Mu.

46. Charles Griffes to Miss Broughton, 19 March 1905, NEE.

CHAPTER 6. The Berlin Years: Summer 1905–Summer 1906

1. Charles Griffes to Clara Griffes, 6 June 1905, NN:Mu. See also ibid., 25 June 1905, NN:Mu. Emil Joël had two brothers, Felix and Philipp, hence Charles's allusion to being considered the Joël's "youngest son." On Emil's siblings, see Charles Griffes to Clara Griffes, 27 January 1907 and 17 September 1906, respectively, NN:Mu.

2. Charles Griffes to Clara Griffes, 5 July 1905, NN:Mu.

3. Ibid., 17 July 1905, NN:Mu.

4. Ibid., 30 July 1905, NN:Mu. In an earlier letter of 5 July, Griffes described the beach at Sassnitz as narrow and stony. Later (on 13 August 1905) he expressed his satisfaction that Sassnitz did not have a sandy beach because that would have attracted rich people who were only interested in sleeping all morning and promenading in the afternoon to show off their fine clothes. He hated such things.

5. Charles Griffes to Clara Griffes, 30 July, 1 August, 2 August, 6 August, and 14 August 1905, NN:Mu.

6. Ibid., 6 August 1905, NN:Mu.

7. Ibid., 13 August 1905, NN:Mu.

8. Ibid., 24 August 1905, NN:Mu.

9. See ibid., 13 August, 18 August 1905, NN:Mu.

10. Ibid., 20 August 1905, NN:Mu.

11. Ibid.

12. Ibid., 4 September 1905, NN:Mu.

13. Ibid., 19 September 1905, NN:Mu.

14. Ibid., 29 May 1905, NN:Mu.

15. These addresses included Kurfürstenstrasse 48, "bei Frau Werner" (fall 1903–summer 1904); Goltz Strasse 28, "bei Frau Scheffel" (summer

1904); Lützow Strasse 44, "bei Fraulein Pfeifer" (fall 1904–summer 1905); Motz Strasse 64, Gartenhaus, "bei Frau Hilpert" (summer–fall 1905); Motz Strasse 16, Gartenhaus 1, "bei Frau Wesche" (fall 1905–summer 1906); and, still at Motz Strasse 16 but in Gartenhaus 3 and with a new landlady, Frau Behrend (fall 1906–summer 1907). Griffes spent his summer vacation in 1904 in the Harz Mountains, that of 1905 in Sassnitz. He was in Elmira during the summer of 1906 and returned to the United States permanently in the summer of 1907.

16. Charles Griffes to Clara Griffes, 30 October 1905, NN:Mu.

17. Charles Griffes to Miss Broughton, 28 October 1905, NEE.

18. Ibid., 21 January 1906, NEE. Three five-part chorale settings, "Passionlied Fünfstimmig, O Haupt voll Blut," "Lobe den Herren," and "Dies ist der Tag," are extant from Griffes's studies with Humperdinck. Neither the Scherzo nor the suite has survived.

19. Charles Griffes to Clara Griffes, 30 October 1905, NN:Mu.

20. Ibid., 7 November 1905, NN:Mu.

21. Charles Griffes to Miss Broughton, 28 October 1905, NEE.

22. Charles Griffes to Clara Griffes, 13 November 1905, NN:Mu.

23. Intermission broadcast with James Fassett, 1954(?), New York Philharmonic. Broadcast tape sent to author by Robert D. Swisher, 21 August 1988.

24. See, for example, Charles Griffes to Miss Broughton, 18 October, 6 December, 21 December 1903, and 26 February 1904, NEE; Griffes diary, 6 April 1912, and 23 October 1915.

25. Charlotte Griffes, interview with author, 28 May 1975 (PI 18:5, 23).

26. Charles Griffes to Clara Griffes, 15 November 1905, NN:Mu.

27. Charles Griffes to Marguerite Griffes, 6 January 1906, NN:Mu.

28. Charles Griffes to Clara Griffes, 22 November 1905, NN:Mu.

29. Ibid., 23 November 1905, NN:Mu.

30. Ibid., 27 November 1905, NN:Mu.

31. Ibid., 4 December 1905, NN:Mu.

32. Ibid., 18 February 1906, NN:Mu.

33. Ibid., 4 December 1905, NN:Mu.

34. Ibid., 16 January 1906, NN:Mu.

35. Charles Griffes to Miss Broughton, 21 January 1906, NEE.

36. As far as I can determine, Griffes had lessons with Humperdinck on 27 October, 3 November, and 10 November 1905; and 8 January, 12 January, 2 February, 23 February, 6 April, and 27 April 1906. See Charles Griffes to Clara Griffes, 30 October 1905; 3, 10, 15 November 1905; 24, 26 January

1906; 4, 25 February 1906; 8 April 1906; and 1 May 1906, NN:Mu. See also Charles Griffes to Marguerite Griffes, 9 January 1906, NN:Mu.

37. Charles Griffes to Clara Griffes, 23 September, 6 October, and 7 November 1906, NN:Mu.

38. Ibid., 25 November 1906, NN:Mu.

39. On Sandra Droucker, see "Limits Great Piano Composers to Five," *New York Times,* 4 November 1912, 11.

40. Charles Griffes to Clara Griffes, 20 August 1910, NN:Mu.

41. Charles Griffes to Miss Broughton, 21 January 1906, NEE.

42. Charles Griffes to Clara Griffes, 19 March, 3 April 1906, NN:Mu.

43. See, for example, ibid., 1 May 1906, in which Charles informed his mother that Emil had a plan so that he could have another year of study in Berlin. Charles did not reveal what the plan was but said he would discuss it with her when he got home.

44. Charles Griffes to Clara Griffes, 23 May 1906, NN:Mu.

45. Ibid., 15 May 1906, NN:Mu.

46. Ibid., 15 April, 15 May, and 1 June 1906, NN:Mu.

47. Original program in author's collection. None of Griffes's arrangements are extant.

48. "Enjoy Piano Recital," *Elmira [Daily] Gazette and Free Press,* 25 July 1906, 5.

49. Charles Griffes to Clara Griffes, 26 February 1907, NN:Mu.

CHAPTER 7. The Final Year in Berlin: August 1906–July 1907

1. See Charles Griffes to Clara Griffes, 18 August 1906, NN:Mu. The letter covers Griffes's entire voyage beginning on 18 August and ending on 26 August.

2. Ibid., 2 September 1906, NN:Mu.

3. Ibid.

4. Ibid., 17 September 1906, NN:Mu.

5. Ibid., 17 September, 23 September 1906, NN:Mu.

6. Ibid., 6 October 1906, NN:Mu.

7. Ibid., 29 October 1906, NEE.

8. Ibid., 7 November, 18 November, and 28 December 1906, NN:Mu.

9. Ibid., 13 January 1907, NN:Mu.

10. Ibid., 27 January 1907, NN:Mu.

11. Ibid., 28 October 1906, NEE.

12. As far as I can determine, Griffes had from two to five piano and harmony students between August 1906 and April 1907. On Griffes's pupils, see Charles Griffes to Clara Griffes, 9 September, 29 October 1906, NEE; 2 September, 6 October, 28 October, 8 November, and 11 December 1906; 27 January, 10 February, 12 February, 8 March, and 28 April 1907, NN:Mu.

13. Charles Griffes to Clara Griffes, 19 March 1906, NN:Mu.

14. Ibid., 8 March 1907, NN:Mu.

15. Ibid., 12 February 1907, NN:Mu.

16. Ibid., 10 February 1907, NN:Mu.

17. Ibid., 8 March 1907, NN:Mu.

18. Ibid., 10 February 1907, NN:Mu.

19. Ibid., 5 May 1907, NN:Mu.

20. Ibid., 28 April 1907, NN:Mu.

21. Ibid., 27 May 1907, NN:Mu.

22. Ibid., 20 June 1907, NN:Mu.

23. Autograph manuscript in NN:Mu.

24. Griffes, for example, wrote Fredy Juel "my almost yearly letter. It always brings back many memories." Griffes diary, 28 June 1912.

25. Ibid., 6 February 1914.

26. Ibid., 13 November 1914.

27. See Edward Maisel, *Charles T. Griffes: The Life of an American Composer,* rev. ed. (New York: Alfred A. Knopf, 1984), 221.

28. Miss Broughton to Clara Griffes, 31 October 1920, NN:Mu.

29. A concert in Emil's memory was presented on Sunday, 1 December [no year given], conducted by Emil's second son, Gerhard. The first of December fell on a Sunday in 1929 and 1935. Since Emil is absent from the family photograph albums in the later years, 1929 seems to be the most likely year of death. Gerhard would have been almost seventeen in December 1929 and almost twenty-three in December 1935. He could have conducted the concert at either age. However, a handwritten note on the program states that Gerhard conducted the concert with only two rehearsals, something more worthy of mention for a precocious seventeen-year-old musician than for a twenty-three-year-old one, it seems to me. Original program in the collection of Natalie Burfoot Billing, Emil's granddaughter.

30. Gary Charles Burfoot (Emil's grandson), interview with author, 21 January 1989. See also "Girl Escapes Deportation," *New York Times,* 24 November 1938, 11, in which Helga Joël (Emil's daughter) states that she was a Lutheran. She was baptized on 9 April 1916. Document in the collection of Natalie Burfoot Billing.

31. "Shoobert Family Entertains Noted Berlin Evacuee," *Sausalito News*, 14 September 1944, 2.

32. Elly Joel [*sic*], certificate of death, Bureau of Records and Statistics, Department of Health, New York, N.Y.

33. Helmer Joël's vita is in the collection of Natalie Burfoot Billing.

34. Natalie Burfoot Billing, telephone interview with author, 2 December 1990.

35. Gerhard Joël's passport is in the collection of Natalie Burfoot Billing.

36. Dennis McGovern, archives assistant, Metropolitan Opera Association, to author, 9 November 1988; Edward Johnson, general manager, Metropolitan Opera Association, to Gerhard Joël, 10 May 1939, in the collection of Natalie Burfoot Billing; J. J. Shubert, Select Theatres Corporation, to Gerhard Joël, 25 March 1944 *(Blossom Time)*; and Theresa Helburn, Theatre Guild, to Gerhard Joël, 25 April 1944 *(Oklahoma!)*, in the collection of Natalie Burfoot Billing.

37. Papers in the collection of Natalie Burfoot Billing.

38. Newspaper clipping, *St. Louis Globe-Democrat*, 1 January 1945, in the collection of Natalie Burfoot Billing; Gerhardt Joël, death certificate, Bureau of Records and Statistics, Department of Health, New York, N.Y. Gerhard Joël's name was sometimes spelled Gerhardt, and he was also known in this country as Joel Gerhard.

39. Helga Joël, immigrant identification card, United States Department of Labor. Issued by the Department of State, American Consulate at Regina, Canada, on 10 October 1939. In the collection of Natalie Burfoot Billing.

40. "Refugee Takes Sinfonietta Baton," unidentified newspaper clipping, Charles T. Griffes clipping file, NN:Mu; Natalie Burfoot Billing, interview with author, 20 January 1989.

41. "Mrs. Burfoot Dies after Long Illness," *New London Day*, 17 March 1965. In the collection of Natalie Burfoot Billing.

CHAPTER 8. Hackley School

1. *The Hackley Annual, 1908*, 13, lists faculty and their titles for the 1907–8 school year. Hazen, a pupil of Rafael Joseffy, Moritz Moszkowski, and S. P. Warren (see *The Hackley Annual, 1907*, 17), had taught at the school since 1900 (*The Hackley Annual, 1906*, "School History," and *The Hackley Annual, 1907*, 13).

2. Report by Headmaster Henry White Callahan to the Hackley Board of Trustees, 3 June 1907, Hackley School archives.

3. George M. Chadwick taught at the University of Colorado in Boulder from 1905 to 1919. Grant James Klausman, "A History of the University of Colorado College of Music, 1877–1951" (Ph.D. diss., University of Colorado, 1967), 80–117. Callahan's mistake is all the more strange given that he himself came to Hackley from Boulder.

4. Marguerite Griffes, interview with author, 10 June 1982 (PI 15:23–24). For the starting date of the 1907–8 school year, see *Hackley Upper and Lower Schools, 1906–1907* (catalog), 4.

5. U.S. Bureau of the Census, *Thirteenth Census of the United States Taken in the Year 1910, Abstract of the Census* (Washington, D.C.: Government Printing Office, 1913), 71, records Tarrytown's population in 1900 as 4,770 and in 1910 as 5,600. According to Jon Gregoire, archives intern, Westchester County Clerk's Office, the New York State census for the year 1905 lists Tarrytown's population as 5,322 (letter to author, 9 February 1989).

6. "The High and the Mighty," *Tarrytown Centennial Album, 1870–1970* ([Tarrytown, N.Y.:] Morgan Press, 1970).

7. Information on Tarrytown's development and businesses from Jeff Canning and Wally Buxton, *History of the Tarrytowns Westchester County, New York from Ancient Times to the Present* (Harrison, N.Y.: Harbor Hill Books, 1975), 70, 95, 72, 98–99, 197, 80, 98, 100, 81–86.

8. "School Days, School Days," *Tarrytown Centennial Album.*

9. "Private Schools Too," *Tarrytown Centennial Album.*

10. *Hackley Upper and Lower School* [sic], [1907–1908] (catalog), 8. The school functions today as a coeducational day school.

11. "Mrs. Hackley's Will: Estate Worth More Than $1,000,000—Many Bequests to Charities," *New York Times,* 7 February 1914, 6.

12. Arthur E. Naething, "History," in *Hackley School: Philosophy, History, Division Descriptions* (Tarrytown, N.Y.: Hackley School, [1986?]), 5–6.

13. Typed list of presidents of the board of trustees, Hackley School archives. "Hackley" (obituary), *New York Times,* 5 September 1913, 9; and "Funeral of Mrs. Hackley: Services Held at Goodhue Memorial Chapel Last Saturday Morning," *Tarrytown Press-Record,* 12 September 1913, 8.

14. Tom Philips, "More Than a Sequence of Buildings . . . Problems of Writing a School History," *Hackley Review* 20, no. 1 (Spring 1985): 14. The first three headmasters would have been Rev. Theodore Chickering Williams, Rev. James Eells, and Dr. Henry White Callahan. See *The*

Hackley Annual, 1906, "Masters" and "School History," and *The Hackley Annual, 1907,* 17.

15. "Mrs. Hackley's Will," 6.

16. *The Hackley Annual, 1906,* "School History." See also *The [Hackley] Annual, 1916,* 11.

17. *The Hackley Annual, 1907,* 13.

18. Ibid., 13–14.

19. Philips, "More Than a Sequence of Buildings," 12; student petition requesting Callahan's removal in favor of Walter Gage, Hackley School archives.

20. *The Hackley Annual, 1909,* 6–7.

21. Elfrieda Van Houten, Office of the Headmaster, Hackley School, to author, 30 November 1988.

22. W. Houston Kenyon, Jr., telephone interview with author, 15 October 1988; *The [Hackley] Annual, 1919,* 13; and Marguerite Griffes, interview with author, 24 July 1969 (PI 3:12–13).

23. Griffes diary, 7 February 1915.

24. Marguerite Griffes, interview with author, 24 July 1969 (PI 3:12).

25. "Charles T. Griffes Succumbs," *Musical Leader* 39, no. 16 (15 April 1920): 383.

26. *Hackley Upper and Lower School,* [1907–1908] (catalog), 9, 22. Money conversions are based on the October 1990 Consumer Price Index using the formula in Gary Greene's article "Understanding Past Currency in Modern Times," *Sonneck Society Bulletin* 13, no. 2 (Summer 1987): 48. Conversion figures for 1907–8 Hackley tuition use the 1908 CPI as a divider.

27. *The Hackley Annual, 1906,* "School History."

28. Information from audits prepared by Walston H. Brown, treasurer, Hackley Board of Trustees, for the years ending 31 July 1908 and 31 July 1919, Hackley School archives.

29. *Hackley Upper and Lower School,* [1907–1908] (catalog), 10.

30. See Hackley annuals, 1908, 109; 1909, 83; 1910, 73; 1911, 76; 1916, 95; 1917, 97; 1918, 103; and 1919, 121.

31. *Hackley School* (Tarrytown, N.Y.: Board of Trustees of Hackley School, 1930), 13.

32. Information on student routine from W. Houston Kenyon, Jr., telephone interviews with author, 15 October 1988 and 23 January 1989; and W. Houston Kenyon, Jr., "Memoirs" (ca. 1985), typescript, 33.

33. Griffes diary, 17 March 1912.

34. In a small notebook in which Griffes recorded his personal property (January 1918), he lists items "in studio in the chapel" and "in bedroom in main building." Notebook in author's collection.

35. Griffes diary, 10 October 1915.

36. Ibid., 12 October 1915.

37. Ibid., 8 October 1912. Years of graduation for all Hackley students cited herein are from *Hackley School Alumni Directory* (Boston: Printed by Spaulding-Moss Co., 1963).

38. Griffes diary, 12 May 1915.

39. On Maud Allan, see Horst Koegler, *The Concise Oxford Dictionary of Ballet* (London: Oxford University Press, 1977), 11. Her name is usually spelled Maude, as it is in Koegler. Griffes and his friend and fellow musician Burnet Tuthill had been guests of Mr. and Mrs. Charles Larned Robinson in Intervale, N.H., in the White Mountains, from 15 to 31 August 1914. Several photographs taken by Griffes during this trip are housed in the Library of Congress.

40. The "pantomime at the Lewisohn's" refers to a "compressed" version of Stravinsky's *Petrouchka* that Griffes and Lily Hyland of the Neighborhood Playhouse were to accompany. On Katherine Sophie Dreier, see *Dictionary of American Biography*, 5th suppl. (1951–55), ed. John A. Garraty (New York: Charles Scribner's Sons, 1977), 184. On Elizabeth Duncan, see Elizabeth Kendall, *Where She Danced* (New York: Alfred A. Knopf, 1979), 60.

41. Mary Dreier had earlier asked Griffes his terms to play at a reception. Griffes diary, 16 February 1916.

42. Only one Blake song, "In a Myrtle Shade," is extant.

43. Griffes diary, 12 January 1916.

44. See *The [Hackley] Annual, 1916*, 9, for all but Cook. For Cook, see *The [Hackley] Annual, 1917*, 7.

45. Harry Cook, interview with author, January 1965.

46. "Editorials," *Hackley* 17, no. 6 (April 1917): 2.

47. Harvey Stevenson to author, 15 March 1965.

48. Ibid., 27 March 1965.

49. W. Houston Kenyon, Jr., to author, 27 April 1965, and telephone interview with author, 15 October 1988.

50. W. Houston Kenyon, Jr., to author, 27 April 1965.

51. Fredrick Y. Smith to author, 16 August 1965.

52. Ibid. Griffes's diary also confirms this. For example, "Developed a film this evening" (31 May 1915). Many of Griffes's photographs are now housed in NN:Mu.

53. Fredrick Y. Smith to author, 16 August 1965.

54. Report by Headmaster Henry White Callahan to the Hackley Board of Trustees, 3 June 1907, Hackley School archives.

55. "Spoke with W. B. [Gage] about next year and the guarantee is raised to $1500" (Griffes diary, 6 April 1915).

56. Edward Maisel, *Charles T. Griffes: The Life of an American Composer,* rev. ed. (New York: Alfred A. Knopf, 1984), 271. From a low (starting) salary of about $500 (in 1907–8) to a high of $1,700 (in 1918–19), Griffes's salary at Hackley ranged in 1990 dollars from about $7,400 (using the 1908 CPI as a divider) to about $13,000 (using the 1919 CPI as a divider).

57. Salaries of academic departments, headmaster's reports, bursars reports, treasurer's reports, approved salary lists, etc., examined by author on 18 November 1988, Hackley School archives.

58. Peter Gibbon, Hackley headmaster, interview with author, 18 November 1988, and Tom Philips, telephone interview with author, 4 December 1988.

59. Peter Gibbon, interview with author, 18 November 1988.

60. Griffes diary, 8 October 1912.

61. Griffes diary, passim. Unfortunately, the Hackley School archives contain no records of private lessons. Term bills do exist, but these are not itemized.

62. Peter Gibbon, interview with author, 18 November 1988. A report prepared for the United States Internal Revenue Service by Walston H. Brown, treasurer of the Hackley Board of Trustees, 30 March 1918 (Hackley School archives), lists fourteen Hackley teachers and identifies twelve as "single." Griffes's name is absent from the list because the music director does not figure on any of the salary schedules in the Hackley School archives after 1907.

63. Griffes diary, 19 January 1915. No one could have foreseen that Charles's death would precede Miss Broughton's.

64. Ibid., 15 March 1915.

65. Marguerite Griffes, interview with author, 10 January 1983 (PI 17:4).

66. Miss Broughton to Arthur Clinton, Elmira College Board of Trustees, 6 May 1916, NEE. She indicates in that letter that she accepted her reappointment to Elmira College at the same salary she received in 1914 and 1915. Her salary, however, climbed steadily, and by 1921 (the year before she died), she was earning $1,800 plus $325 room and board. Information from a typed list of Elmira College faculty salaries for 1920–21 and 1921–22, NEE. See

also Miss Broughton to Dr. Frederick Lent, president of Elmira College, 3 March 1921, NEE.

67. Marguerite Griffes, interview with author, 13 September 1973 (PI 6:19).

68. Miss Broughton to Dr. Frederick Lent, 17 June 1921, NEE. Elmira College catalogs from 1891–92 through 1916–17 list Miss Broughton in the School of Music. She appears for the first time as professor of Spanish in the 1917–18 catalog and appears for the last time (still as professor of Spanish) in the 1921–22 catalog. The catalogs never identify her as teaching German.

69. "Death Claims Miss Broughton," *Elmira Star-Gazette*, 7 June 1922, 5.

70. Griffes diary, 18 March 1915, and 3 April 1916.

71. Marguerite Griffes to author, 14 September 1965. If Griffes had kept up the rate of savings indicated in his diary, he could have accumulated close to $2,000 before his death. Miss Griffes also once identified the amount Charles saved as $200 (interview with author, 1 January 1983 [PI 17:4]). That amount could have been what remained in Griffes's account after he repaid Miss Broughton the sum he owed her. My effort to locate Griffes's Tarrytown bank records was unsuccessful. The reference to St. Aubyn's article is to Frederic St. Aubyn, "Just Mention My Name in Elmira," *Elmira Telegram*, 8 November 1964, 7B, written as publicity for the Elmira College Griffes Festival held on 20–22 November 1964, which Miss Griffes attended.

72. For a different view, see Maisel, *Charles T. Griffes*, 95 and 347 nn. for line 22 (p. 94) and line 23 (p. 95). Maisel informed me that in a "Pocket Miscellany" (see ibid., 338), Griffes noted the following: "To Mother for Summer 1915, July, August, September, $154.72; Summer 1916, to Mother July, August, September, $154.69." Edward Maisel, telephone interview with author, 10 April 1989. This could indicate, I believe, that Griffes sent his mother about $52.00 each month during those two years, which would have amounted to $624.00 a year. However, the odd amounts—$154.72 and $154.69—could also indicate that these were not for monthly support but for some other purpose.

73. G. Schirmer, statement of royalties, in author's collection.

74. Marguerite Griffes, untaped interview with author, 22 June 1977 (TD, 11); and Marguerite Griffes, interview with author, 13 September 1973 (PI 6:30).

75. Griffes diary, 5 January 1915.

76. On Thursday, 7 October 1915, for example, Griffes took the 8:32 A.M. train for New York, saw pianists Alexander Lambert and Paolo Martucci, had lunch with Mr. Meyer from G. Schirmer and played him some of his compositions, played for Laura Elliot and a friend of hers and joined them for tea, had dinner with the Bancrofts, and then went to the studio of a friend, Grace Freeman, and played some Debussy and Strauss. Finally, he "took the 12.35 [midnight] train back and had to walk up the hill in a pouring rain. It wasn't worth while." Griffes diary, 7 October 1915.

CHAPTER 9. Building a Career: New York City, 1909–1918

1. U.S. Bureau of the Census, *Thirteenth Census of the United States Taken in the Year 1910, Abstract of the Census* (Washington, D.C.: Government Printing Office, 1913), 71, lists the population of New York City as 4,766,883; see also *The Encyclopaedia Britannica,* 11th ed., s.v. "New York (City)."

2. Data on New York from *The Encyclopaedia Britannica,* 11th ed., s.v. "New York (City)."

3. Information in this paragraph from Richard Aldrich, *Concert Life in New York, 1902–1923* (New York: G. P. Putnam's Sons, 1941). See also *Baker's Biographical Dictionary of Musicians,* 7th ed., rev. Nicolas Slonimsky (New York: Schirmer Books, 1984); and the *New Grove Dictionary of American Music,* ed. H. Wiley Hitchcock and Stanley Sadie (London: Macmillan Press, 1986), s.v. "Flonzaley Quartet" and "New York."

4. On Adolf Bolm, see Horst Koegler, *The Concise Oxford Dictionary of Ballet* (London: Oxford University Press, 1977), 80. See also Helen Caldwell, *Michio Ito: The Dancer and His Dances* (Berkeley and Los Angeles: University of California Press, 1977), ix, 3; Alice Lewisohn Crowley, *The Neighborhood Playhouse: Leaves from a Theatre Scrapbook* (New York: Theatre Arts Books, 1959); "Arturo Giovannitti Dies at 75; Poet, Long-Time Labor Leader," *New York Times,* 1 January 1960, 19; and "Mrs. Laura M. Elliot, a Teacher of Voice, Pupil of de Reszke Trained Many Notables of Stage," *New York Times,* 10 June 1940, 17.

5. Griffes diary, 11 April 1912.

6. Ibid., 13 April, 6 May 1912.

7. Ibid., 17 July 1912.

8. Ibid., 9 August 1912.

9. Ibid., 30 November 1912.

10. Charles Griffes to Gottfried Galston, 30 July 1913. German type-script sent to author by Edward Maisel.

11. Griffes diary, 3 April 1914. I have been unable to find a program for this concert or an earlier performance. Griffes dedicated *The Lake at Evening* to Hodgson.

12. Griffes diary, 9 May 1914.

13. Ibid., 5 May 1914.

14. Ibid., 21 October 1914.

15. Ibid., 7 November 1914.

16. Ibid., 24 November 1914.

17. Ibid., 30 January 1915.

18. Ibid., 4 February, 5 February, and 6 March 1915.

19. Ibid., 11 March 1915. Griffes's first visit to the Busonis was on 2 May 1907. See Charles Griffes to Clara Griffes, 5 May 1907, NN:Mu.

20. Royalty agreement in author's collection.

21. Griffes diary, 11 May, 14 May 1914.

22. Ibid., 15 May 1915.

23. Ibid., 20 May, 26 May, 7 June, and 14 August 1915.

24. Ibid., 30 May, 8 June, 14 June, and 16 June 1915.

25. A. Walter Kramer, "A New Note in Our Piano Music," *Musical America* 23, no. 5 (4 December 1915): 37.

26. Griffes diary, 4 December 1915.

27. A. Walter Kramer, "New Music—Vocal and Instrumental," *Musical America* 23, no. 6 (11 December 1915): 44.

28. Griffes diary, 20 June, 22 June, and 24 June 1915.

29. Ibid., 6 July 1916. See also return address on letters and postcards in NN:Mu.

30. "Mrs. Laura M. Elliot," 17; Griffes diary, 13 November, 2 December 1915.

31. Griffes diary, October, November, and December 1915, passim.

32. Ibid., 7 October 1915.

33. Ibid.

34. Ibid., 9 October 1915.

35. Ibid., 16 October 1915. On Charles Cooper, see Charles Cooper clipping file, NN:Mu.

36. Original program in author's collection.

37. Griffes diary, 25 October 1915. On Indiana-born Noble Kreider, see "Krieder, Noble," supplementary biographical index, NN:Mu. On Griffes's first meeting with Lewis Isaacs, see Griffes diary, 31 March 1914.

38. Griffes diary, 6 November, 9 November, 8 December, and 28 December 1915.

39. Ibid., 11 January 1916.

40. Original program in author's collection.

41. Griffes diary, 23 February 1916.

42. Sylvester Rawling, in *Evening World* [New York], 24 February 1916, 19.

43. Griffes diary, 26 April 1916.

44. Original program in author's collection.

45. Griffes diary, 12 April 1916.

46. Original program in author's collection; Griffes diary, 24 November 1915.

47. "Helen Stanley Is Heard with Barrere [*sic*] Ensemble," *New York Tribune,* 20 December 1916, 11.

48. Royalty agreement in author's collection.

49. Griffes diary, 23 August 1916.

50. Ibid., 1 April, 4 April 1916.

51. Information on Ratan Devi and Ananda Coomaraswamy from the Ballet-Intime publicity booklet, NN:Da, and Ratan Devi clipping file, NN:Mu.

52. Griffes diary, 6 May 1916.

53. Ibid., 13 May 1916.

54. Harriette Brower, "Rudolph Ganz as Musical Editor," *Musical America* 24, no. 9 (1 July 1916): 35.

55. Griffes diary, 30 December 1916.

56. Ibid., 3 June 1916.

57. Ibid., 11 October 1916.

58. Richard Burbank, *Twentieth Century Music* (New York: Facts on File, 1984), 78. Peter Ostwald, *Vaslav Nijinsky: A Leap into Madness* (New York: A Lyle Stuart Book, 1991), 142–43, writes that Monteux's refusal to conduct was not because Strauss was German but because of the chaos surrounding the preparation of the ballet—chaos due mainly to the dancer-choreographer, Nijinsky.

59. Crowley, *The Neighborhood Playhouse,* xix.

60. Ethan Mordden, *The American Theatre* (New York: Oxford University Press, 1981), 56.

61. Ibid., 60–61.

62. Griffes diary, 6 April 1916.

63. Ibid., 6 May 1917; and Crowley, *The Neighborhood Playhouse,* 43.

64. Griffes diary, 22 June 1916.

65. Ibid., August–December 1916, passim.

66. Original program in NN:Th. Subsequent performances were held on 11, 12, 17, 18, 22, 24, 25 February; 24, 25, 31 March; and 1, 8 April 1917.

67. Paul Rosenfeld, "Mr. Griffes en Route," *Seven Arts* 1 (April 1917): 673–74.

68. Griffes signed contracts for the labor song "These Things Shall Be" and the op. 10 songs on 22 March 1917 and 10 September 1917, respectively. Royalty agreements in author's collection.

69. Griffes diary, 6 October, 24 October 1917.

70. "Schirmer Issues Griffes Compositions," *Musical Leader* 35, no. 6 (7 February 1918): 151.

71. Original program in author's collection.

72. Original program in NEE.

73. Information from New Nixon Theatre announcement (Atlantic City) and Booth Theatre program (New York), NN:Da. *Assyrian Dance,* the title given on the New York program, is the same as *A Trip to Syria.*

74. Original program in NEE.

75. George Amberg, *Ballet in America: The Emergence of an American Art* (New York: Duell, Sloan and Pearce, 1949), 23.

76. Tulle Lindahl clipping file, NN:Da.

77. Frederick H. Martens, "Folk Music in the 'Ballet-Intime,'" *New Music Review and Church Music Review* 16, no. 191 (October 1917): 764–65.

78. Ibid., 765.

79. "Adolph Bolm Moving Spirit of Charming Organization; Chas. T. Griffes Writes Splendid Music for Itow—Roshanara, Ratan Devi, and Other Artists Seen," *Musical Leader* 34, no. 9 (30 August 1917): 211.

80. Griffes diary, 6 October, 26 October, and 27 October 1917.

81. Sigmund Spaeth, "Music: Carnegie Hall Recital by Alice Gentle—Eva Gauthier Sings Some New Songs," *Evening Mail* [New York], 2 November 1917, 6.

82. H. K. M., "New Songs and Novel Manners," *Boston Evening Transcript,* 5 November 1917, 13.

83. *Encyclopedia of American History: Bicentennial Edition,* ed. Richard B. Morris (New York: Harper & Row, 1976), 330.

84. Marguerite Griffes, interview with author, 18 January 1982 (PI 11:17).

85. Charles Griffes to Burnet Tuthill, 3 November 1918, DLC.

86. When the songs were reissued in 1945, Schirmer changed the title to *Five Poems of the Ancient Far East.* The royalty agreement signed by

Griffes on 10 September 1917 listed them as *Five Chinese and Japanese Songs*. Royalty agreement in author's collection.

87. A. Walter Kramer, "Five Poems of Ancient China and Japan," *Musical America* 27, no. 19 (9 March 1918): 36.

88. The 10 September 1917 royalty agreement that Griffes signed with G. Schirmer, Inc., for the publication of his op. 10 songs also included provisions for the publication of "In a Myrtle Shade," "Waikiki," and "Phantoms" (with opus number but no collective title indicated). Royalty agreement in author's collection.

89. Griffes signed the contract for the publication of "Sorrow of Mydath" and "The Rose of the Night" (with no opus number or collective title indicated) on 23 February 1918. The former was not published until 1920, as no. 2 of *Two Poems by John Masefield;* the latter appeared later in 1918 as no. 3 of the op. 11 Fiona Macleod songs. It was not until 8 June 1918 that Griffes signed the contract for "The Lament of Ian the Proud" and "Thy Dark Eyes to Mine" (with no opus number or collective title indicated), issued as nos. 1 and 2 of the op. 11 songs.

90. Original program in author's collection.

91. "Griffes Heard at MacDowell Club," *Musical Leader* 35, no. 10 (7 March 1918): 262.

92. Sylvester Rawling, in *Evening World* [New York], 27 February 1918, 19.

93. Herbert F. Peyser, "Give Program of Works by Charles T. Griffes," *Musical America* 27, no. 19 (9 March 1918): 4.

94. Marion Bauer, "Charles T. Griffes as I Remember Him," *Musical Quarterly* 29 (July 1943): 377.

95. "New York Notes," *Christian Science Monitor*, 2 March 1918, 22.

96. J. V., "A Chat with Rudolph Ganz," *Musical Courier* 77, no. 4 (25 April 1918): 10.

97. Harriette Brower, "'More Love for Music Here Than in Europe' Declares Bauer," *Musical America* 29, no. 11 (11 January 1919): 17.

98. A. Walter Kramer, "'In a Myrtle Shade,' 'Wai Kiki,' 'Phantom,'" *Musical America* 27, no. 22 (30 March 1918): 40.

99. Original program in author's collection.

100. Herbert F. Peyser, "Ultra-Moderns Rule at Gauthier Recital," *Musical America* 28, no. 1 (4 May 1918): 48.

101. Max Smith, "Greta Masson Pleasing in First Recital Here," *New York American*, 23 April 1918, Social Side of City Life section.

102. Sigmund Spaeth, "Music: Some Novel Songs," *Evening Mail* [New York], 23 April 1918, 8.

103. Original program in author's collection.

104. Original program booklet in author's collection.

105. Original program in author's collection.

106. Caldwell, *Michio Ito,* 132.

107. Original program in author's collection.

108. Original programs in author's collection. Meakle and Greenough were students of Eugene Heffley.

109. Edward Maisel, *Charles T. Griffes: The Life of an American Composer,* rev. ed. (New York: Alfred A. Knopf, 1984), 233.

CHAPTER 10. The "Big Year": New York City, 1919

1. G. Schirmer, statement of royalties, in author's collection. The statement indicates royalties of $48.70 plus an additional sum for the op. 10 songs, which Schirmer indicated separately.

2. Original programs for all concerts cited are in author's collection.

3. Griffes diary, 12 February 1916.

4. Original program in NEE. The spelling of Votitchenko varies. The concert program reads Sasha Votichenko, whereas his *New York Times* obituary (31 October 1971) has Sacha Votichenko. A signed (autograph?) photo of Votitchenko appearing on the 23 February program reads Sasha Votitchenko, which is the spelling used in this book.

5. Original program in Vera Janacopulos clipping file, NN:Mu. On Vera Janacopulos, see "Vera Janacopulos in Recital," *Musical Leader* 37, no. 14 (3 April 1919): 327.

6. The van Dresser concert took place on 24 March 1919. *Philadelphia Orchestra Program,* 19th season, 1918–19, 807. Original program in the Philadelphia Orchestra Association archives.

7. Katharine Lane, "With the Musicians: Vera Janacopulos Sings," *Evening Mail* [New York], 24 March 1919, 4.

8. A. Walter Kramer, "Vera Janacopulos Presents New Songs," *Musical America* 29, no. 22 (29 March 1919): 44.

9. "Vera Janacopulos in Recital," 327.

10. On Janacopulos's singing, see Kramer's review in *Musical America* (n. 8 above) and "Vera Janacopulos, Soprano," *Musical Courier* 78, no. 13 (27 March 1919): 26.

11. The version for voice and piano bears a 1918 copyright and had probably been issued in late 1918 or early 1919. The royalty agreement for "The Rose of the Night" is dated 23 February 1918, that for "The Lament of Ian the Proud" and "Thy Dark Eyes to Mine" 8 June 1918. Royalty agreements in author's collection.

12. A. Walter Kramer, "Three Poems by Fiona Macleod," *Musical America* 30, no. 2 (10 May 1919): 40.

13. Original program in NEE.

14. Originally called the Lambord Choral Society, the society changed its name to the Modern Music Society in 1914. *New Grove Dictionary of American Music*, ed. H. Wiley Hitchcock and Stanley Sadie (London: Macmillan Press, 1986), s.v. "Modern Music Society."

15. Frances R. Grant, "Applaud Griffes Works," *Musical America* 29, no. 24 (12 April 1919): 45.

16. "Flonzaleys Play American Work," *Musical Leader* 37, no. 15 (10 April 1919): 350.

17. Louise Varèse, *Varèse: A Looking-Glass Diary*, vol. 1, *1883–1928* (New York: W. W. Norton & Co., 1972), 140.

18. James Gibbons Huneker, "Music: A New Symphony Orchestra," *New York Times*, 12 April 1919, 13. On the orchestra's sponsors and projected concerts, see 1919 spring season brochure, in author's collection.

19. "Hugo Riesenfeld, Music Conductor," *New York Times*, 11 September 1939, 19.

20. Frances R. Grant, "Bolm Urges a Cycle of Russian Opera," *Musical America* 29, no. 23 (5 April 1919): 4.

21. Original program in author's collection.

22. Clive Barnes, "They Forgot to Dance," *New York Post*, 4 May 1988, 32.

23. On *Salut au monde*, see Alice Lewisohn Crowley, *The Neighborhood Playhouse: Leaves from a Theatre Scrapbook* (New York: Theatre Arts Books, 1959), 124. Griffes lived to complete only one of the six Duo-Art recordings (agreement in author's collection). See *Duo Art Piano Music: A Classified Catalog of Interpretations of the World's Best Music Recorded by More Than Two Hundred and Fifty Pianists* (New York: Aeolian Company, 1927), 46, 306, which lists only *The White Peacock* (as no. 64930). A. Walter Kramer, "Honor Griffes' Memory," *Musical America* 33, no. 6 (4 December 1920): 48, also states that Griffes recorded only *The White Peacock*. On the Coolidge festival, see Charles Griffes to Elizabeth Sprague Coolidge, 26 August 1919, DLC, in which Griffes accepts Mrs. Coolidge's invitation to attend the festival

and asks her to send the tickets to him at 12 West Forty-sixth Street, since he planned to be there well into September. From Pittsfield, Griffes wrote his mother: "The concerts are beautiful, and there is an interesting crowd of people up. I get away tomorrow night. . . ." Charles Griffes to Clara Griffes, postcard, 26 September 1919, NN:Mu.

24. "Personalities," *Musical America* 28, no. 13 (27 July 1918): 18.

25. Georges Barrère to Charles T. Griffes, postcard, 16 September 1919. Photocopy sent to author by Edward Maisel.

26. Burnet C. Tuthill to author, 7 November 1964. Tuthill attended the festival with Griffes.

27. *New Grove Dictionary of American Music,* s.v. "New York."

28. Amy Fay to Melusina ("Mudkins"), 23 December 1908, quoted in S. Margaret William McCarthy, *More Letters of Amy Fay: The American Years, 1879–1916* (Detroit: Information Coordinators, 1986), 80–81.

29. Richard Aldrich, "Music: The New York Symphony Orchestra," *New York Times,* 17 November 1919, 20.

30. "New American Work at Symphony Concert," *New York Tribune,* 17 November 1919, 9.

31. "Symphony Society Hears New Work," *New York Herald,* 17 November 1919, pt. 2, 8.

32. Henry T. Parker, "New Music, Liked Music and a Problem," *Boston Evening Transcript,* 15 November 1920, 15.

33. "Reviews and New Music," *Musical Courier* 85, no. 22 (30 November 1922): 51.

34. Lawrence Gilman, "A Notable American Work to Be Revived: Griffes' 'Kubla Khan,'" *New York Herald Tribune,* 30 November 1924, sec. 7–8, 18. Original program for 11 December 1924 performance in author's collection.

35. Marguerite Griffes, interview with author, 13 September 1973 (PI 6:41).

36. Ibid., 23 July 1969 (PI 2:1), and 13 September 1973 (PI 6:40–41).

37. Ibid., 23 July 1962 (PI 2:2).

38. Charlotte Griffes, interview with author, 28 May 1975 (PI 18:12–13, 15).

39. Charles Griffes to John Meyer, 27 November 1919, quoted in Edward Maisel, *Charles T. Griffes: The Life of an American Composer,* rev. ed. (New York: Alfred A. Knopf, 1984), 296, 297, 298. Maisel calls John Meyer "Dan Martin."

40. Marguerite Griffes, interview with author, 13 September 1973 (PI 6:42, 43).

41. *Boston Symphony Orchestra Programmes*, 39th season, 1919–20 (28, 29 November 1919), 473–74.

42. Philip Hale, " 'Kubla Khan' at Symphony; Orchestra Gives First Performance of Griffes's Fantastic Work; Audience Twice Recalls Composer," *Boston Herald*, 29 November 1919, 11.

43. Henry T. Parker, "Voice of the Orient: Means of the Occident; Symphony Concert; a Notable New Piece from Mr. Griffes," *Boston Evening Transcript*, 29 November 1919, pt. 2, 8.

44. "Mme Homer Sings with the Symphony; New American Composer Has a Brilliant Introduction," *Boston Daily Globe*, 29 November 1919, 10.

45. Olin Downes, "American Music by Symphony; Griffes' Work Pleases Audience—Miss Homer, Soloist," *Boston Post*, 29 November 1919, 9.

46. Charlotte Griffes, interview with author, 28 May 1975 (PI 18:12).

47. Charles Griffes to John Meyer, 27 November 1919, quoted in Maisel, *Charles T. Griffes*, 298.

48. James Gibbons Huneker, "Music: The Band from Boston Plays," *World* [New York], 5 December 1919, 15.

49. "Coleridge Poem, Translated into Music, a Success; Exceptional Merit Shown by Griffes, American Composer; Boston Symphony Plays Piece," *New York Tribune*, 5 December 1919, 11.

50. Richard Aldrich, "Music: The Boston Symphony Orchestra," *New York Times*, 5 December 1919, 13.

51. Pitts Sanborn, "Music: New Piece by Griffes Done by Boston Symphony," *Globe and Commercial Advertiser* [New York], 5 December 1919, 13.

52. Marguerite Griffes, interview with author, 10 January 1983 (PI 17:9), and 13 September 1973 (PI 6:42, 44, 45).

53. Ibid., 13 September 1973 (PI 6:42–43, 44–45).

54. Charles Griffes to A. Walter Kramer, 10 December 1919, quoted in A. Walter Kramer, "Charles T. Griffes: Cut Down in His Prime, a Victim of Our Barbarous Neglect of Genius," *Musical America* 32, no. 4 (22 May 1920): 39.

55. Charles Griffes to Miss Broughton, 13 December 1919, NN:Mu.

56. Marguerite Griffes, untaped interview with author, 9 January 1983 (TD, 58–59), and 22 June 1977 (TD, 9).

57. *Philadelphia Orchestra Program*, 20th season, 1919–20 (19, 20 December 1919), 311, 313.

58. The *Notturno für Orchester,* not related in any way to the piano *Notturno* (op. 6, no. 2), was most likely an arrangement of an earlier piano piece, as were *The White Peacock, Clouds,* and *Bacchanale.* Original program in author's collection.

59. Griffes diary, 13 November 1915.

60. "Christmas Concert by the Orchestra," *Philadelphia Public Ledger,* 20 December 1919, 11.

61. "Philadelphia Orchestra: Brahms' Symphony in E Minor Feature of Yesterday's Programme," *Philadelphia Inquirer,* 20 December 1919, 12.

CHAPTER 11. Illness, Death, and Aftermath

1. Marguerite Griffes, untaped interview with author, 22 June 1977 (TD, 9).

2. Marguerite Griffes, interview with author, 18 January 1982 (PI 11:7), 13 September 1973 (PI 6:45), and 24 July 1969 (PI 3:12).

3. Ibid., 24 July 1969 (PI 3:17).

4. Charles Griffes to John Meyer, 18 January 1920, quoted in Edward Maisel, *Charles T. Griffes: The Life of an American Composer,* rev. ed. (New York: Alfred A. Knopf, 1984), 312. Maisel calls John Meyer "Dan Martin."

5. Marguerite Griffes, interview with author, 24 July 1969 (PI 3:13).

6. Ibid., 22 May 1981 (PI 9:21).

7. Marguerite Griffes, untaped interview with author, 5 June 1983 (TD, 88).

8. Marguerite Griffes, interview with author, 14 September 1973 (PI 7:2–3).

9. Royalty agreement in author's collection.

10. Original programs for all concerts identified in this paragraph in author's collection.

11. Marguerite Griffes, interview with author, 24 July 1969 (PI 3:7).

12. Maisel, *Charles T. Griffes,* 320. Hospital address from 1920 Manhattan telephone directory. Neither the Loomis Sanatorium records nor the New York Hospital records from this period are extant. In 1952 the Loomis Sanatorium became the Liberty-Loomis Hospital, and as of 1983 records more than seven years old were destroyed. Nancy McGay, Sullivan County Historical Society, Hurleyville, N.Y., telephone interview with author, February 1983. New York Hospital has been located at 525 East Sixty-eighth Street since 1932. The hospital generally kept its records for a maximum of twenty

years. Dorothy Brown, officer of records, New York Hospital, interview with author, 18 January 1980.

13. Marguerite Griffes, interview with author, 18 January 1982 (PI 11:8).

14. Information on Griffes's operation and death from Marguerite Griffes, interview with author, 24 July 1969 (PI 3:18–19), and 18 January 1982 (PI 11:9); Marguerite Griffes, untaped interview with author, 22 June 1977 (TD, 11); Maisel, *Charles T. Griffes,* 323; and "Funerals: Charles T. Griffis [*sic*]," *Elmira Star-Gazette,* 12 April 1920, 15. The obituary from the *Star-Gazette* also appeared in the *Elmira [Daily] Advertiser,* 13 April 1920, 3.

15. Laura Elliot to Elizabeth Sprague Coolidge, no date, DLC. The letter must have been written between 19 January and 20 March 1920, while Griffes was at Loomis Sanatorium, since Mrs. Elliot commented that Griffes "was taken to a sanatorium where the proper drainage and treatment could be given."

16. "C. T. Griffes, Well Known as Composer, Is Dead," *New York Tribune,* 10 April 1920, 6.

17. "Funerals: Charles T. Griffis [*sic*]," 15.

18. "Charles T. Griffes Succumbs," *Musical Leader* 39, no. 16 (15 April 1920): 383.

19. "In Memoriam Charles Tomlinson Griffes." Original typescript, dated 10 April 1920, initialed by Miss Broughton, in author's collection.

20. D. J. T., "Does Griffes's Sad Experience Await Others? Frances Nash Points Out False Pathos in Public's Attitude toward the Late Gifted Composer—How the Need of Bread Blighted His Work—The Part of the Executive Artist in Preparing the Way for Creative Art," *Musical America* 33, no. 12 (15 January 1921): 35.

21. A. Walter Kramer, "Charles T. Griffes: Cut Down in His Prime, a Victim of Our Barbarous Neglect of Genius," *Musical America* 32, no. 4 (22 May 1920): 39–40.

22. Lawrence Gilman, "Griffes Recalled," *New York Herald Tribune,* 24 May 1931, sec. 8, 6.

23. Noble Kreider, "The Story of 'The American Debussy' Charles T. Griffes," *Etude* 62, no. 7 (July 1944): 379, 380.

24. "Charles T. Griffes Succumbs," 383.

25. Richard Aldrich, "Aid for American Composers," *New York Times,* 18 April 1920, sec. 6, 3.

26. *The Encyclopedia Americana,* international ed., s.v. "American Academy in Rome."

27. "Tributes to Charles T. Griffes, American Composer," *Musical Leader* 39, no. 23 (3 June 1920): 623.

28. Original program in author's collection.

29. Original program in author's collection.

30. Typewritten copy in author's collection. On Gilman's tribute, see A. Walter Kramer, "Honor Griffes' Memory," *Musical America* 33, no. 6 (4 December 1920): 48.

31. Original program in author's collection.

32. Kramer, "Honor Griffes' Memory," 48.

33. Griffes Group publicity flyer in author's collection.

34. Original program of Aeolian Hall concert in author's collection.

35. "Lucy Gates Joins Griffes Group," *Musical Courier* 88, no. 1 (3 January 1924): 16.

36. *Boston Symphony Orchestra Programmes*, 40th season, 1920–21 (31 December 1920 and 1 January 1921), 598, 600, 602, 604. Original program of Carnegie Hall concert in author's collection.

37. Richard Aldrich, "Music: The Boston Symphony Orchestra," *New York Times*, 9 January 1921, 12.

38. *Minneapolis Symphony Orchestra Program*, 18th season, 1920–21 (31 December 1920), 215–16.

39. Original program in author's collection. Although the program does not indicate that this was Morris's debut, the *New York Times* review clearly notes that it was. "Harold Morris Appears; Young Texas Pianist and Composer Wins Last [Large?] Audience at Debut," *New York Times*, 13 January 1921, 18.

40. Original program in author's collection.

41. Original program in author's collection.

42. "Barrere Ensemble Plays Novelties," *Musical America* 33, no. 18 (26 February 1921): 30.

43. Original program in author's collection. Although the program does not list the Intermezzo, Mary Selena Broughton mentioned its addition in a handwritten note and also wrote, "The Intermezzo which has not been published, I liked the best of all." The manuscript (see n. 44 below) is lost.

44. Original program of the Stamford concert in author's collection ("Stamford, Conn." is added in ink). I do not have a program of the Town Hall recital but know of no earlier New York performance. There were at least four reviews of Hodgson's concert. See, for example, Oscar Thompson, "Music: Leslie Hodgson Brings Back Works of Griffes in Piano

Recital of Sincerity and Taste," *New York Evening Post,* 23 November 1933, 34, which mentions the Intermezzo, "still in manuscript."

45. See "Damrosch Plans Cycle; to Give Series Showing Historic Growth of Symphonic Music," *Musical America* 32, no. 4 (22 May 1920): 40.

46. Original program in author's collection.

47. See "25,000 Out to Hear Ten Sunday Concerts," *New York Times,* 28 November 1921, 16, which briefly covers the Schmitz concert and mentions Griffes's *Fountain.*

48. Original program in author's collection. Subsequent performances took place on 23, 29, 30 April and 6, 7, 13, 14 May. Dates from Neighborhood Playhouse scrapbook, NN:Th.

49. See Clara Griffes to Miss [Irene?] Lewisohn, 4 March 1920, NN:Mu.

50. Clara Griffes to Miss Lewisohn, 28 February 1920, NN:Mu. The salutation does not identify which Lewisohn, but it seems likely that the letter was meant for Irene because she and Griffes worked on the score together.

51. Ibid., 4 March 1920, NN:Mu.

52. See "Edmond W. Rickett, Savoyard Expert," *New York Times,* 16 March 1957, 19; and Alice Lewisohn Crowley, *The Neighborhood Playhouse: Leaves from a Theatre Scrapbook* (New York: Theatre Arts Books, 1959), 125 n. 1.

53. Crowley, *The Neighborhood Playhouse,* 124–25.

54. Ibid., 125.

55. Information from original program and script in author's collection.

56. Crowley, *The Neighborhood Playhouse,* 121–22.

57. Ibid., 124.

58. See score in NN:Mu.

59. See, for example, Katharine Spaeth, "Opera and Concert: Salut au monde," *Evening Mail* [New York], 24 April 1922, 10.

60. Information from original program in author's collection.

61. Deems Taylor, "Music: 'Salut au monde,'" *World* [New York], 24 April 1922, 7.

62. Marion Bauer, "Charles T. Griffes as I Remember Him," *Musical Quarterly* 29 (July 1943): 375.

63. William Treat Upton, "Some Recent Representative American Song-Composers," *Musical Quarterly* 11 (July 1925): 407. See also idem, "The Songs of Charles T. Griffes," *Musical Quarterly* 9 (July 1923): 314–28.

64. Frederick Jacobi, "Forecast and Review: In Retrospect," *Modern Music* 4, no. 2 (January–February 1927): 32, 33.

65. Edward Robinson, "The Life and Death of an American Composer," *American Mercury* 30, no. 119 (November 1933): 347, 348.

66. Ibid., 346.

67. Aaron Copland, *Music and Imagination* (Cambridge: Harvard University Press, 1952), 102–3.

68. Aaron Copland and Vivian Perlis, *Copland: 1900 through 1942* (New York: St. Martin's/Marek, 1984), 32.

69. Peter G. Davis, "A Deluge of Musical Americana," *New York Times,* 4 July 1976, sec. 2, 1, 13.

70. Donal Henehan, "Winerock, Pianist, Plays Program of Americana," *New York Times,* 30 September 1974, 52.

71. Peter G. Davis, "Bruce Eberle, Pianist Based in San Francisco," *New York Times,* 9 April 1978, 52.

72. John Rockwell, "Disks Pay Hommage to Griffes's Music," *New York Times,* 23 January 1983, sec. 2, 22.

CHAPTER 12. Stylistic Overview

1. A. Walter Kramer, "Charles T. Griffes: Cut Down in His Prime, a Victim of Our Barbarous Neglect of Genius," *Musical America* 32, no. 4 (22 May 1920): 39.

2. A. Walter Kramer, "A New Note in Our Piano Music," *Musical America* 23, no. 5 (4 December 1915): 37.

3. "Artist Needs No Patriotic Aid: Compositions of Charles Griffes, Brought to Attention Here by Boston Symphony, Able to Stand without Label of 'American,'" *Evening Sun* [New York], 19 December 1919, 10.

4. Griffes indicated that he used an authentic Chinese melody in "So-fei Gathering Flowers" on the autograph manuscript in DLC.

5. Winthrop P. Tryon, "Mme. Eva Gauthier, an Internationalist of the Musical World," *Christian Science Monitor,* 31 March 1923, 14.

6. See ibid. and Avery Strakosch, "Lived in a Sultan's Harem to Glean Java Folk Songs," *Musical America* 21, no. 16 (20 February 1915): 15.

7. A sketchbook in NN:Mu contains some of the melodies Griffes transcribed from Gauthier's notebooks of Javanese traditional melodies. A second notebook, dated November 1917 by Griffes, contains some Japanese melodies that Griffes may have received from Gauthier. They are not so identified, however. See Donna K. Anderson, *The Works of Charles T. Griffes: A Descriptive Catalogue* (Ann Arbor: UMI Research Press, 1983), 481–83.

8. Information from Griffes diary, passim, and from Harold Wand's appraisal of Griffes's library prepared after the composer's death. Copy in author's collection.

9. For an excellent overview of Griffes's use of synthetic scales (including the one given in ex. 9), and for an in-depth study of *The Kairn of Koridwen* and the Piano Sonata, see Jonathan Lee Chenette, "Synthetic Scales, Charles Griffes, and the *Kairn of Koridwen*" (Ph.D. diss., University of Chicago, 1984).

10. Quoted in Edward Maisel, *Charles T. Griffes: The Life of an American Composer,* rev. ed. (New York: Alfred A. Knopf, 1984), 363 n. for line 32 (p. 187). *Pierrot Lunaire* (1912) is scored for speaker, flute (alt. piccolo), clarinet (alt. bass clarinet), violin (alt. viola), cello, and piano.

11. See Anderson, *Griffes: Descriptive Catalogue,* 379–410, for a discussion of the Indian material used in the various versions of the two string quartet movements.

12. "Artist Needs No Patriotic Aid," 10.

13. See entries in Griffes diary for 28 March 1912 ("Spent an hour in the afternoon at the Nichols'. . . . I played my 'Lake at Evening.' . . ."), 7 June 1915 ("Gave [Mr. Pinter] the title which I chose for No. 2 of the 'Tonepictures,' 'The Vale of Dreams'"), and 16 May 1912 ("I started to revise 'Night Winds,'" but began to wonder if it were worth while and dropped it again").

14. The royalty agreement Griffes signed on 12 March 1915 lists the three pieces only as "Three Tone Pictures, Op. 5, Nos. 1, 2 and 3" (no individual titles). Royalty agreement in author's collection.

15. Griffes diary, 26 May 1915. The "combination from Fiona MacLeod" that Griffes found for *Barcarolle* was "A Record" and "Motherhood," both from William Sharp's *Poems* (Fiona Macleod was Sharp's pseudonym). The Paul Verlaine verses for *Notturno* are from *La Bonne Chanson,* no. 6. The royalty agreement Griffes signed for *Three Tone-Pictures* (see n. 14 above) also includes the *Fantasy Pieces,* listed as "Notturno, Op. 6, No. 2," "Scherzo, Op. 6, No. 3," and "Barcarolle, Op. 6, No. 1." There is no indication in the agreement that the set would be called *Fantasy Pieces.*

16. The royalty agreement of 11 December 1916 lists only the titles of the four compositions. It includes no collective title and no opus number. Royalty agreement in author's collection.

17. See autograph manuscript of *The Night Winds* in DLC.

18. On the composition dates of *De Profundis,* see Griffes diary, 18 November 1915 ("started a new piece in g Minor"), and 7 December 1915 ("fin-

ished up my new piece in g minor"). The autograph manuscript in NN:Mu is dated November 1915, but Griffes didn't actually copy out the manuscript until late May 1916. See Griffes diary, 29 May, 30 May 1916.

19. Undated brochure in author's collection.

20. Quoted in Josef Rufer, *The Works of Arnold Schoenberg: A Catalogue of His Compositions, Writings and Paintings,* trans. Dika Newlin (London: Faber and Faber, 1962), 34.

21. Marion Bauer, "Charles T. Griffes as I Remember Him," *Musical Quarterly* 29 (July 1943): 356.

22. Marguerite Griffes, interview with author, 13 September 1973 (PI 5:13).

23. Information on Griffes's library from a notebook containing his record of books purchased between 1903 and 1919, in author's collection, and from Harold Wands's appraisal of Griffes's library prepared after the composer's death. Copy in author's collection. Some of these books and some not listed in the notebook are in the author's collection; several are in NEE, and several are in NN:Mu, circulation department.

24. *The Dictionary of National Biography,* suppl. 1901–11, ed. Sir Sidney Lee (London: Oxford University Press, 1920), s.v. "Sharp, William."

25. Gilbert Chase, *America's Music: From the Pilgrims to the Present* (New York: McGraw-Hill Book Co., 1955), 520. Subsequent editions of Chase's text (1966 and 1987) omit the scale entirely. Jeanne Behrend includes a similar scale in her jacket notes for Allegro ALG 3024 (American Piano Music Series, vol. 1).

26. Chenette, "Synthetic Scales," 17.

27. Arthur Berger, "The Tarrytown Impressionist," *New York Review of Books* 32, no. 10 (13 June 1985): 29. Similar scales may be found in David H. Cope, *New Directions in Music,* 5th ed. (Dubuque, Iowa: W. C. Brown Publishers, 1989), 11, and Maisel, *Charles T. Griffes,* 273.

28. Dean Luther Arlton, "American Piano Sonatas of the Twentieth Century: Selective Analysis and Annotated Index" (Ed.D. diss., Teachers College, Columbia University, 1968), 188. Hoon Mo Kim Pratt, "The Complete Piano Works of Charles T. Griffes" (D.M.A. diss., Boston University, 1975), 158, discusses a similar scale.

29. See Anderson, *Griffes: Descriptive Catalogue,* 301.

30. For a description of the manuscript sketch and fair copy of the Sonata in NN:Mu and NEE, respectively, see ibid., 291–306.

31. See Anderson, *Griffes: Descriptive Catalogue,* 343–61, 369–74, and 452–65.

32. *Boston Symphony Orchestra Programmes*, 39th season, 1919–20 (28, 29 November 1919), 474–75.

33. Karl Krueger, *The Musical Heritage of the United States: The Unknown Portion* (New York: Society for the Preservation of the American Musical Heritage, 1973), 203.

34. Pai Ta-Shun, "The Artist's Precept," in *Chinese Lyrics* (Shanghai: Kelly & Walsh, 1916), 23. Griffes's copy in author's collection. Pai Ta-Shun was the pseudonym of Frederick Peterson (1859–1938).

35. André Gide, "Concerning Influence in Literature," trans. Blanche A. Price, in *Pretexts: Reflections on Literature and Morality by André Gide*, ed. Justin O'Brien (New York: Dell Publishing Co., 1959), 28.

Index

Page references in bold indicate music examples. All musical works are by Griffes unless otherwise indicated.